THE GOLDEN VALLEY

a visual biography
of the garw

SEREN is the book imprint of
Poetry Wales Press Ltd.,
Nolton Street, Bridgend, Wales

www.serenbooks.com
facebook.com/SerenBooks
twitter: @SerenBooks

Text and Photographs
© Phil Cope 2021

ISBN 9781781726334

A CIP record for this title is available
from the British Library.

The publisher works with the financial
assistance of the Welsh Books Council.

Designed for Seren
by Phil Cope
phil.cope66@gmail.com

Printed in the Czech Republic
by Akcent Media Ltd.

acknowledgements and thanks
Although I take full responsibility for
everything herein, I have been greatly
assisted in my efforts by many people and
organistions without whose help **The
Golden Valley** would have been a much
slimmer and less interesting volume.

These have included Dr Wyn Price whose
knowledge, inspiration and authority have
supported my efforts more than anyone;
my walk companions and best critics,
Robert Minnhinnick, Richard 'Cuffy' Evans,
Angela Graham, Julian Cason and Stephen
Thomas; Karl Luxford, the Garw Valley
Community Ranger, both for the hard work
and care he is providing for the Valley's
parks and wild places, as well as his help-
ful hints of sites for me to search out and
record; Des Gibson, who revealed new
round barrow sites by flying his drone in
the hills above our homes; the painter
Kevin Sinnott, portrait artist George
Farmer, lovespoon maker Siôn Llewellyn,
and the late Merlin Madog; Anthony and
Nicola Thomas of the Ffaldau Institute;
filmmaker John Geraint; Selwyn Jones and
Aled Jenkins of Corilla Plastics; Andy
Bowdler and Chris Adams, Bridgend
Valleys Railway Company Ltd; Ann Harris,
Garw Valley Community Council; Naomi
Harris, Electoral Services, Bridgend County
Borough Council; Gerald Jarvis, Ann M
Leitch and C/TH Davies, Garw Valley
Heritage Society; Kirsty Williams of Kirsty's
K9 Cwtches; Rob and Karen Cowell of
Fforchwen Farm; and Bernard Ingram,
Grafton Radcliffe, Susan Wedlake, Michael
Clubb, David Pinches, Ian Black, Alex
Bowen and AH Williams.

The Golden Valley
is dedicated to
Aeron Lleision-Jones
my first grandchild
born beautiful
to Laura and Aled
22 July 2020

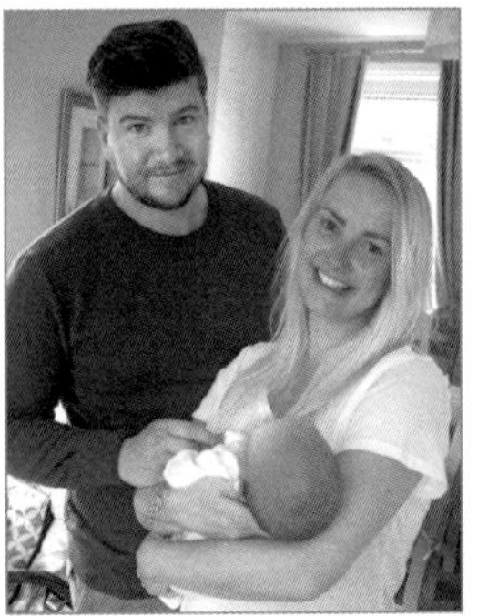

THE GOLDEN VALLEY

a visual biography
of the garw

PHIL COPE

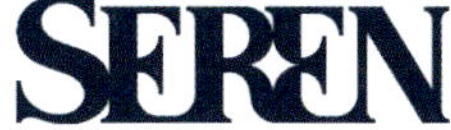

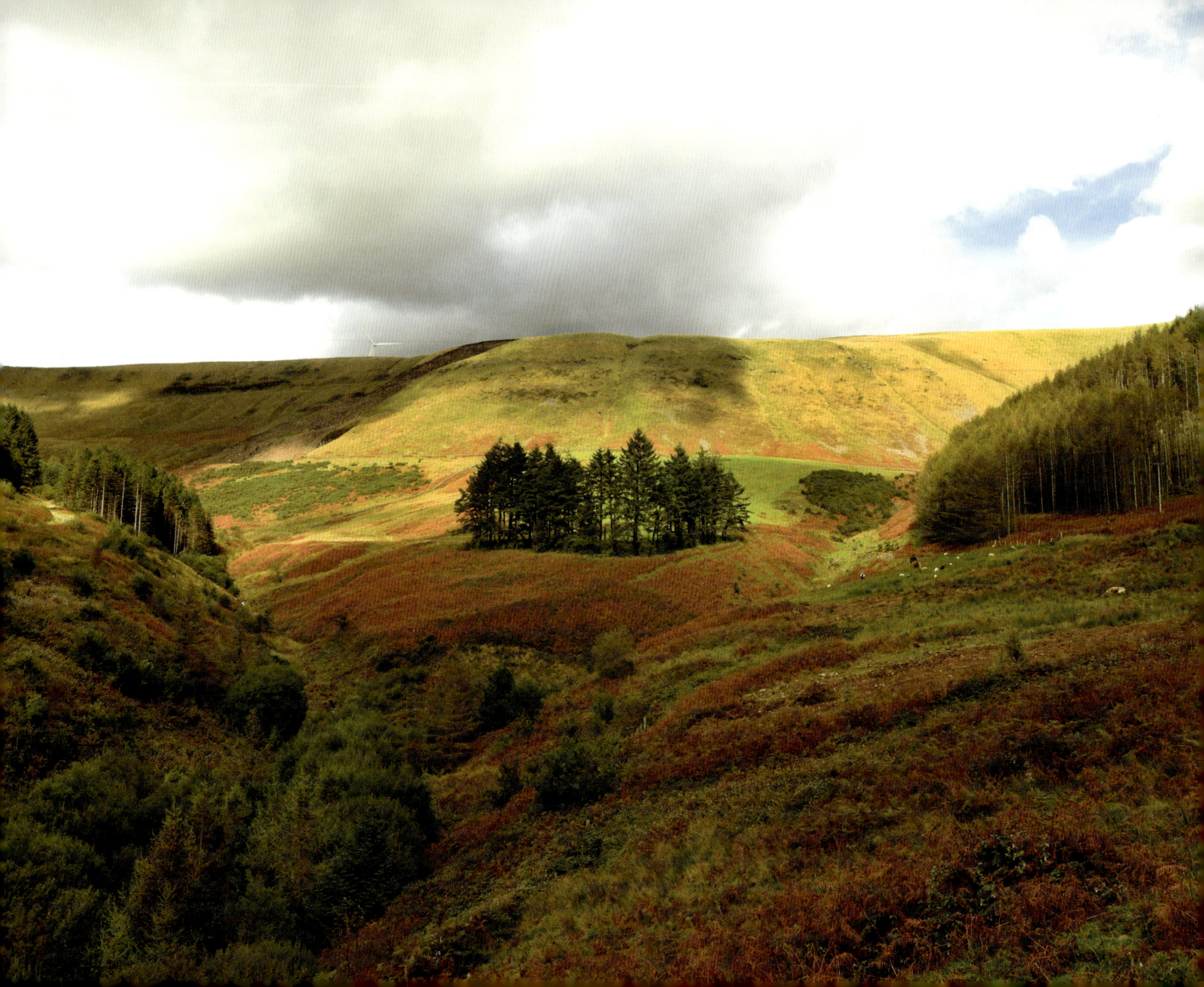

INTRODUCTION: *a hundred springs*

If you search for the source of the River Garw, you'll be disappointed.

Just like the profusion of events that have contributed to the often-troublesome history of this small Valley, Afon Garw has countless origins.

Flowing from scores of springs high up on the slopes of its surrounding hills, and joined by dozens of tributaries, the Garw's brief journey terminates at the confluence, just beyond Bryngarw House and Park, with its more broad-chested neighbour, Afon Ogwr / the River Ogmore.

site of
the old Carn reservoir,
at the head of
the Garw Valley

But along the Garw's six mile fall, it murmurs a rich library of tales. Some begin at the time of the formation of the coal measures millions of years ago; or at the land's later sculptings by the river's constant undercutting of the softer rocks that determined the Garw's fundamental topology, making this, one of the steepest-sided valleys in South Wales.

It passes, along the way, Stone and Bronze Age presences, in an area once rich in native trees, roamed by bears, wolves and foxes, deer and red squirrels, its main river and tributaries filled with salmon, trout and sewin. It would also hear the faint memories of the monastery (or *llan*) founded by St Ceinor in the fifth century (leading to the naming of present-day Llangeinor); and of the twelfth century Norman-built church dedicated to St David in Bettws – itself raised on much earlier Christian foundations – both sitting like spiritual sentinels high up on either side of the lower reaches of the Garw.

The river flows below Tynton Farm, the birthplace of Richard Price [1723-91], 'the apostle of liberty'; and beside the home of Daniel James [1848-1920] who, while living in the Garw, penned the poem that was to become the celebrated hymn, 'Calon Lân'; and it might even breathe in something of the spirit of educationalist, suffragist and Labour Party activist, Fanny Margaret Thomas [1868-1952].

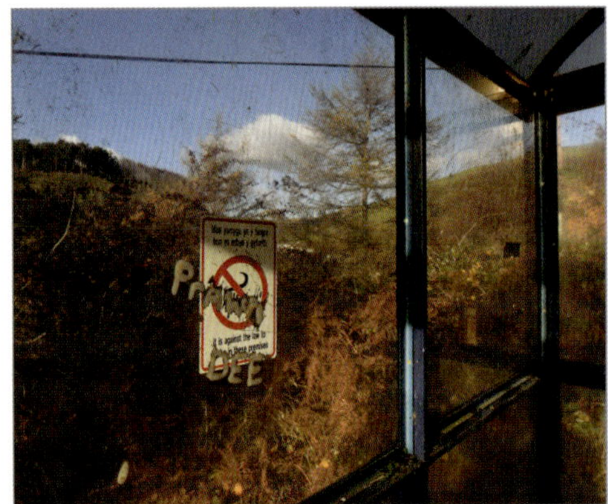

Dominating much of our story, of course, are the rough carvings into the land's skin for coal, following its exploitation on an industrial scale in the late 1800s; and, then, within less than one hundred years, this dangerous trade's demise.

Today, the river and its streams run through the bold statements of the reclamation schemes of the late 1980s and early '90s which modified some of the waters' courses, created lakes, and pushed the landscape a little way towards a quieter green, though never fully erasing all of its scars.

Situated at the centre of the South Wales Coalfield, north of Bridgend, and squeezed between its much larger Valley neighbours of the Llynfi and the Ogmore, the Garw offers a microcosm of the Valleys as a whole. Its unique beauty and its many rich stories – though often hidden in the overgrowth of nature and of time – extend much deeper than its coalmining years.

What we see today, and what **The Golden Valley** in turn interrogates, laments and celebrates is the result of a millennia-long dialogue between the forces of nature and of humankind. The landscape's artistry has been partnered, compromised and sometimes insulted by human industry and greed, all of these multiple shades of experience and meaning piled, layer upon layer here, in what Robert Minhinnick has described as a "psychedelia of sight" *.

left:
Braich y Cymer bus shelter

opposite:
Llygaid y Ffynhonnau,
one of the sources of the Garw river,
above the site of the Ocean / Garw colliery

* from 'At the Cairns above Blaengarw', 2020 (a poem Robert kindly dedicated to me after one of my guided walks)

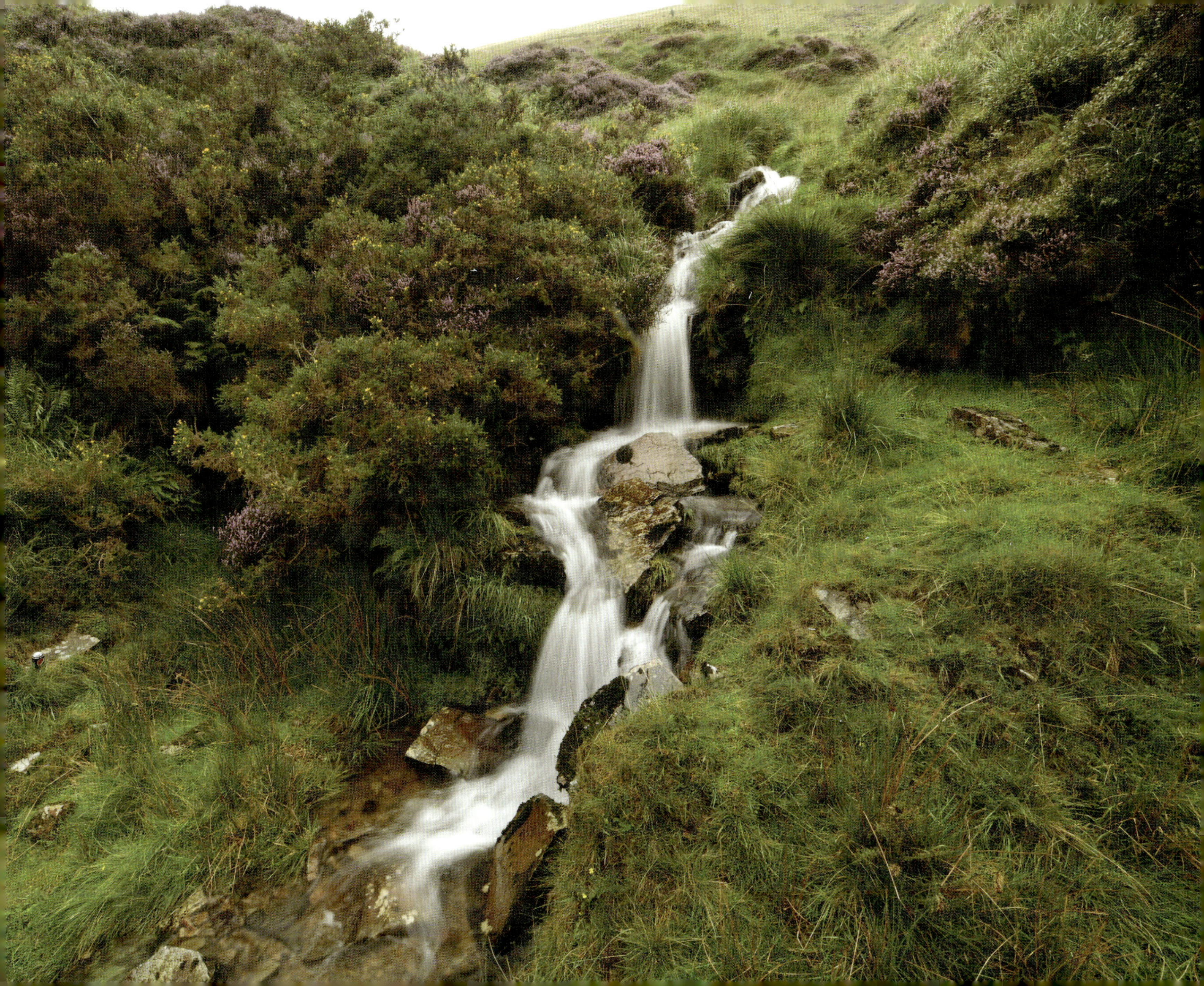

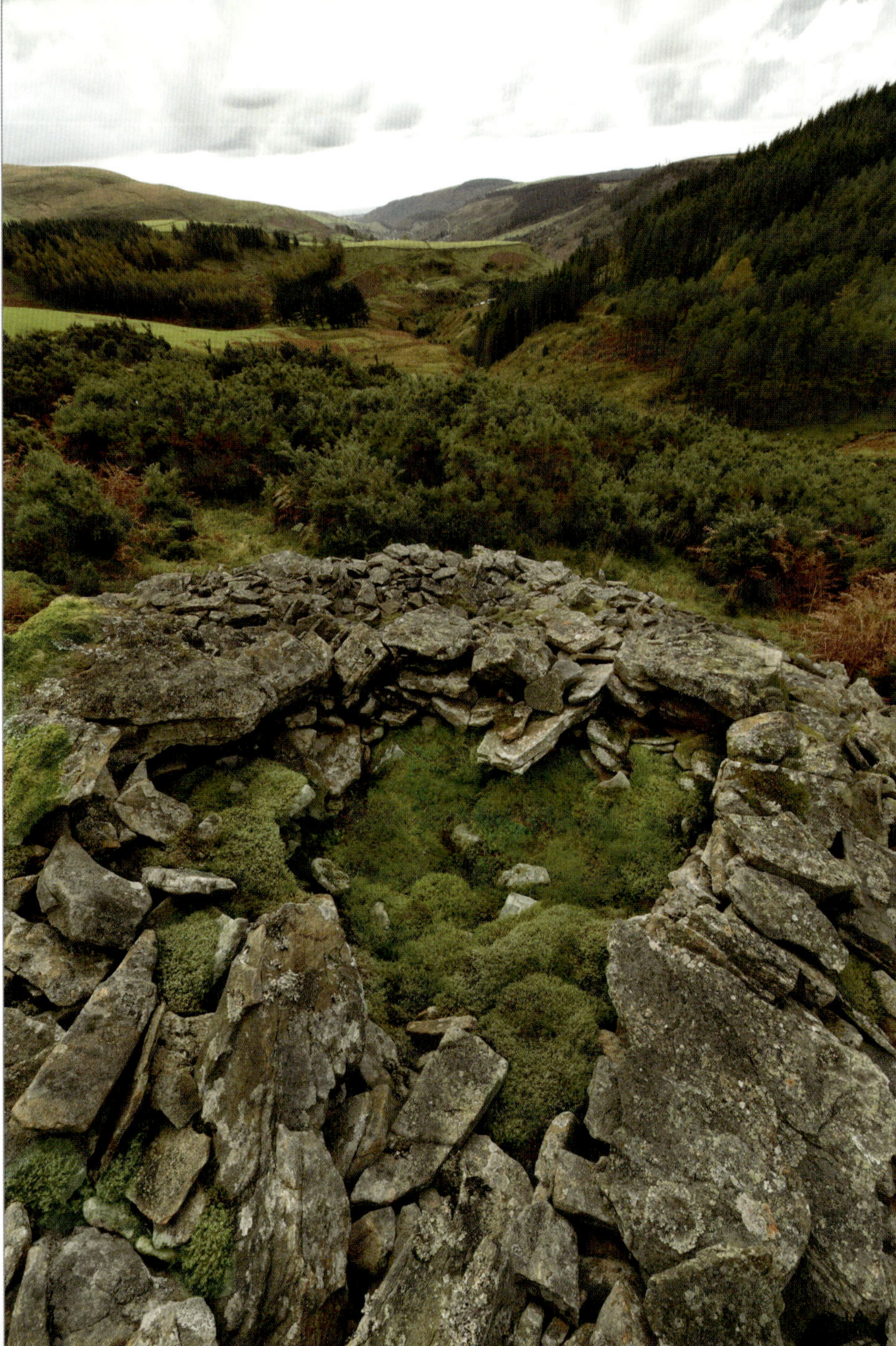

BEFORE COAL:
our lending library of water, earth and stone

340 million years ago, the land we now know as Wales was much nearer to what we now call the equator. Dense tropical forests grew tall and were subsequently drowned as sea levels rose, crushing trees and plants below deep layers of water and mud, a process repeated over many millennia, transforming this rich sediment first into peat, and then to seams of coal.

The latest of the Ice Ages to scour and sculpt this area concluded its southern slide a relatively-recent 10,000 years ago, since which time the Garw's rivers and streams have continued to shape our hills and valleys, leaving the towering walls of Mynydd Moelgilau and Moel Cynhordy rising to the west; Mynydd Llangeinwyr in the east; and Mynydd Blaengarw, Mynydd Y Gelli and Mynydd Caerau shaping our terminal northern boundaries.

The Garw's steep-sided bowl – its name translating as 'rough', 'harsh' or 'unrefined' – gives birth to its main river through a serious of amniotic springs, eternally reforming.

And high above these waters, on plateaux with almost always the very best of views and the oldest of ideas on how to live and die, are the remains of burial chambers and ancient forts.

the mossy mattress
and lichen-patterned
pillows of the
long barrow above Carn,
at the head of
the Garw Valley

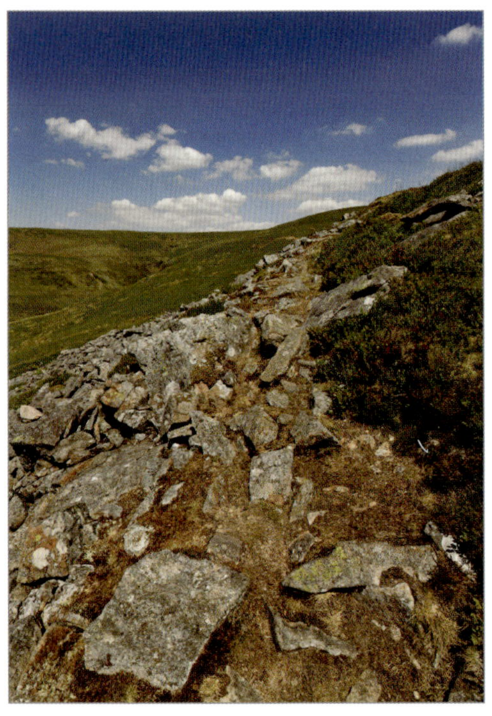

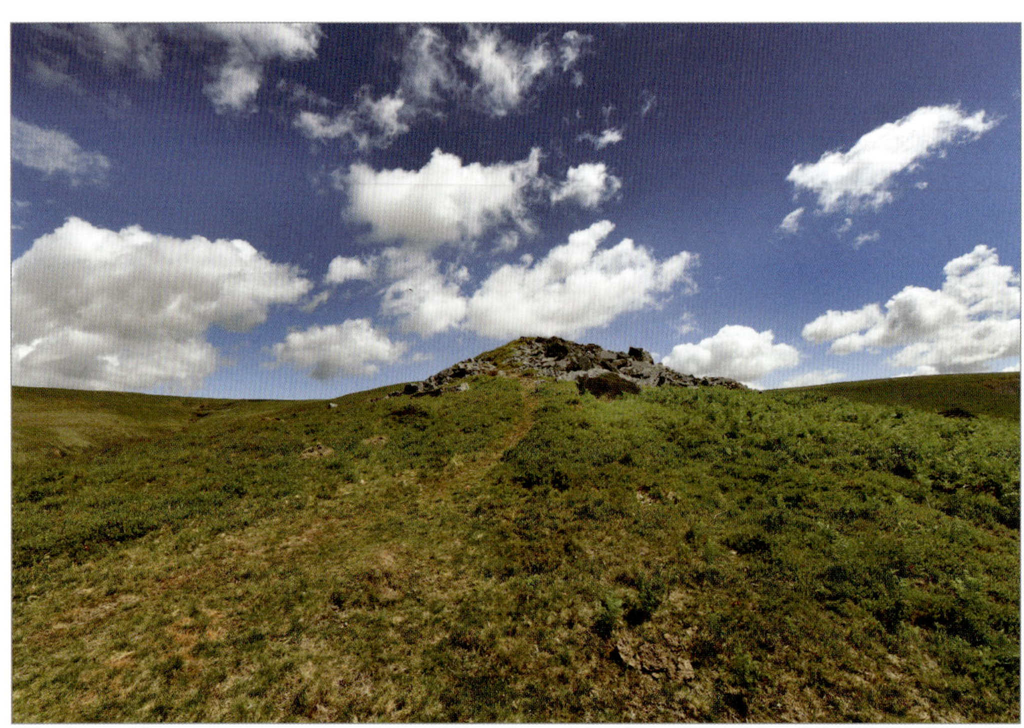

above and opposite:

one of the impressively-situated round barrows above Nant Fforchwen

These ancient round and long barrows were usually sited on the skyline "announcing to any intruder that the spirits of the ancestors were watching over the communal homeland".

(from *Landscape Encyclopaedia*, 2004, Richard Muir)

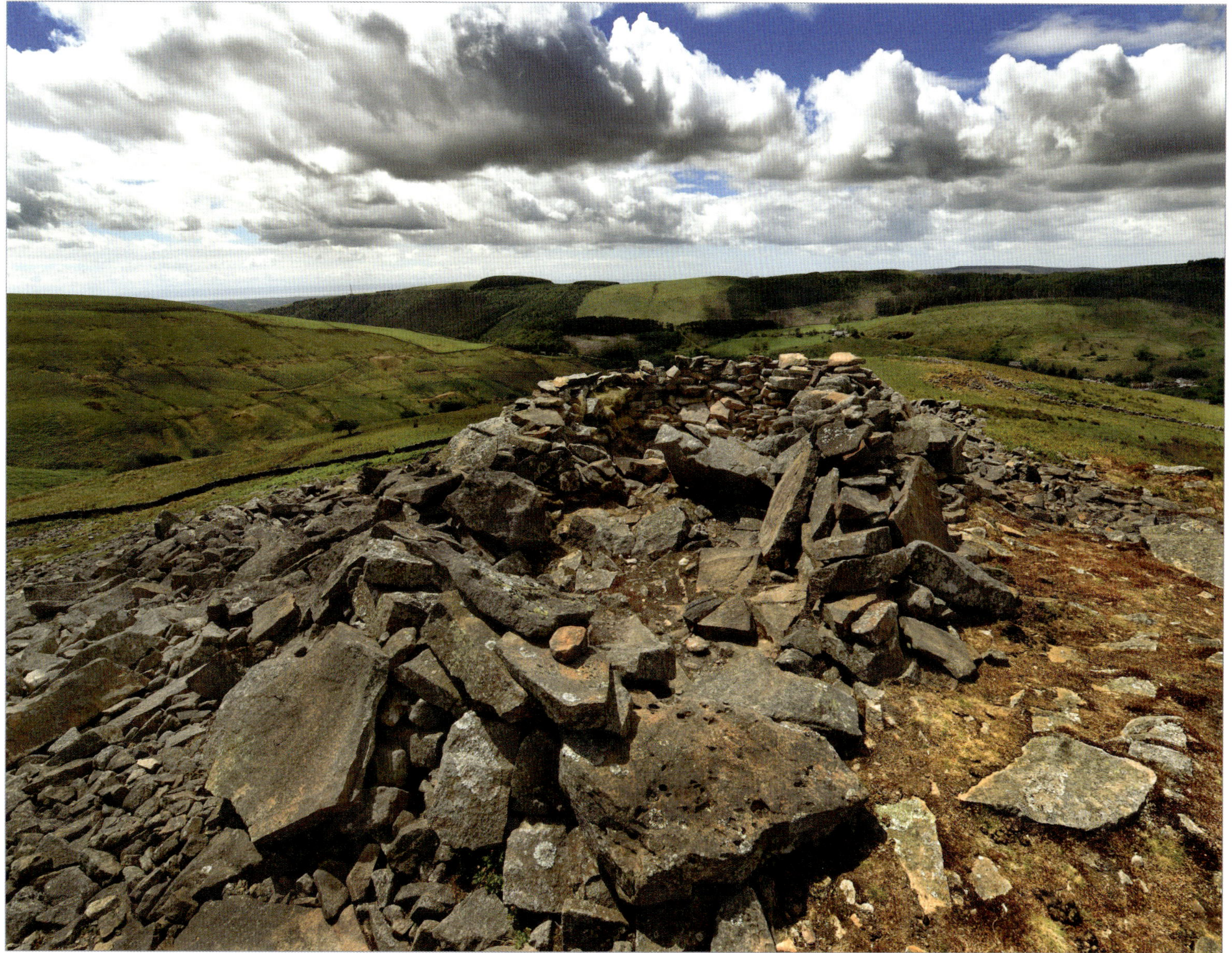

Often unmarked on modern maps, these round and long barrows were once the sacred sites of the loose network of Bronze Age people we now know as the Silures who arrived in this area some 3-4,000 years ago.

They made their homes and buried their dead on Garw's mountain tops, sometimes accompanied on their way to whatever afterlife they believed in by copper daggers and spearheads, flint knives and decorated beakers (often deliberately broken), alongside a little food for the journey … and, on the rarest of occasions, a cape made from gold.

Most of these sites were and still are covered by earthen mounds, though some have been partially revealed by a combination of early archaeology and the fierce undressing of the mountain winds.

They hold the very deepest of our histories, only available today by walking high above the Valley floor, or searching deeper still within our imaginations:

RHEDDI'S VIEW
Fforchwen barrows
Moel Garn, Garw Valley
[OS Explorer map no.166: SS 914 916]

Old Hegna always preached that
*'Every man must learn
at least six things if
granted a full life'.*

I found that if you wished to
bring down a bird, you had to
aim at where it was going
not where it was,
that the sun always rose
even when it didn't,
that *her* old tales didn't make
the storms
or cold disappear but
would sometimes warm the heart,
that we should caress as many things
in our small world as we could, and
that no stone could
be broken perfectly
unless it wanted to be broken,

and that these rocks,
pushed down on ancient sleds of ice,
arrived here long before our people,
and that it was our job to
re-arrange them
into circles and straight lines.

*

But as a child, I failed to see why
on my harvest's fifth anniversary,
I had to hurl three of
our polished, treasured stones
in one direction, as high and far as
my young arms could manage
to mark the beginnings of
some other kind of mountain here.

I learned much later that
where they landed was to be
my tomb,
added to each birthday season by
the blue stained hands of
family and friends
to make an easy bed after my death
for all my weathered bones
and ashes, my bird-picked
and burned remains.

*

I passed the place most every day
to gather water from
the rock pool's eye, and always in
the company of our mountain winds
… though this gathering pile meant
nothing much to me back then.

I loved most of all the views
out beyond the rivers to
the waves on which our Hegna said
we had arrived, sick,
and hungry most for solid ground
and elevation, to dream
our new beginnings slowly into life.

*

The days back then were always
measured by
the distance you could
or could not see,
although we knew deep down
the sky belonged to
cloud and rain, to sun and moon,
to eagle, swift and crow.

And I threw many other stones,
of course …
to scare a deer,
to kill a rabbit or a bird,
and once, much later on,
a man.

I used to sit up here at night
and watch the movement of
the stars, some racing wild,
some crawling now like me, and
others, falling from the sky.

And as I too grew old,
slower now and nearly blind,
this place assumed
a new identity,
a different power, where –
no longer striding rock to rock –
my body shed its influence
though strangely felt much heavier,
weighed down it seemed
by air alone, until
I slipped and spilled my body's red
one night into these stones,
a day or two beyond
my twentieth season, and
well before that darkening world
of men arrived more skilled in
war and weapons than we were.

A boy with my old water job
found me up here, drained pale and
broken as our granite.

But Hegna always said that
everything we touch or see
or walk upon
has its beginning and
would one day find its end,
and that, in any case,
we all were living somewhere tiny,
insignificant, wedged tight between
conception and destruction,

up to the river's sources and
down to the hostile plain and sea,
enclosed by wooded hills of
wolves and bears and fear.

I'd tried to follow Hegna's tutoring
and touched all of
these stones up here,
rode them through the air, heard
their songs in rain and storm,
observed their colours changing,
listening in to their conversations
with passing, nesting, creeping,
grazing things.

*

Mine always was an unmarked grave
of course, but when you climb up to
my destiny of rock,
rest and listen for a while,
and try to feel
a whisper of what's left of me
up here.

Sit and watch the sun's rise and fall,
illuminating then extinguishing
these boulders,
and feel the heat or rain or wind
upon your skin, and
these sharp foundation stones
– my bones –
cutting into your bare feet.

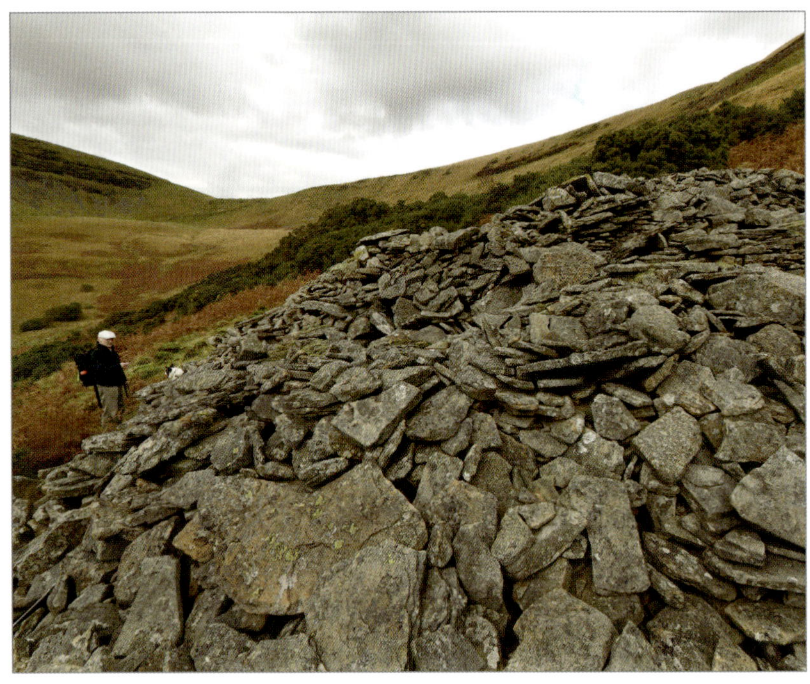

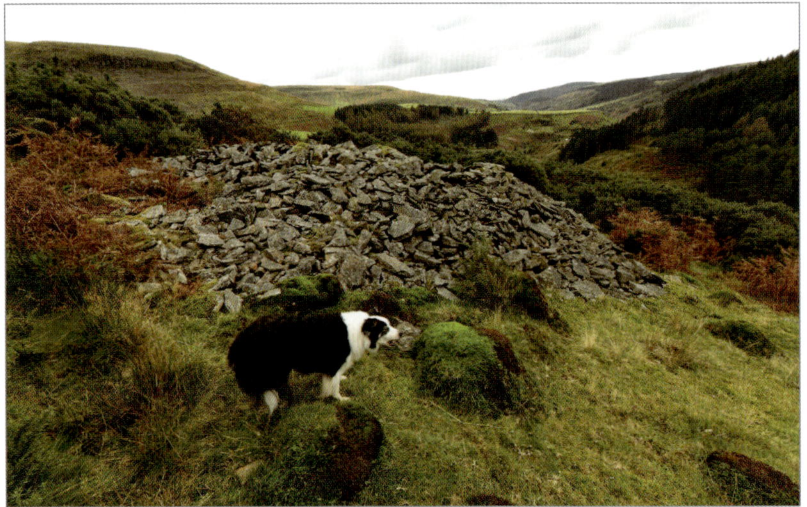

one of the three long barrows above Carn, at the head of the Valley:

Stephen Thomas' dog, Poppy, would not stop barking, here … at the spirits of the ancient dead, perhaps.

opposite:

a further selection of the Garw Valley's round and long barrows, with a *bullaun*, a (probably man-made) rock-cut ceremonial basin from the Fforchwen cairns area, at its centre

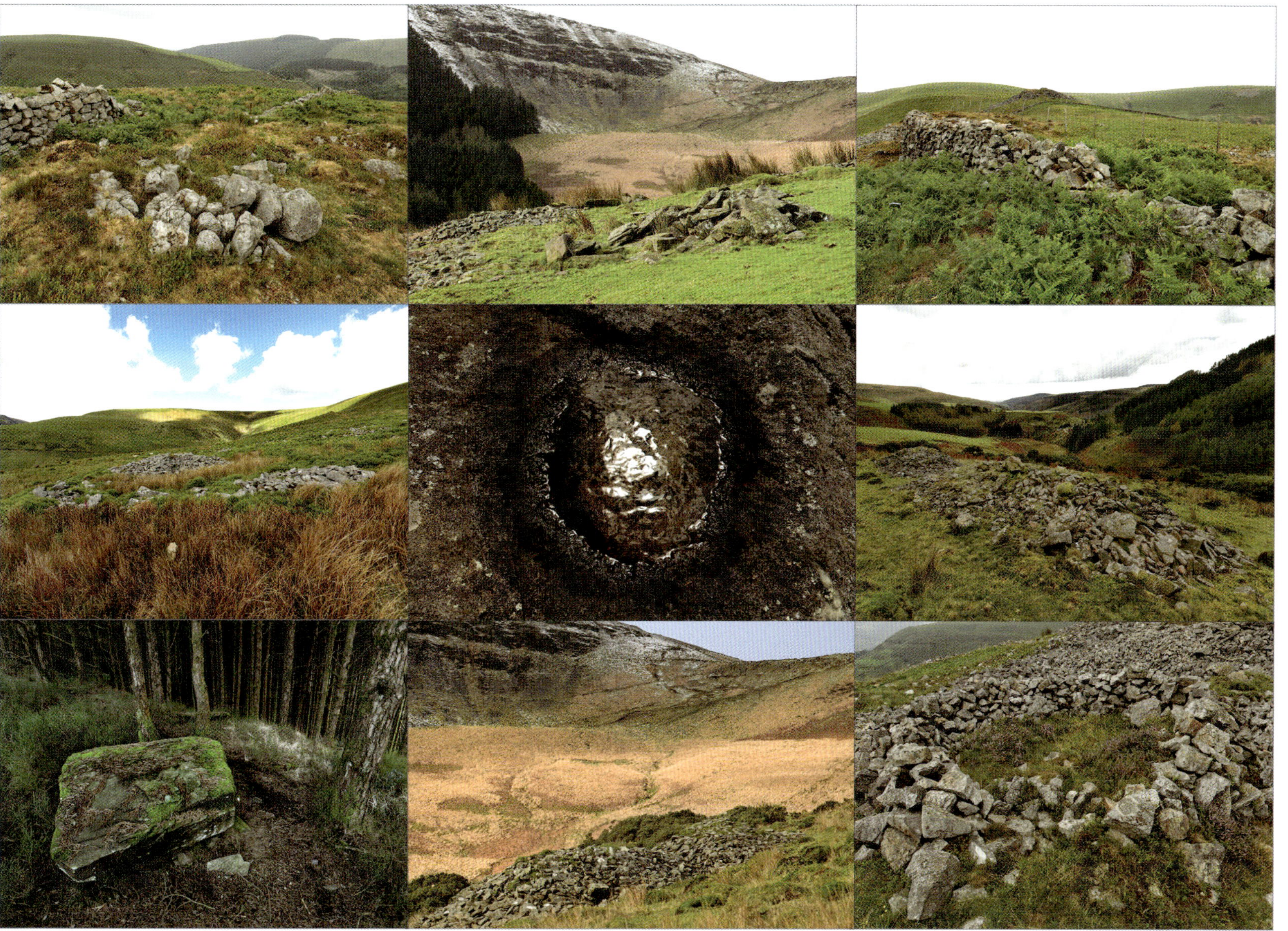

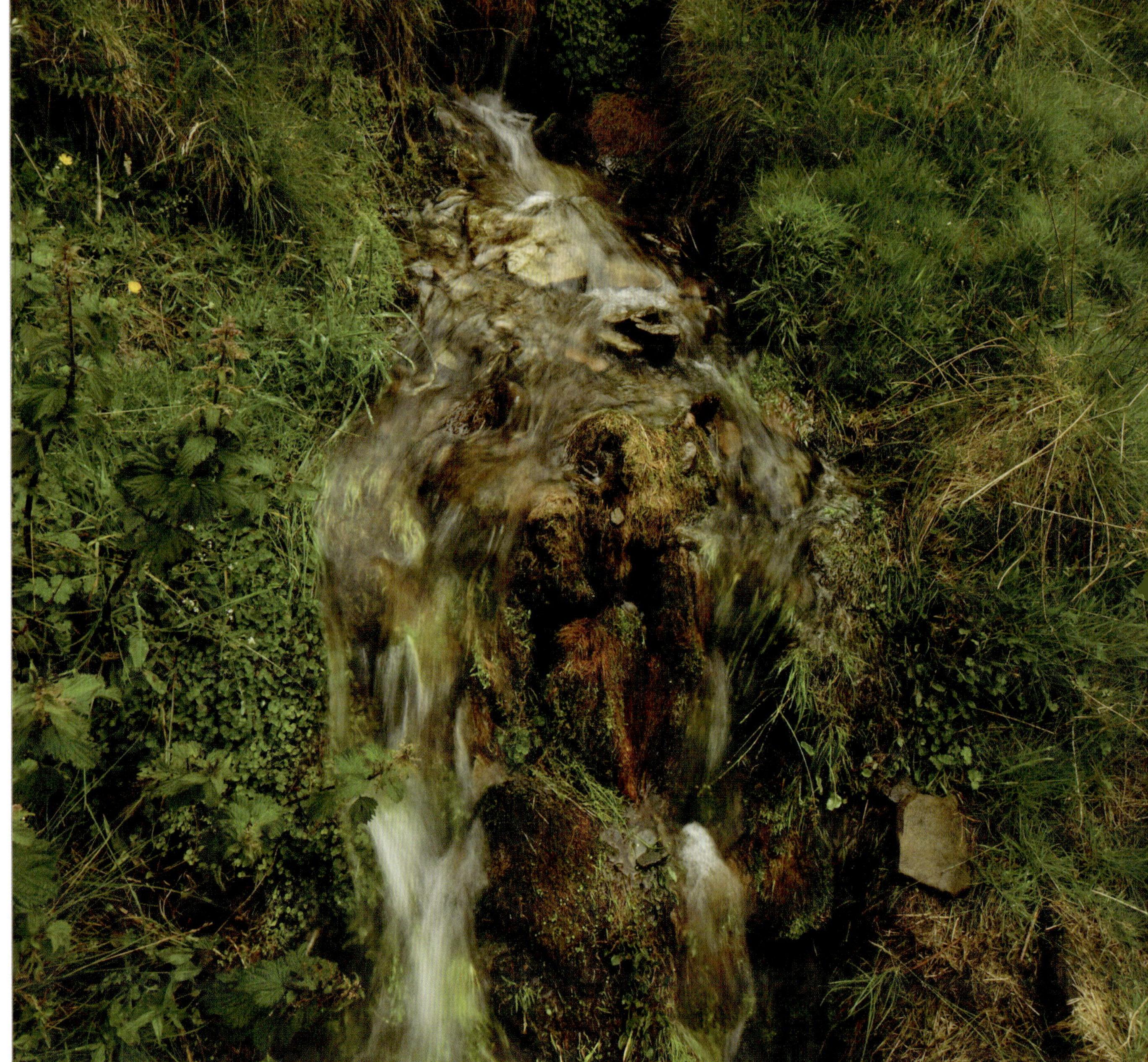

Although I've claimed that it would be impossible to locate the single source of the Garw river, if I was pushed, I'd have to choose this spring, above Carn at the head of the Valley.

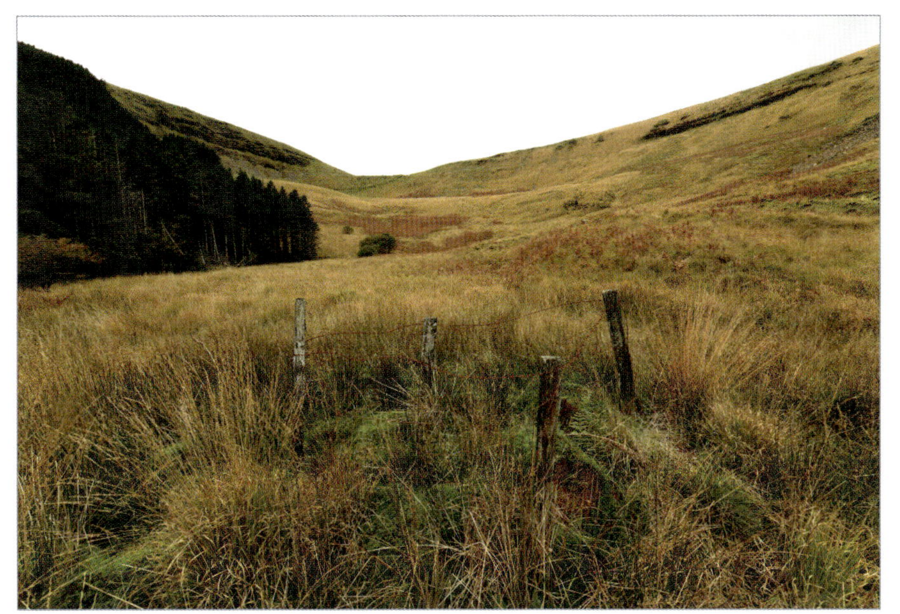 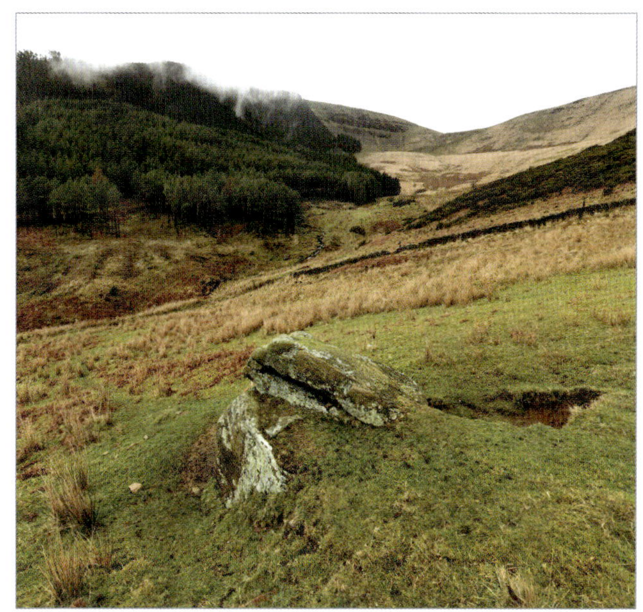

left to right:

another of the springs above Carn,
fenced this time for safety;
and one of my special rocks to
visit, which I have named
the 'Revolution (or Union) Stone'

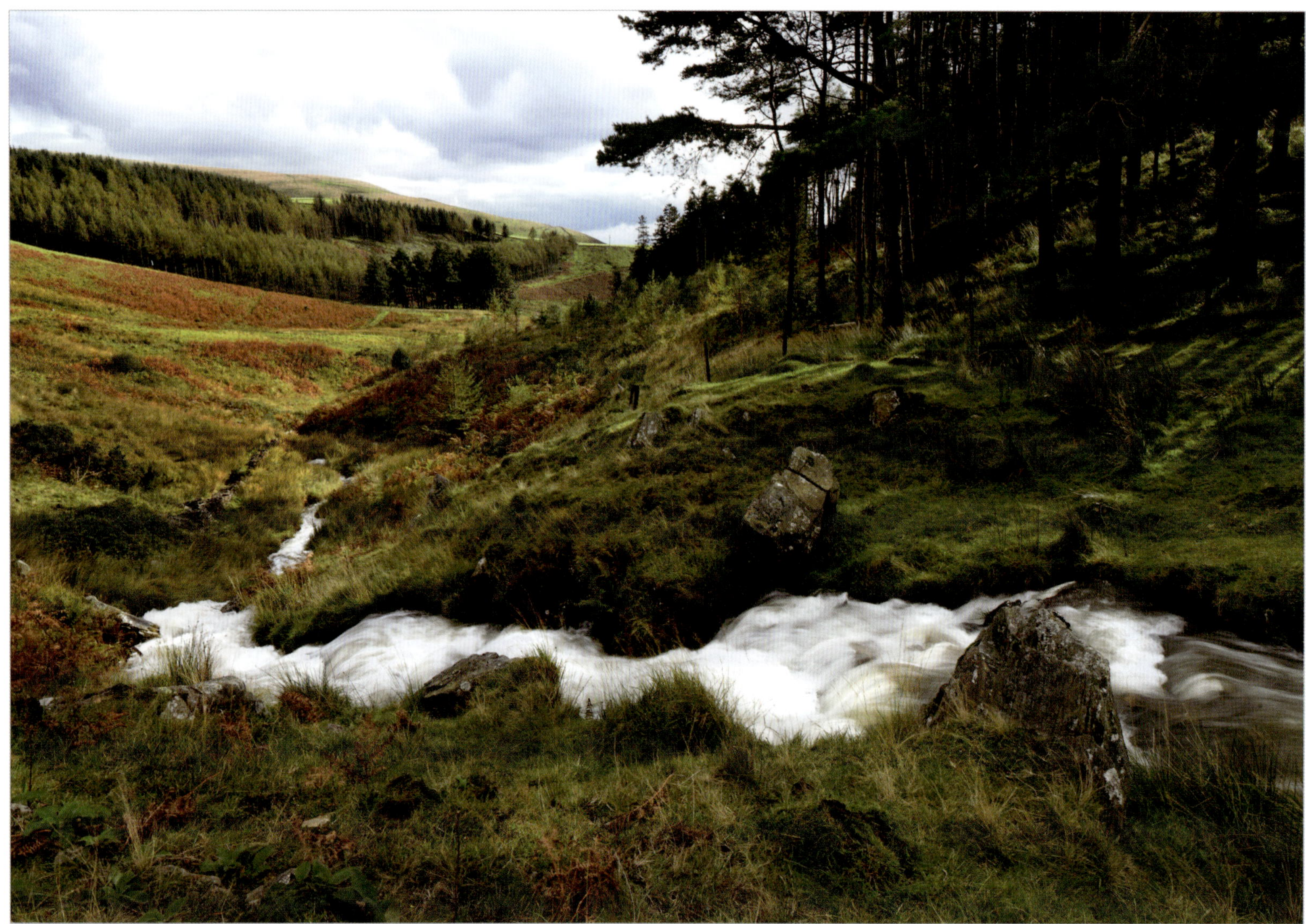

the stream which flows from my favourite source of the Afon Garw,
above Carn

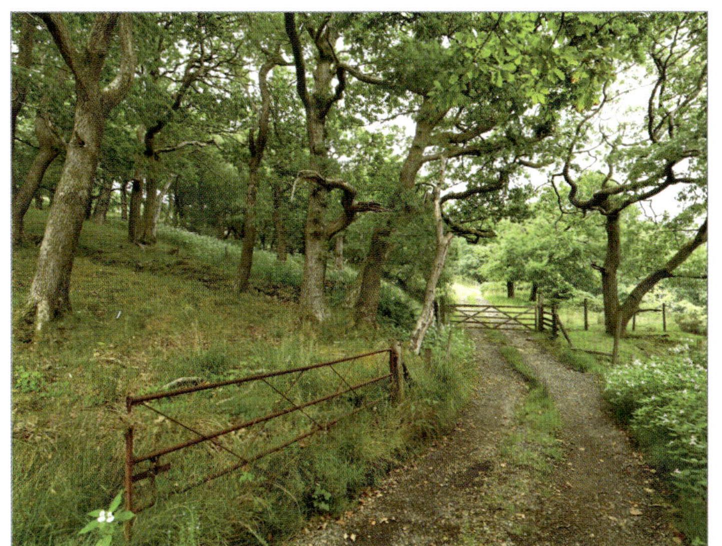
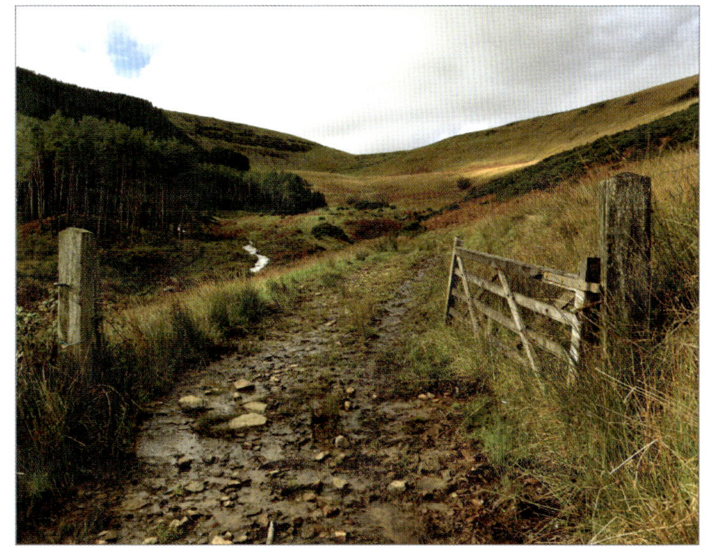
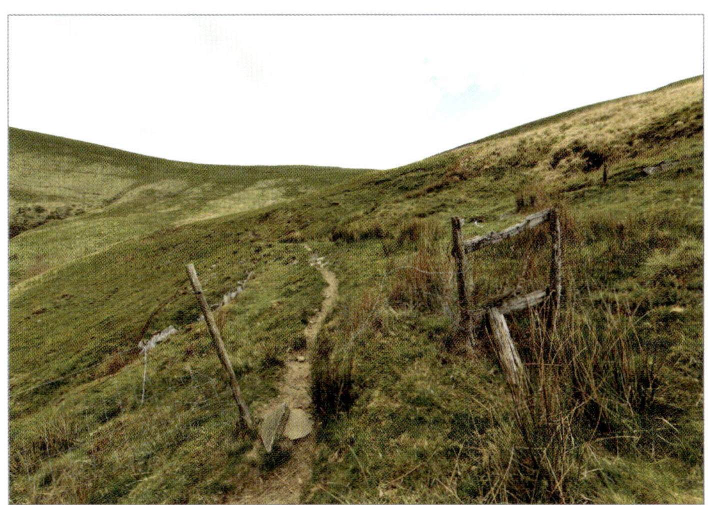
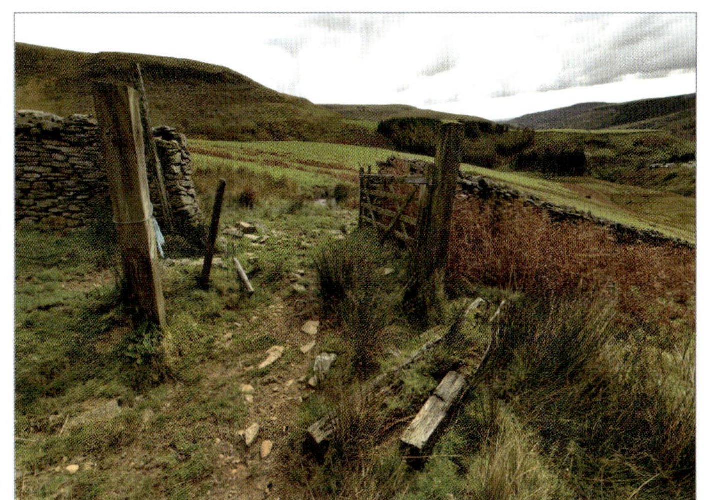

a small selection of farmland gateways and paths
in the upper Garw

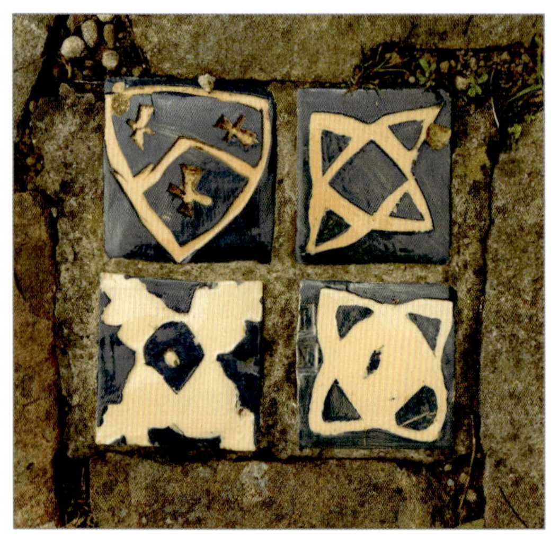

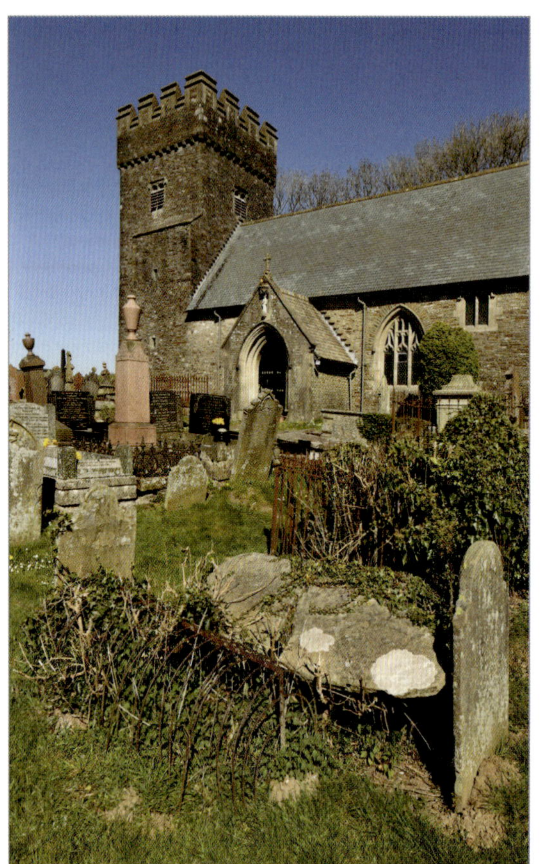

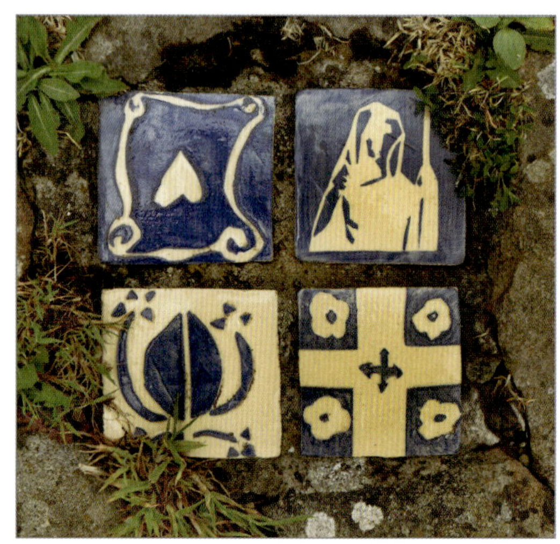

St Cein's Church, Llangeinor,
founded by St Ceinor (or Cein)
in the fifth century:

note the caged grave ...
to prevent the devil from
stealing the body!

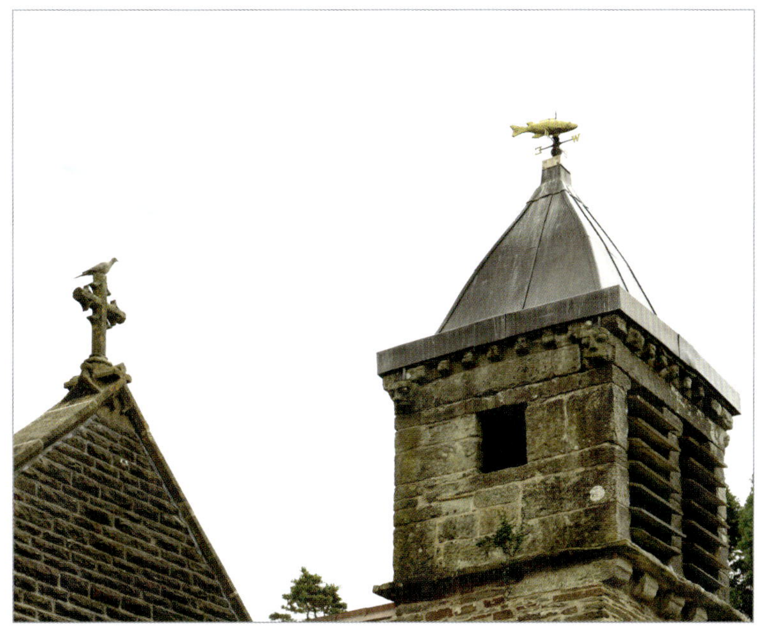

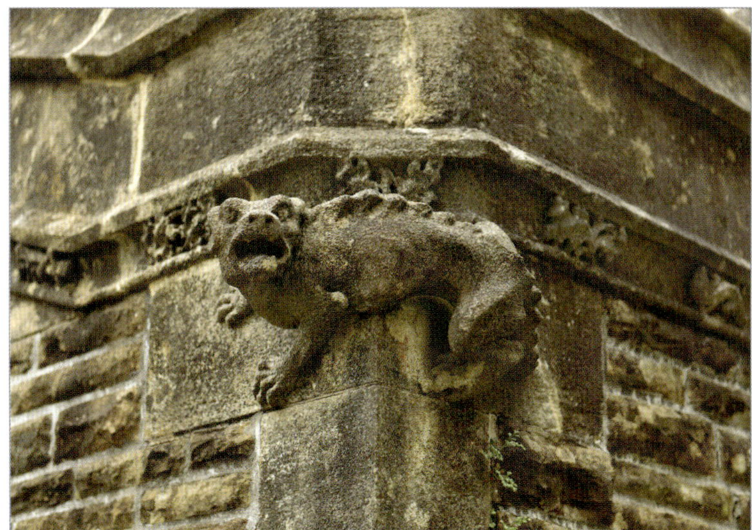

details from
the twelfth century
St David's Church
in Bettws:

note the unusual
fish weather-vane.

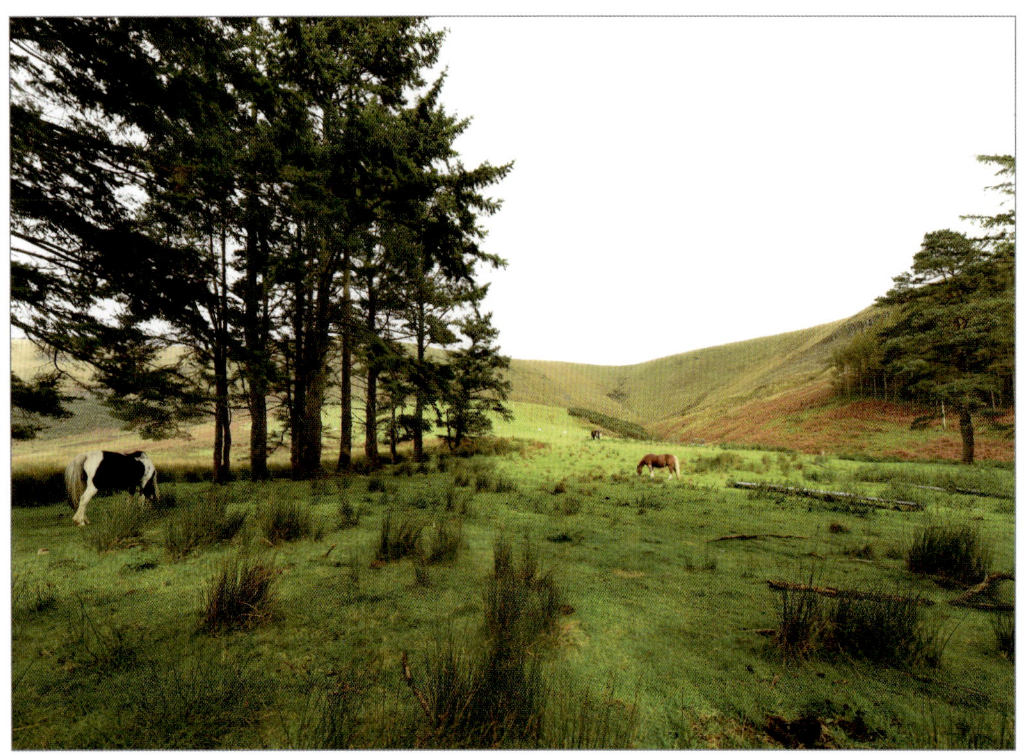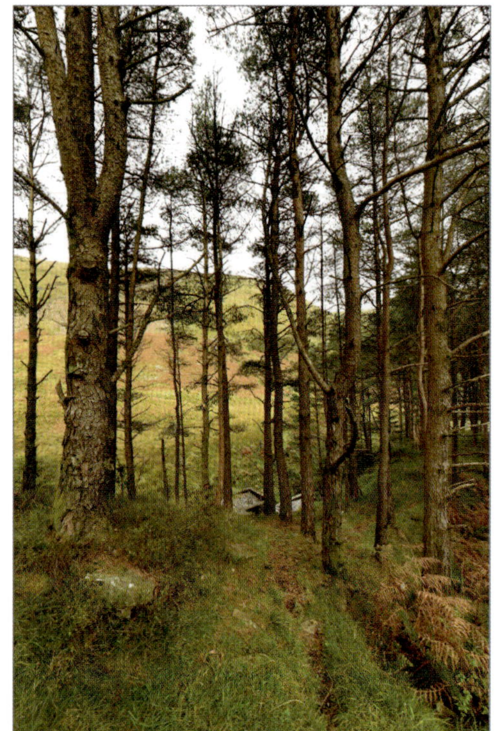

left to right:

the site of the old Carn reservoir;
and the higher three pools reservoir,
viewed through the trees on the forestry path above Carn

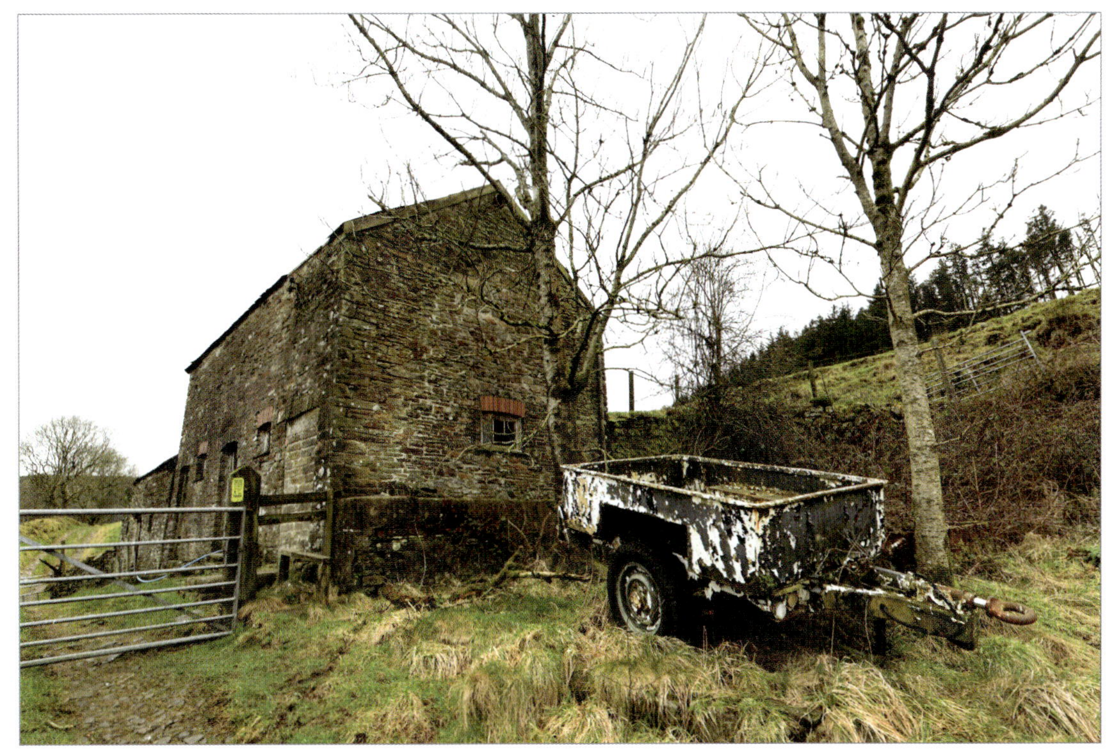

Braichycymer Farm

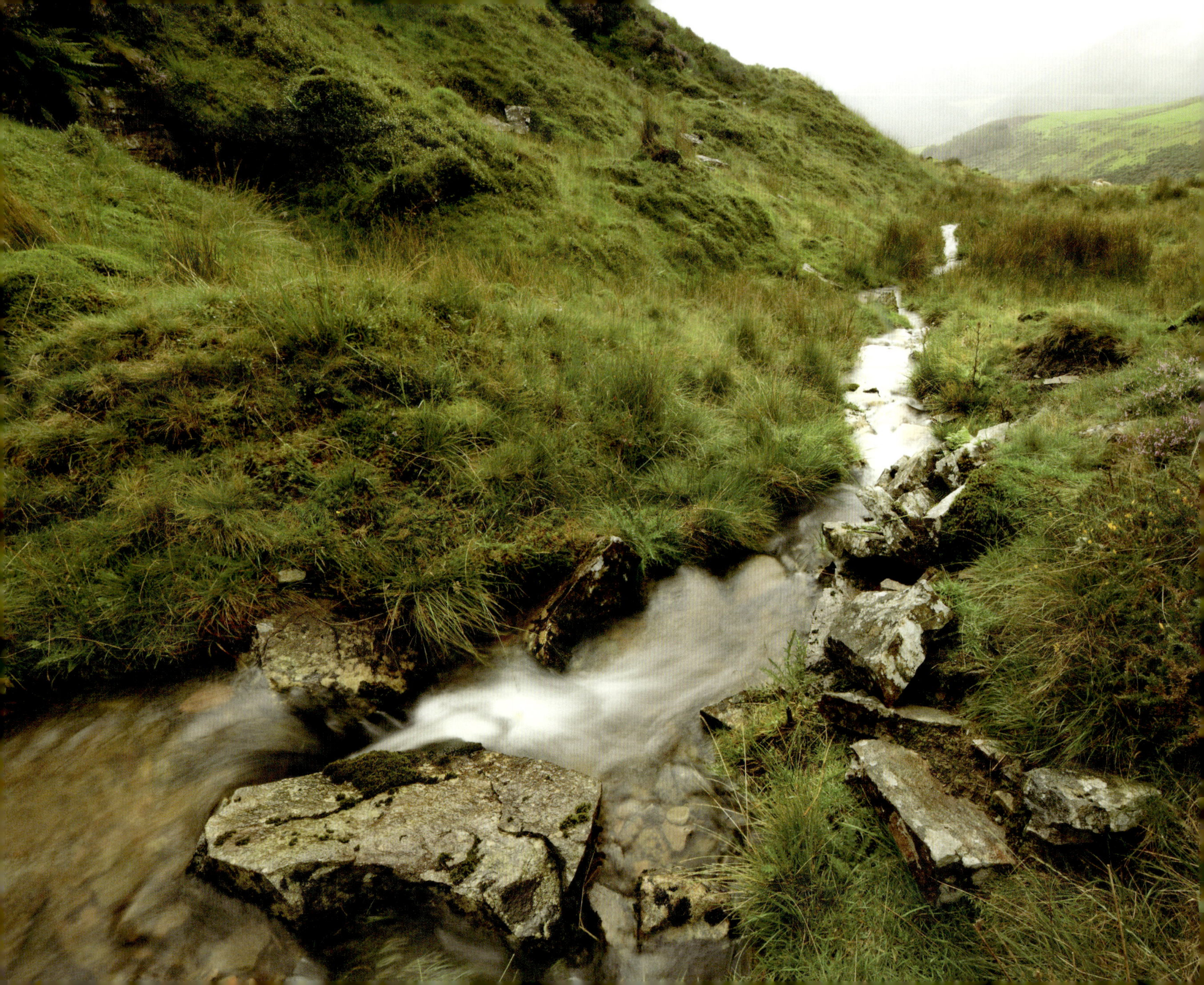

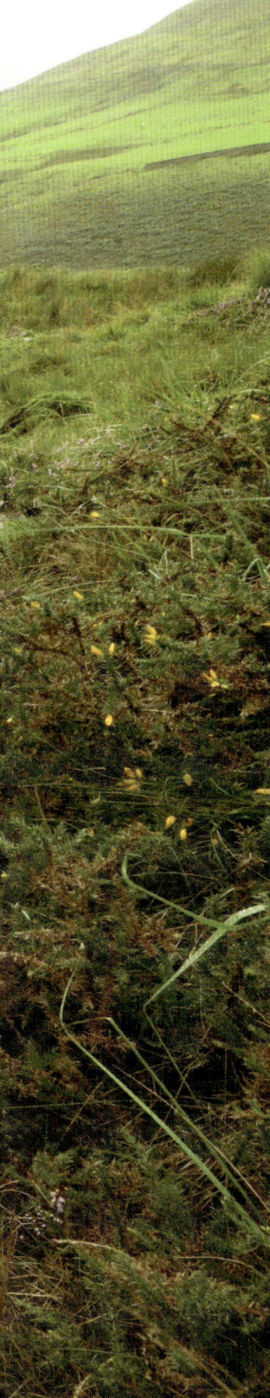

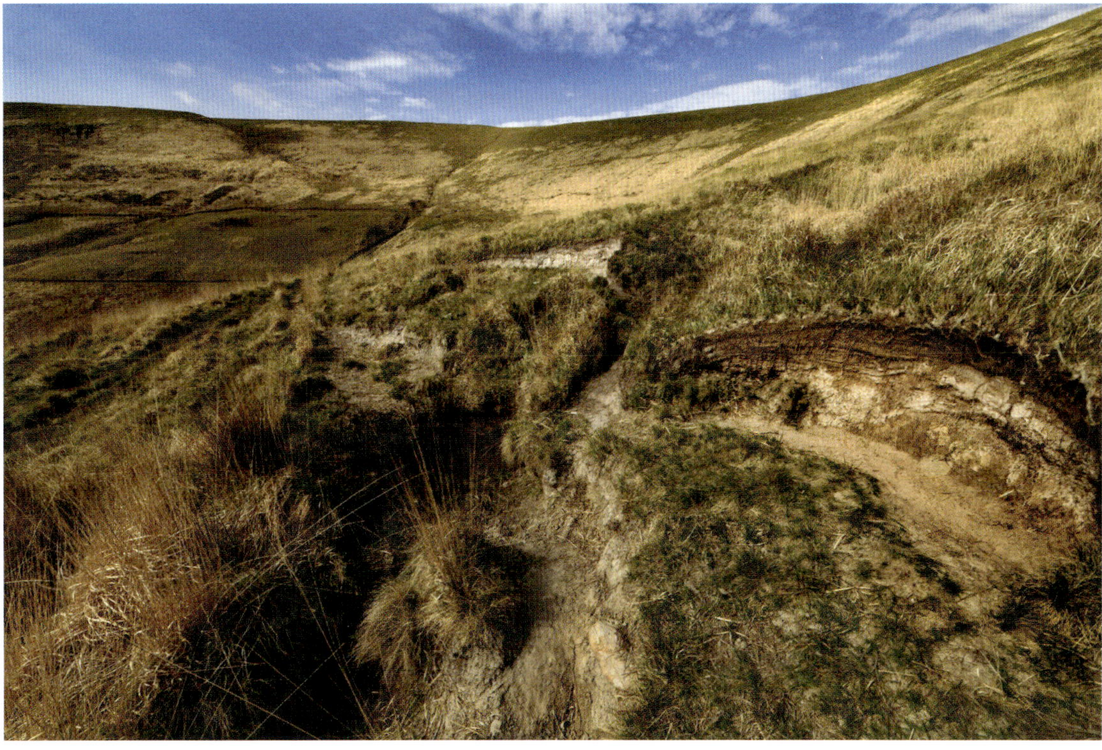

opposite and above:

spring flowing from Llygaid y Ffynhonnau;
and sheep scrape, near the summit
of the Nant Hir valley,
above the site of the Ocean / Garw colliery

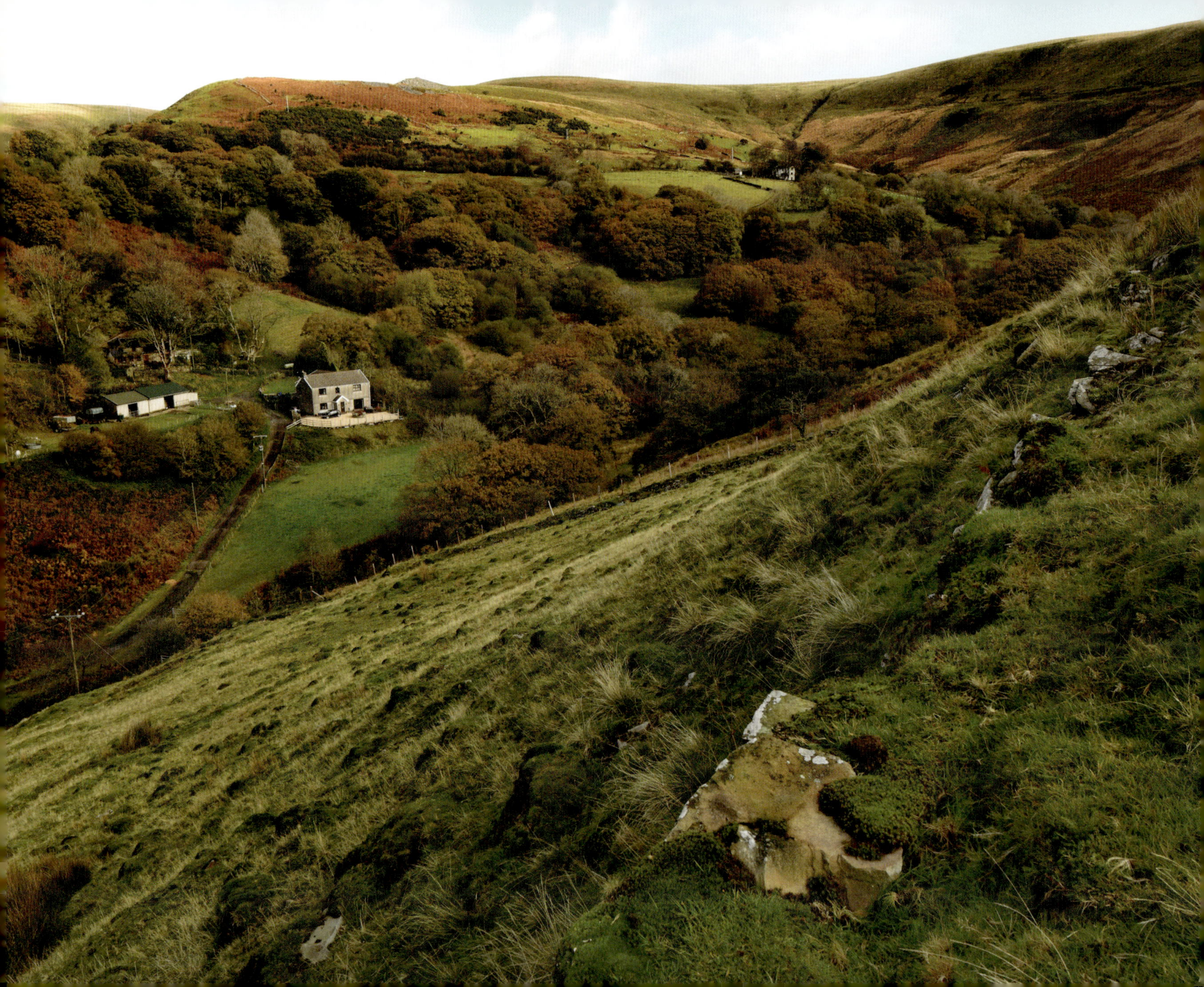

opposite:

Nant Fforchwen, above the village of Pontycymer:

In the years before the serious exploitation of coal, thickly-wooded hills would have supported a handful of small sheep farms (like at Fforchwen).

The Nant Fforchwen brook is best known locally for its crossing point at Forchlas – two railway sleepers stretching between its banks – and for the fact that it was once used to fill Pontycymer's swimming baths, which were closed in the 1970s after a polio scare (and have since been demolished).

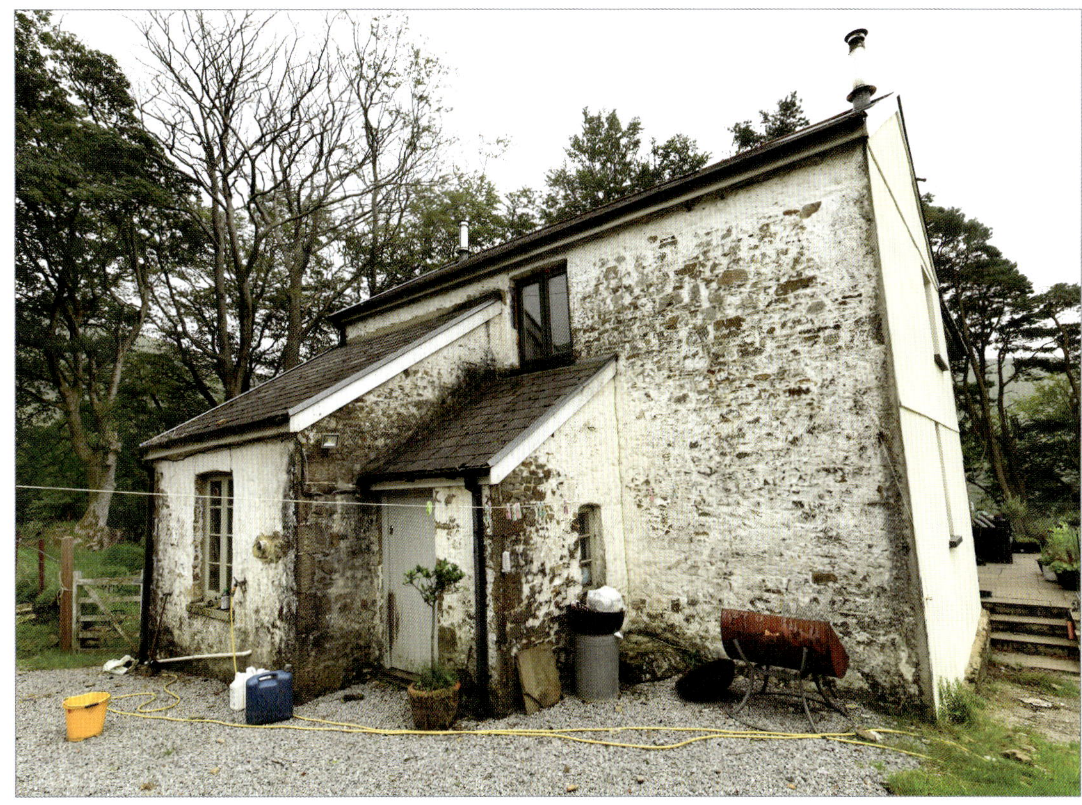

Fforchwen Farm was the subject of a documentary series produced and directed by Eric Styles for BBC Wales in the early 1990s. Entitled *Last Days At Fforchwen*, it told the story of Tom Hopkin, a shepherd here for over 50 years at the point when he was about to give up farming and move to a new house lower down the Valley. Jack Azeratti, the owner of the Station cafe in Pontycymer said of Tom who never married: "the animals took the place of a family".
(All six episodes of *Last Days* are avaible to view on *YouTube*.)

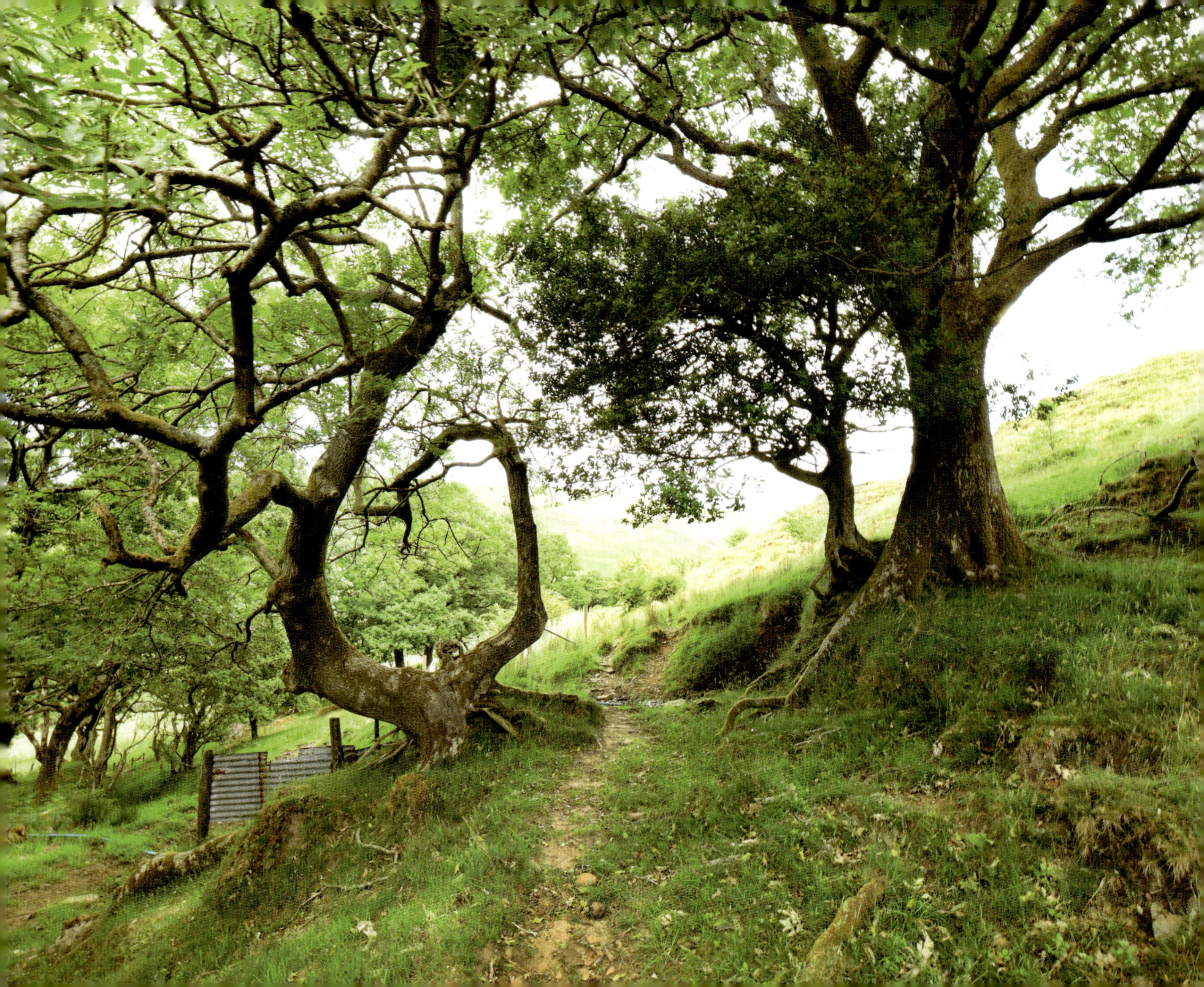

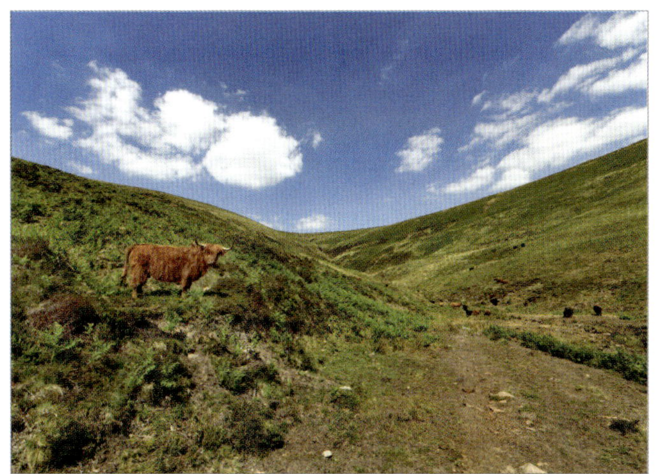

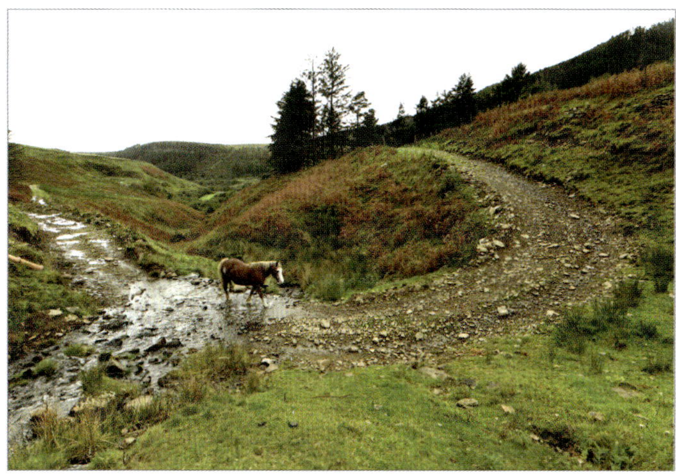

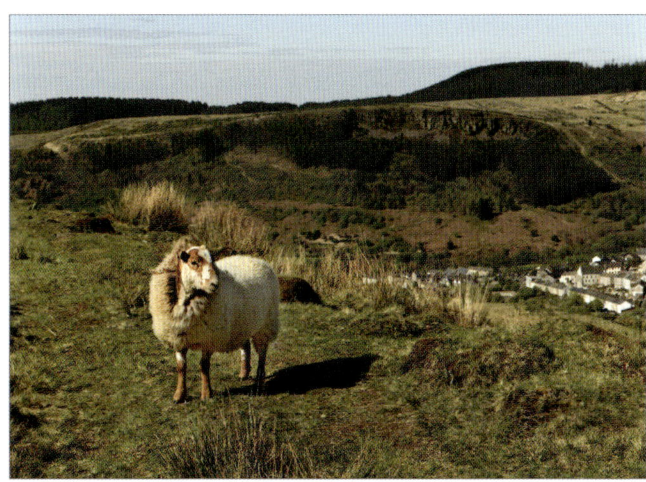

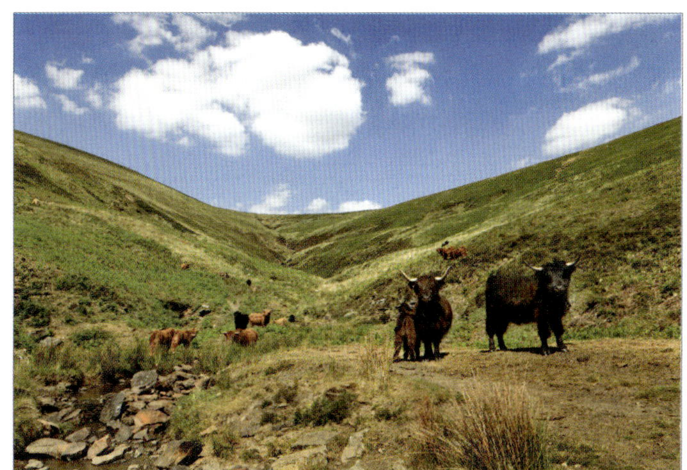

opposite:

Gelli'r-onn farm,
above Gelliron cemetery

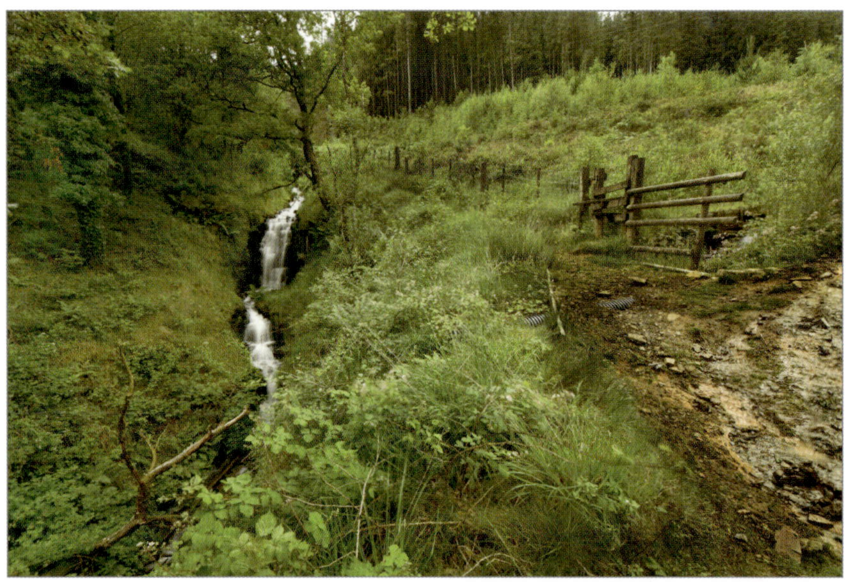

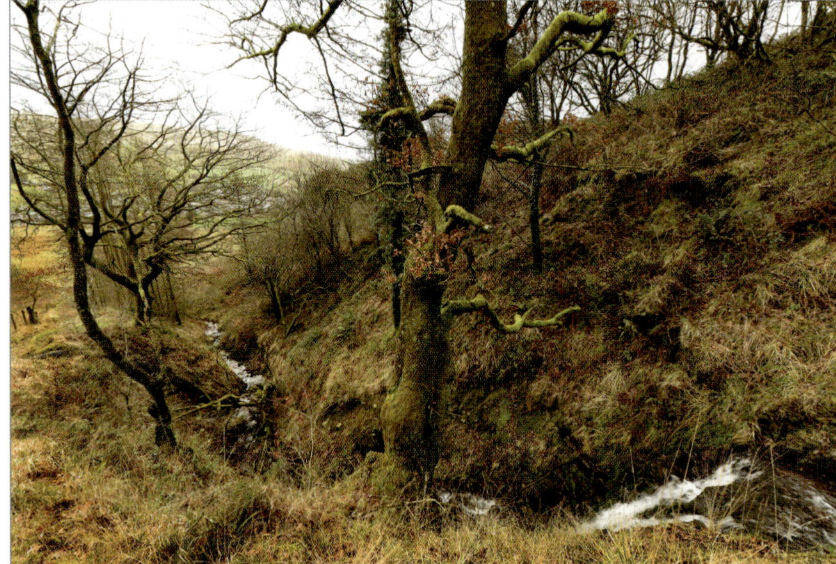

Nant Gwinau:

This brook above Blaengarw is best known in the local area for its impressive waterfall and now defunct reservoir.

The long tradition of farming practised by our earliest ancestors continued in the Garw, largely uninterrupted, for the next four thousand years, up to the mid nineteenth century when the Valley accommodated fewer than a hundred inhabitants.

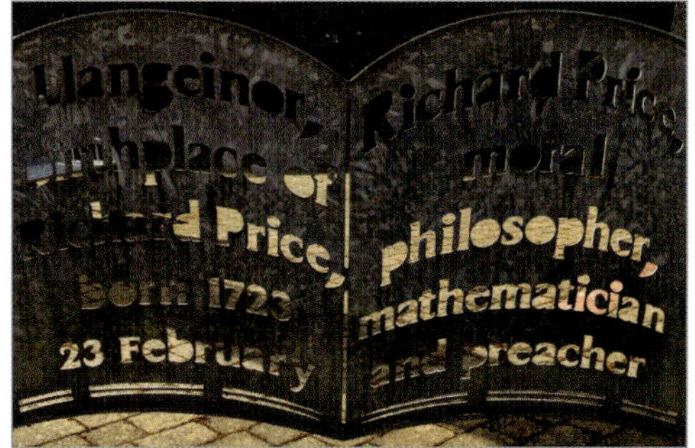

part of the memorial to Dr Richard Price, Llangeinor Square

Though born on a farm in the Garw, our most famous resident was to make his mark not on the soil but in the world of ideas. Richard Price [1723–91] was a political thinker, internationalist, humanist, libertarian writer and philosopher. He was a supporter of the American and French Revolutions, and described by his close friend Benjamin Franklin as "the foremost production of human understanding that this century has afforded us".

His Enlightenment ideas seem as relevant today as they were when developed in the late eighteenth century. He wrote:

A scheme of government may be imagined that shall, by annihilating property and reducing mankind to their natural equality, remove most of the causes of contention and wickedness.

from *Four Dissertations*, 1772

And these words, taken from his *Discourse on the Love of our Country*, published in 1790, offer an albeit overly-optimistic commentary on both his times as well as the struggles the Valley of his birth was to face less than a hundred years after his death:

Take warning all ye supporters of slavish governments and slavish hierarchies! …

You cannot now hold the world in darkness. Struggle no longer against increasing light and liberality.

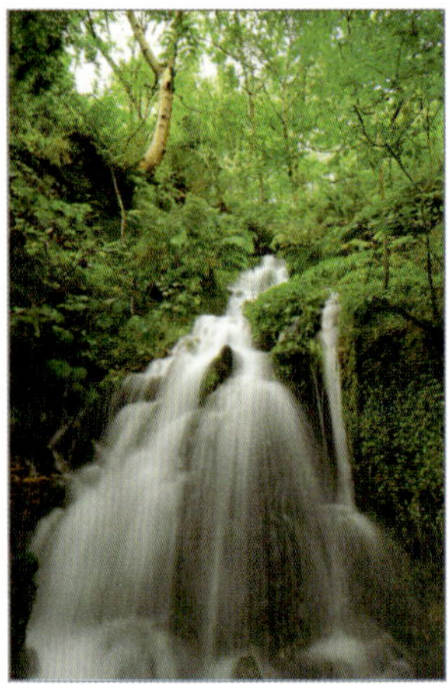

The Garw Valley was,
and still is, a land of
springs, streams,
rivers and waterfalls.

I've learned that,
after rain, you need to wait
two days for a waterfall
or well's fullest response,
following their often-
lengthy underground
journeys before sufficient
pressure releases their
erupting power.

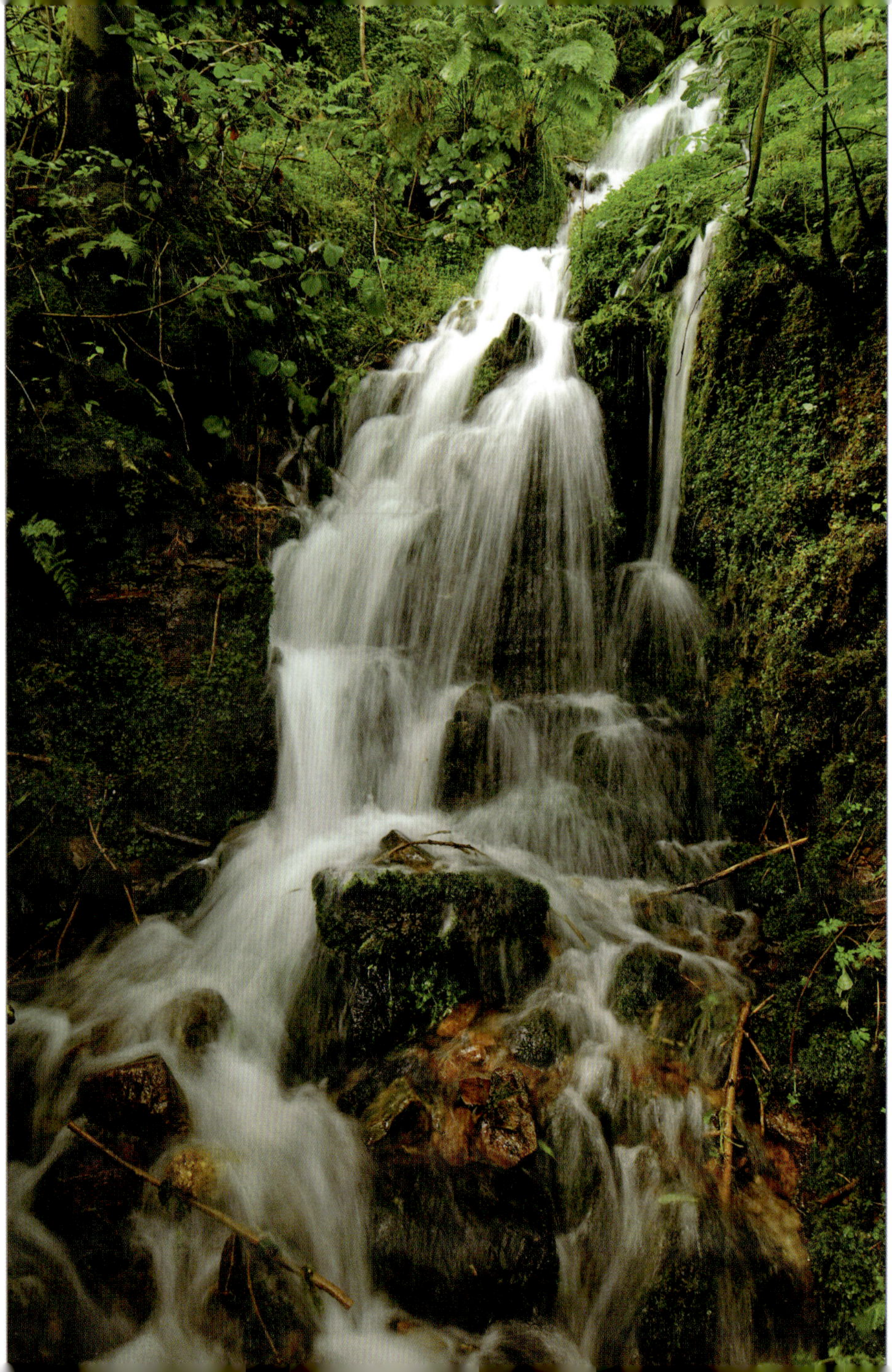

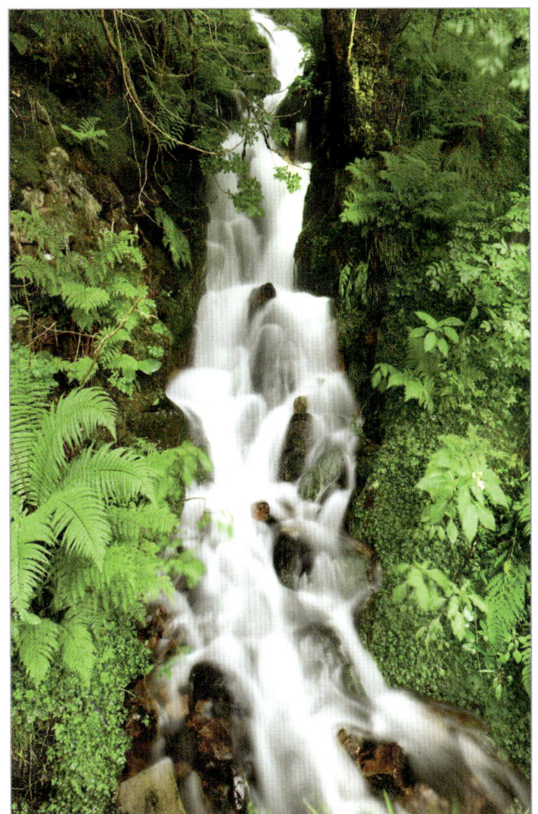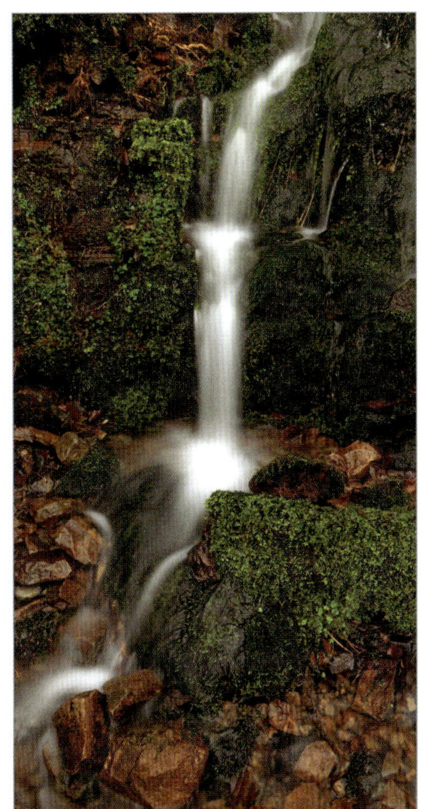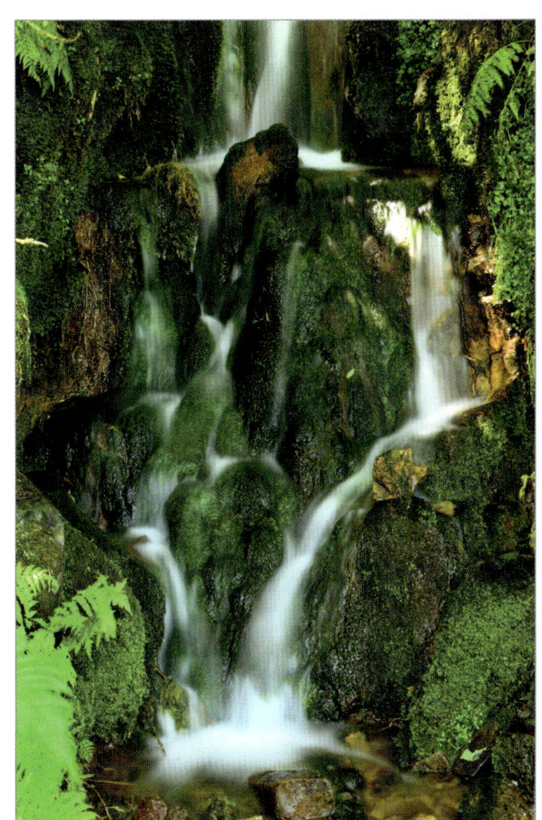

opposite and above:
The waterfalls of Sweetwells near Pontyrhyl
supplied drinking water for many years
to this part of the Valley.

Cwm Garw Fechan,
above the village
of Pontyrhyl:

This small valley with
its narrow river, wooden
footbridge and impres-
sive waterfall was once
a picturesque nature
reserve, though today a
combination of neglect
and industrialised
forestry mean that its
charms are less easy –
though, with a few
scrambles, not
impossible – to find.

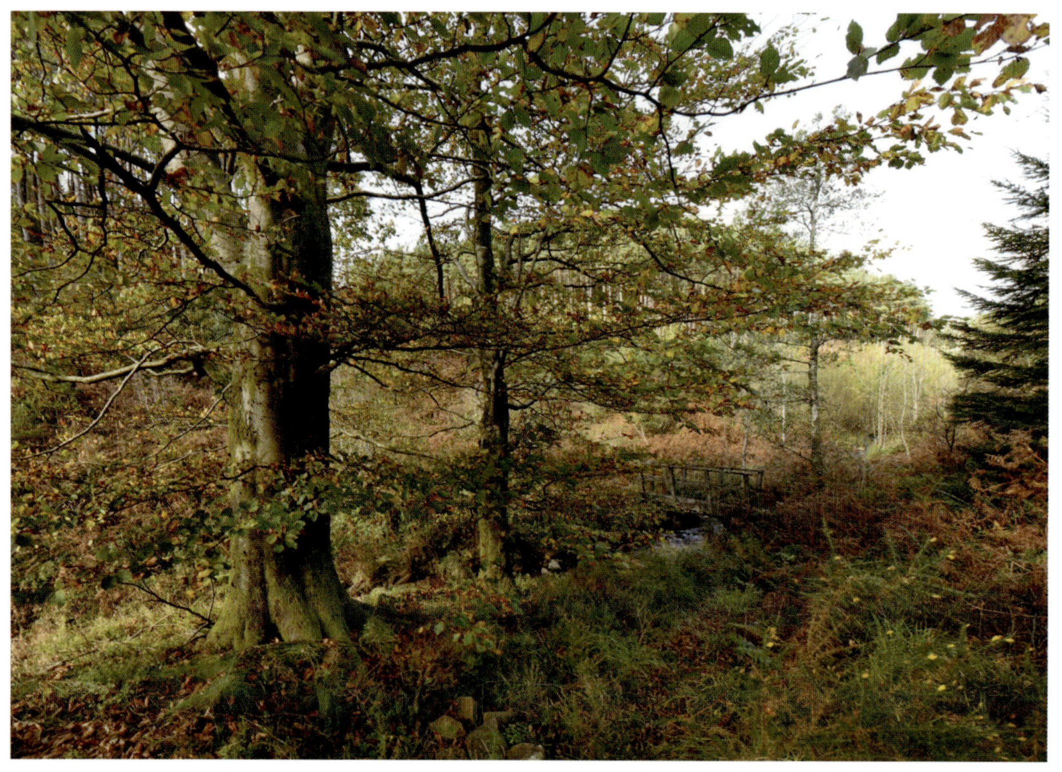

opposite:

Cwm Garw Fechan
falls

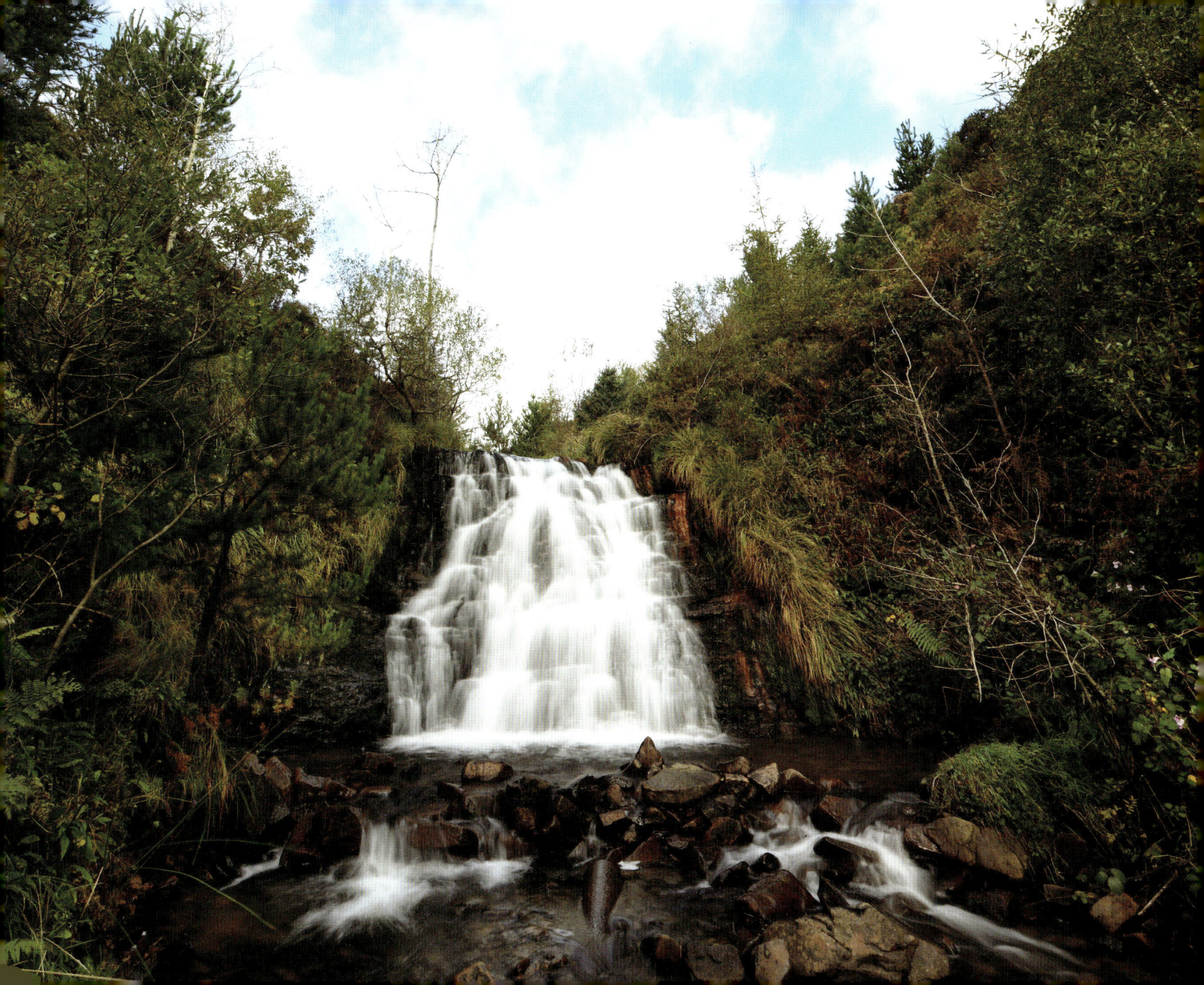

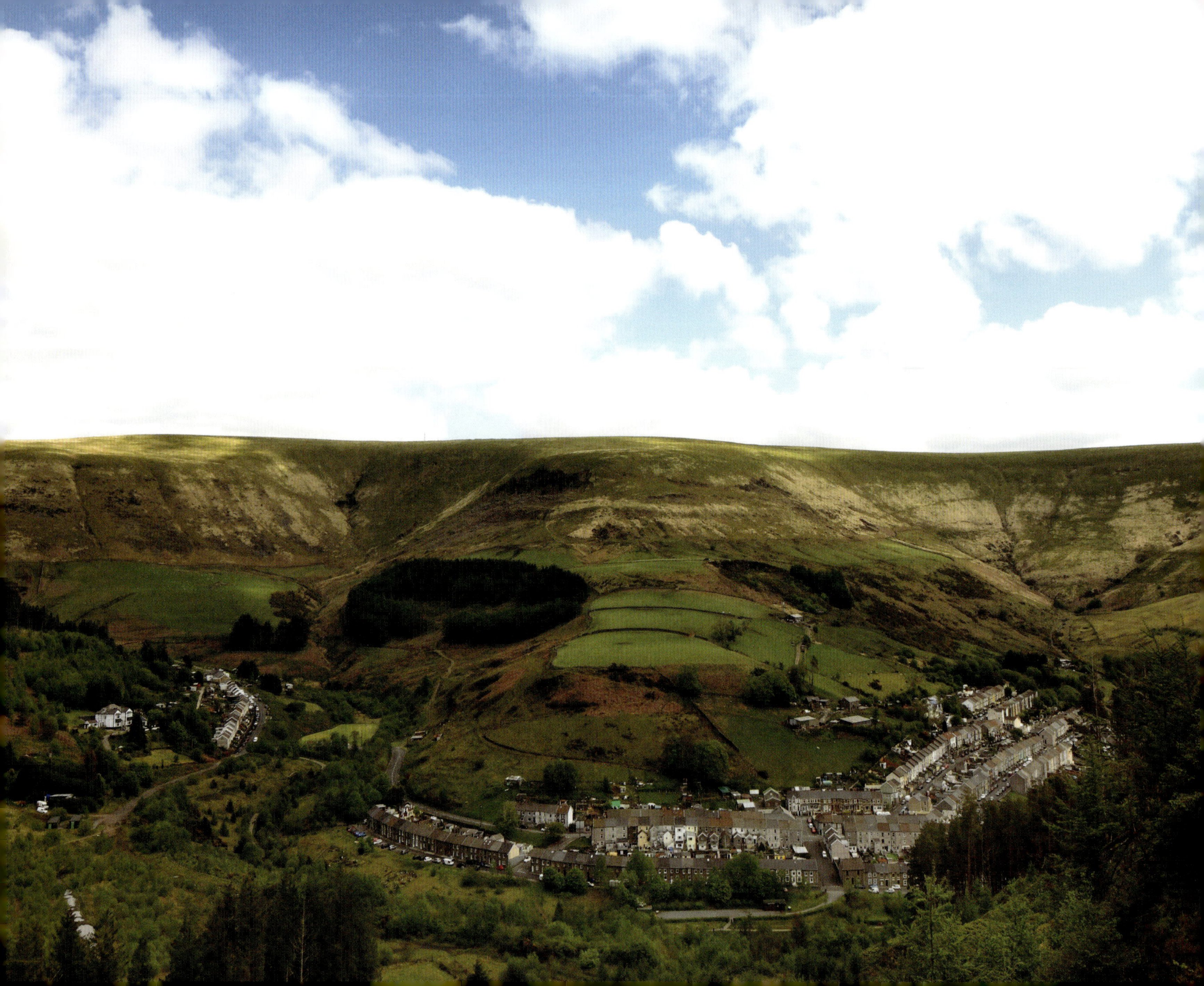

A BRIEF HISTORY OF MINING:
comradeship and suffocation *

* from the poem *Heritage* by Dannie Abse

Carn and upper Blaengarw:

The distinctive style of Valleys' terraced housing was dictated by the contours of the land.

Although digging for coal had been practised on a subsistence level for millennia, with evidence of mining by local monks cutting into the sides of the hills to heat their churches, alongside the numerous signs still to be found of early domestic 'levels', it was not until the nineteenth century that our hunt for this 'black gold' was raised to a hellish scale.

In 1851, the Valley had just 78 inhabitants, all engaged in farming. Their peace was soon to be shattered, however, by the quest for coal to fuel the world's first Industrial Revolution.

In 1865, a party of 'sinkers' working for the Ffaldau Coal Company arrived to establish the first pit in the Garw, and during the following years, thousands of men and their families poured into the area, speeded by the laying of the Garw Valley railway line from Bryn-menyn in 1872, and the building of hundreds of homes in which to shelter them.

By 1891, in excess of 6,000 people were crowded into the upper reaches of the Garw, coming from throughout Wales and beyond, a large town's worth of people crammed into a narrow rural valley … and this number was to more than double by the end of that decade. Pits sprang up at the places where coal was easiest to reach, and schools, churches, shops, pubs and workmen's halls and institutes were built.

The Valley's once-rich flora was trampled, its fauna mostly expelled, and its fish stock choked in a soup of chemicals and coal dust.

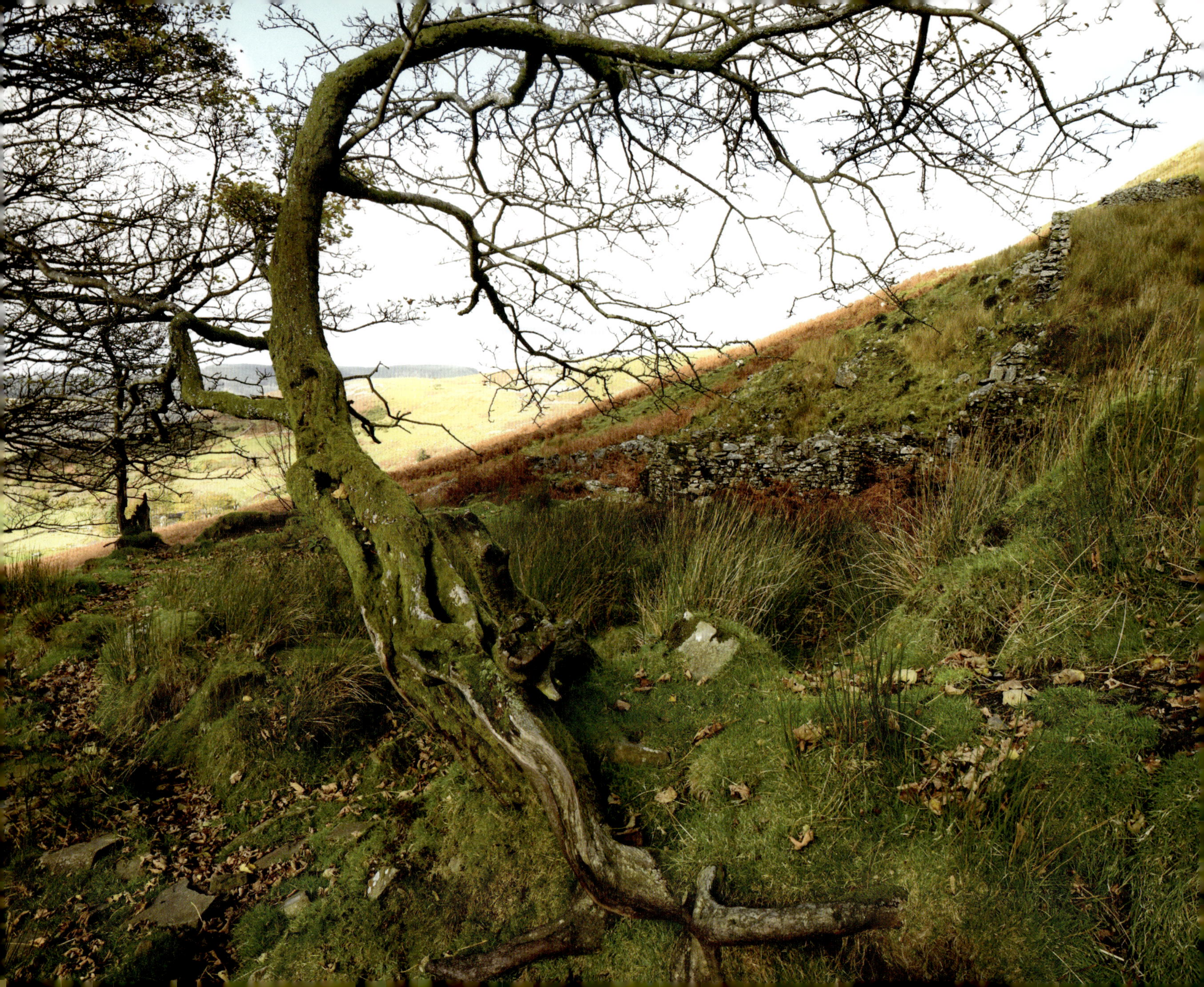

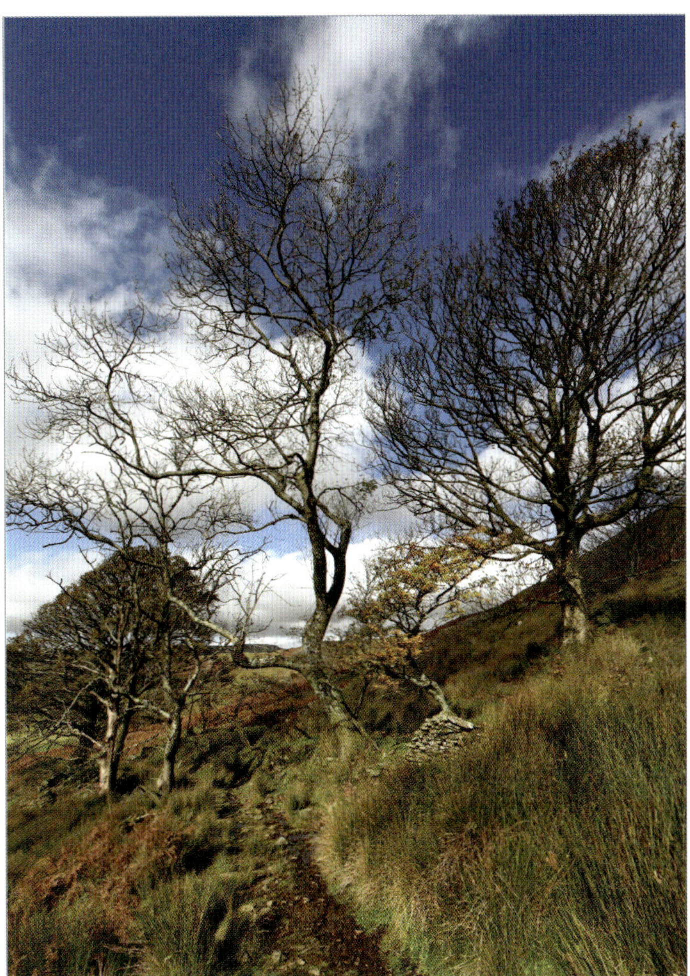

During the early days of coalmining, the Valley resembled a frontier settlement, with few facilities for its workers.

The miners who sank the earliest pits or drove the 'slants' were accommodated in two wooden huts on the banks of the Gelliron stream, or here, high above Nant Fforchwen.

Mine owners rarely built houses for their workers until coal extraction had been guaranteed.

Calculating the number of pits in the Garw Valley depends upon your definition of a 'pit'.

Using local historian Dr Wyn Price OBE as my guide (in this and much else), and distinguishing between the deep pits which produced huge quantities of steam coal and those smaller undertakings (known as 'slants', 'drifts' or 'adits') dug for house coal, we can be confident that there were six, or perhaps even seven, deep mines here: the Ffaldau, the Braichycymer (later to become an extension of the Ffaldau), and possibly the much lesser-known 'House Coal Pit', all in Pontycymer; the International and the Garw (or Ocean) in Blaengarw; and the Lluest No.1 and the ill-fated Lluest No.3 in Pontyrhyl.

In addition, there were five drift mines in the upper Valley: in Pontycymer, the Victoria (which later also became an extension of the Ffaldau); the Darran Fawr and the Glengarw, in Blaengarw; the Duchy No.3, in Pantygog; and the New Braichycymer, in the Garw Fechan; as well as four others in the lower Valley (the Cedfyn-Rhondda, Butcher's Main Slant and Gwern Llwyn, in Bettws; and the Bryn-y-Wrach, in Llangeinor). *

Men often walked miles to their places of work, to sometimes be faced by a further two-mile trek underground which could take another two hours before they arrived at their stalls. Originally cutting by hand with pick-axes, they worked eight hour shifts, six days a week, some seams being no more than two feet nine inches high, the coal having to be won by lying sideways or on their stomachs, often in half a foot of water, with the constant fear of a roof fall.

This was the time of the fiction of early promises, when the uncomfortable compromise between the necessities of finding paid work to feed and house your family ... and of safety – economics versus well-being, replicated for many now during Covid-19 – opened the floodgates to human danger and to the despoliation of the land.

The coal industry throughout South Wales thrived, making huge profits for its owners, though not without tragedy for its workers. Mining was a dangerous occupation especially in its early days, a significant number of men being lost to coal's exacting extraction each and every year.

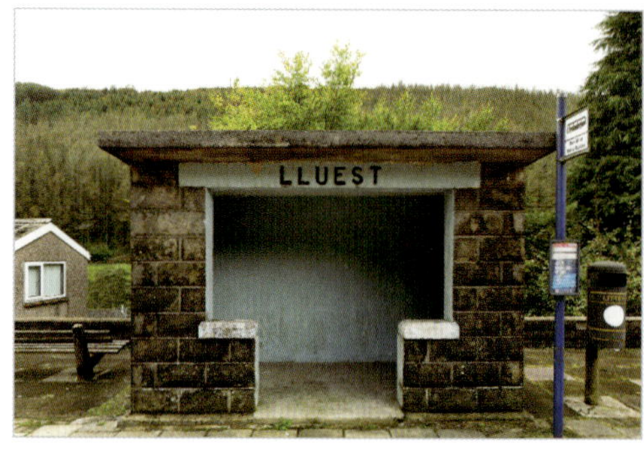

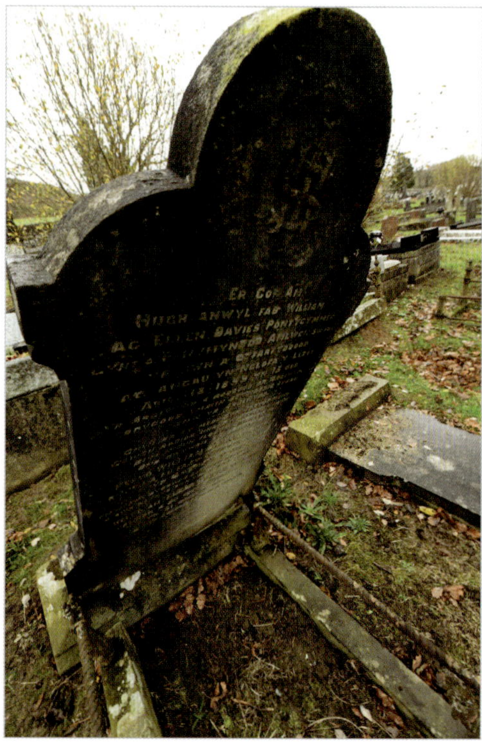

* based on information from NCB records, 1976, held at the Glamorgan Records Office

And for those who avoided the explosions and the regular rock falls, there were the lingering horrors of silicosis and pneumoconiosis:

Ted, my other brother, died full of pneumoconiosis, chock-a-block he was. He didn't have a bit of wind, he was full of it. Ted was young; forty-two he was when he died, and he left six or seven kids. Nothing for it, no compensation then, see.
William Gibson
from *The Valleys Autobiography: a people's history of the Garw, Llynfi and Ogmore valleys*, Valley & Vale, 1992

They had to chip his lungs. They were like solid stone. Chip his lungs to take the samples.
Jill John
from *The Valleys Autobiography*

The Garw, as one of the smallest of South Wales' coalmining valleys, never experienced disasters comparable in terms of the losses of life to places like Cilfynydd (where 276 men were killed in 1894), the Universal colliery, Senghenydd (with 439 dead in 1913), and Aberfan, where 116 children and 28 adults were buried beneath the colliery spoil tip which engulfed the village school in 1966.

But, two hours after midnight on Friday 19 August 1899, nineteen men and boys were killed in an explosion that devastated the Lluest No.3 colliery. An accumulation of gas had been ignited by a naked flame, in what the *Western Mail* described as a "baptism of fire".

It was 'fortunate' that the blast occurred during the early hours of the morning before the dayshift had arrived, when a much larger number of workers would have been present.

It was nothing to see two or three funerals a week, see 'em walking down, carrying the coffin … well, it was part of our living.
Louis Thomas
from *The Valleys Autobiography*

… boys that were killed had nothing … a horse was valued at fifty pounds but the boy was not valued at all.
Bryn Price
from *The Valleys Autobiography*

opposite:

The Welsh inscription on this gravestone in the Gelliron Cemetery in Pontycymer translates as:

IN MEMORY OF HUGH,
LOVING SON OF WILLIAM AND
ELLEN DAVIES, PONTYCYMER,
RECENTLY FROM
PENYMYNYDD AMLWCH,
WHO MET HIS DEATH IN
THE LLEST [sic.] COAL MINE
ON AUGUST 18TH
AT THE AGE OF 13.

The minimum age for going underground at that time was 14.

In the same disaster, Abendego Williams was horribly mutilated on just his second day underground, after returning home from Philadelphia because he felt mining conditions in the USA were too dangerous.

William Williams, another Lluest colliery survivor, was known after the tragedy as Billy 'One Arm'.

And as for the women, for most there were few options beyond the role of housewife:

… if the girls didn't have no alternative, it was to 'domestic service' … I went to London. I was fourteen and a fortnight.
Gwennie Ley Jones
from *The Valleys Autobiography*

… it was 'slavery' … for nothing, because your wage was nothing, terrible, doing all the donkey work, the dirty work. You'd have six shillings a week if you were lucky. You had to live in, you'd be there at their beck and call.
Gwyneth Fricker
from *The Valleys Autobiography*

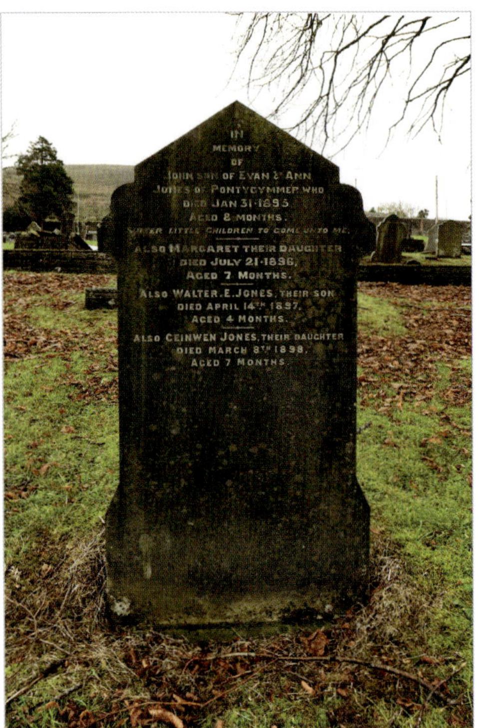

This gravestone in Gelliron cemetery illustrates the harsh realities of the early days of coalmining, the Jones family losing their son John aged 8 months in 1895, daughter Margaret aged 7 months in 1896, another son Walter aged 4 months in 1897, and another daughter Ceinwen aged 7 months in 1898.

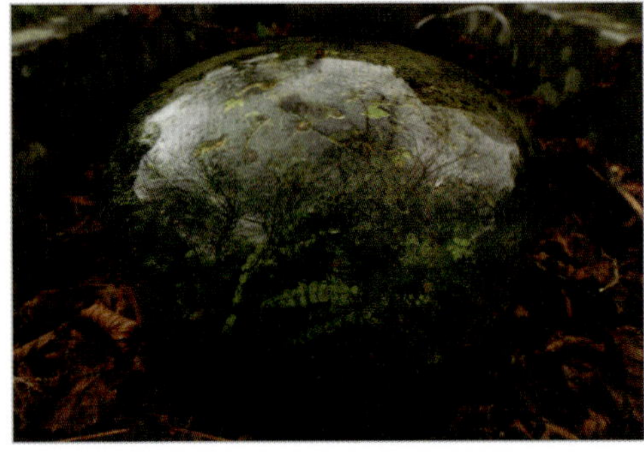

opposite:
Tabernacle Welsh Congregationalist Chapel, Meadow Street / Alexandra Road, Pontycymer

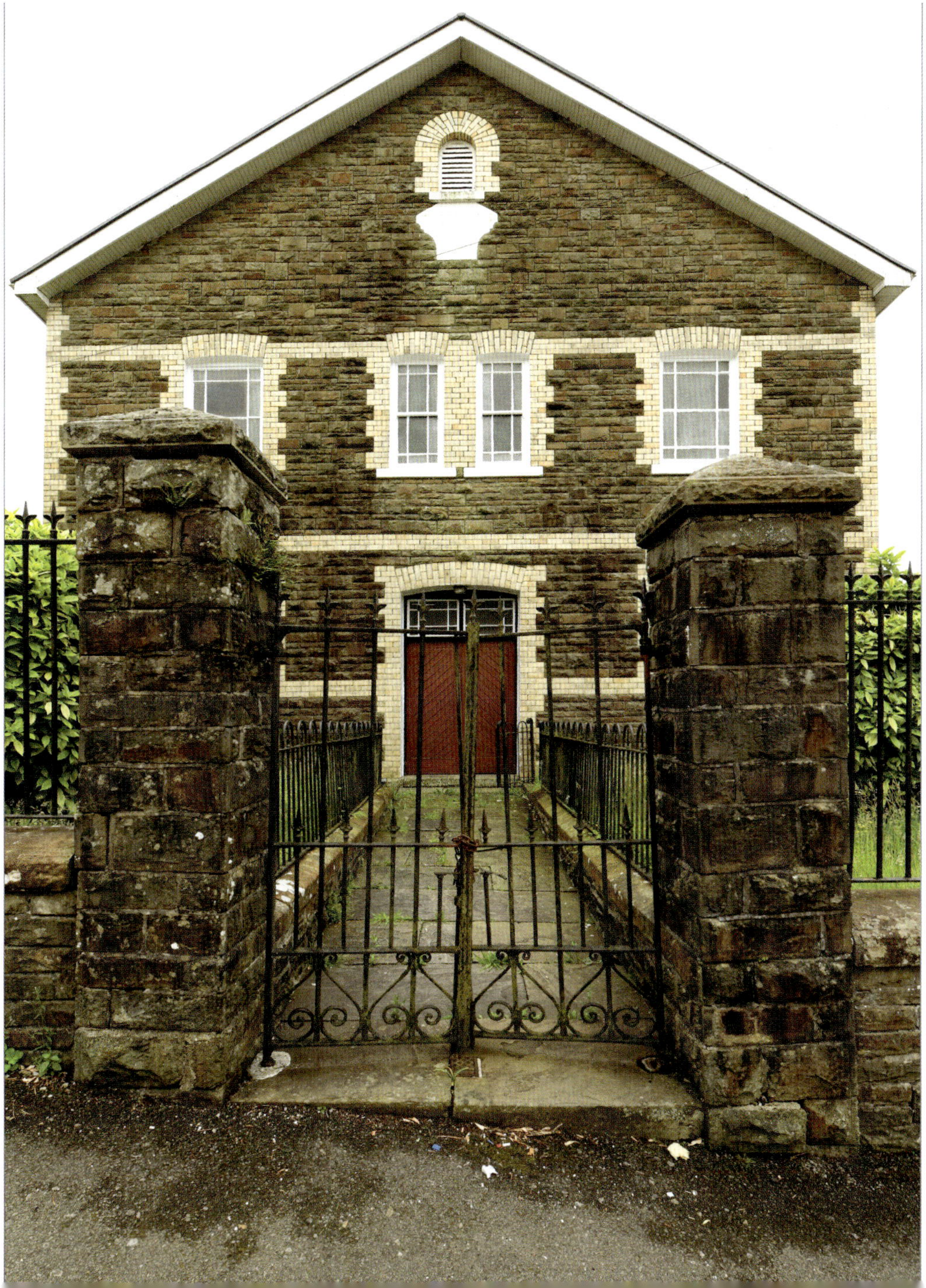

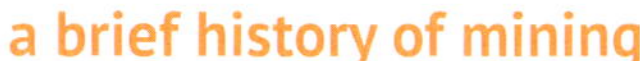

Churches of every denomination played a central part in Valley life, offering a temporary spiritual escape from these harsh realities. The chapel was the meeting place at which to explore the bigger questions of faith and morality and, much too often, to say a final goodbye to loved ones taken too soon by coal.

Religious fervour reached its peak during the great evangelist Evan Roberts' 1904 'Revival'. On his three-day visit to Pontycymer, *'the Welsh Wesley'* was said to have eaten very little food and only slept for one hour.

In the words of Merlin Madog:

"Drunks, blaggards, vagabonds and ladies with children out of wedlock attended religious gatherings, confessed their sins and asked God for forgiveness."
from *Whilst The Valley Sang 1900-1914*, 2009

By 1909, however, the numbers of churchgoers had returned to pre-Roberts' levels, the men in particular reverting in droves back to their previous life-styles of hard and dangerous work, pub and tobacco.

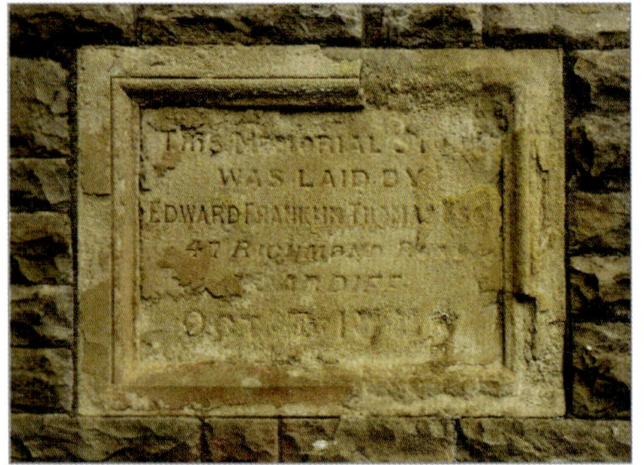

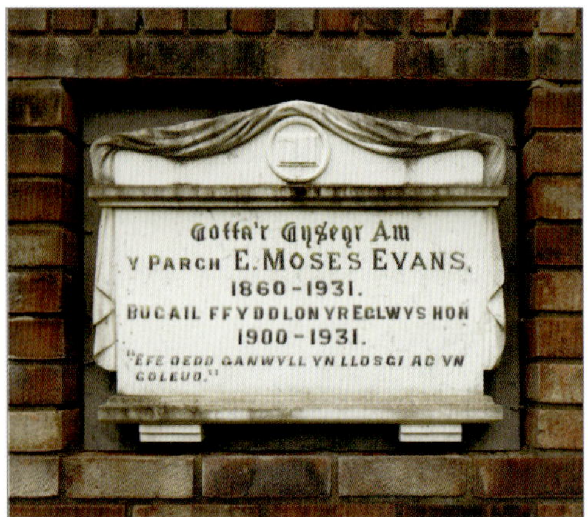
Coffa'r Cysegr Am
Y Parch E. Moses Evans,
1860 – 1931.
Bugail Ffyddlon yr Eglwys Hon
1900 – 1931.
"Efe oedd ganwyll yn llosgi ac yn
goleuo."

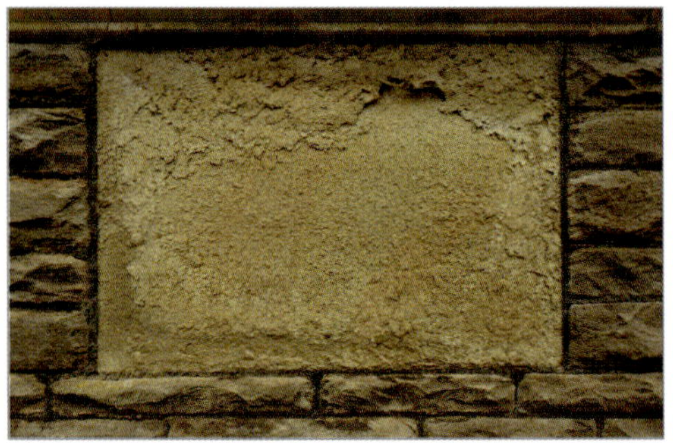

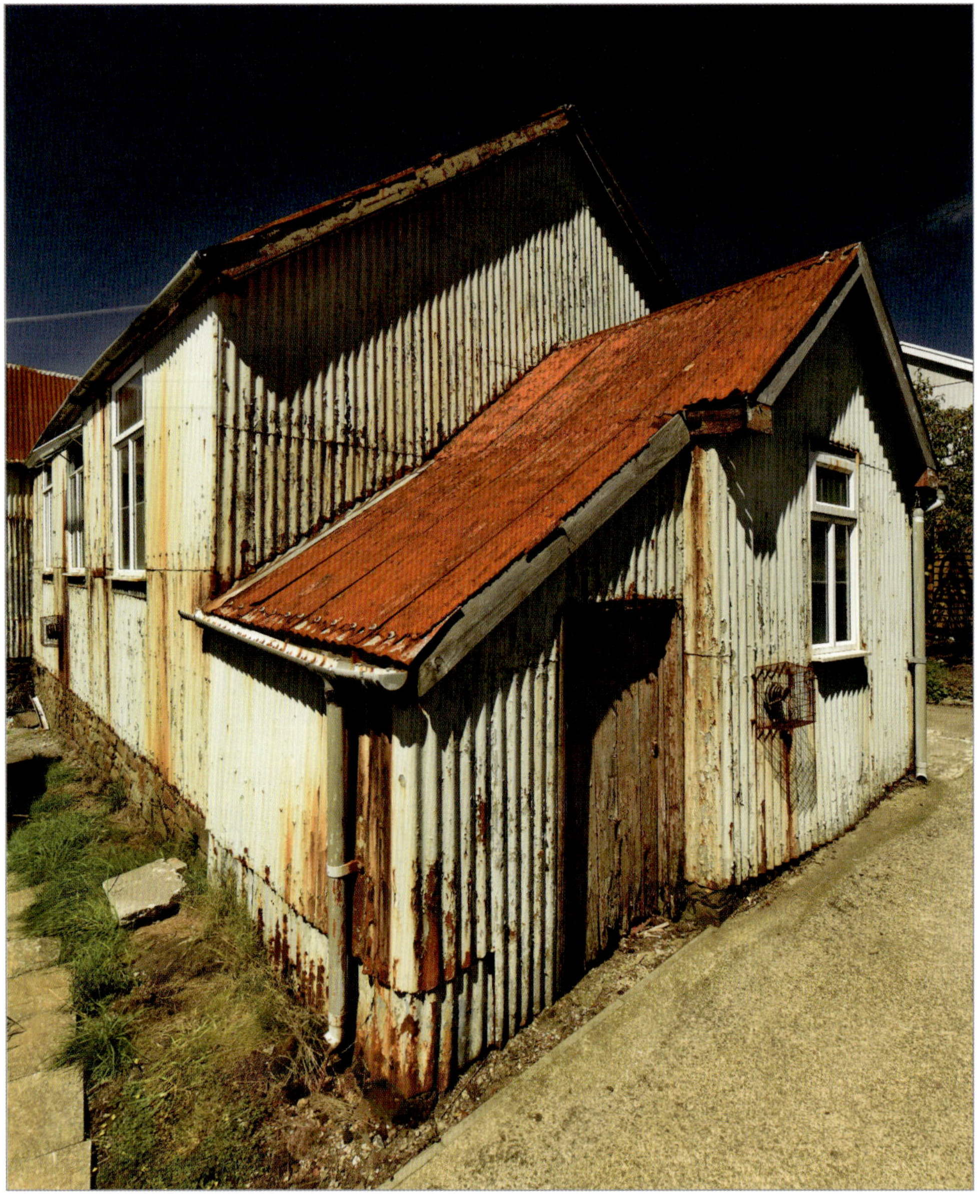

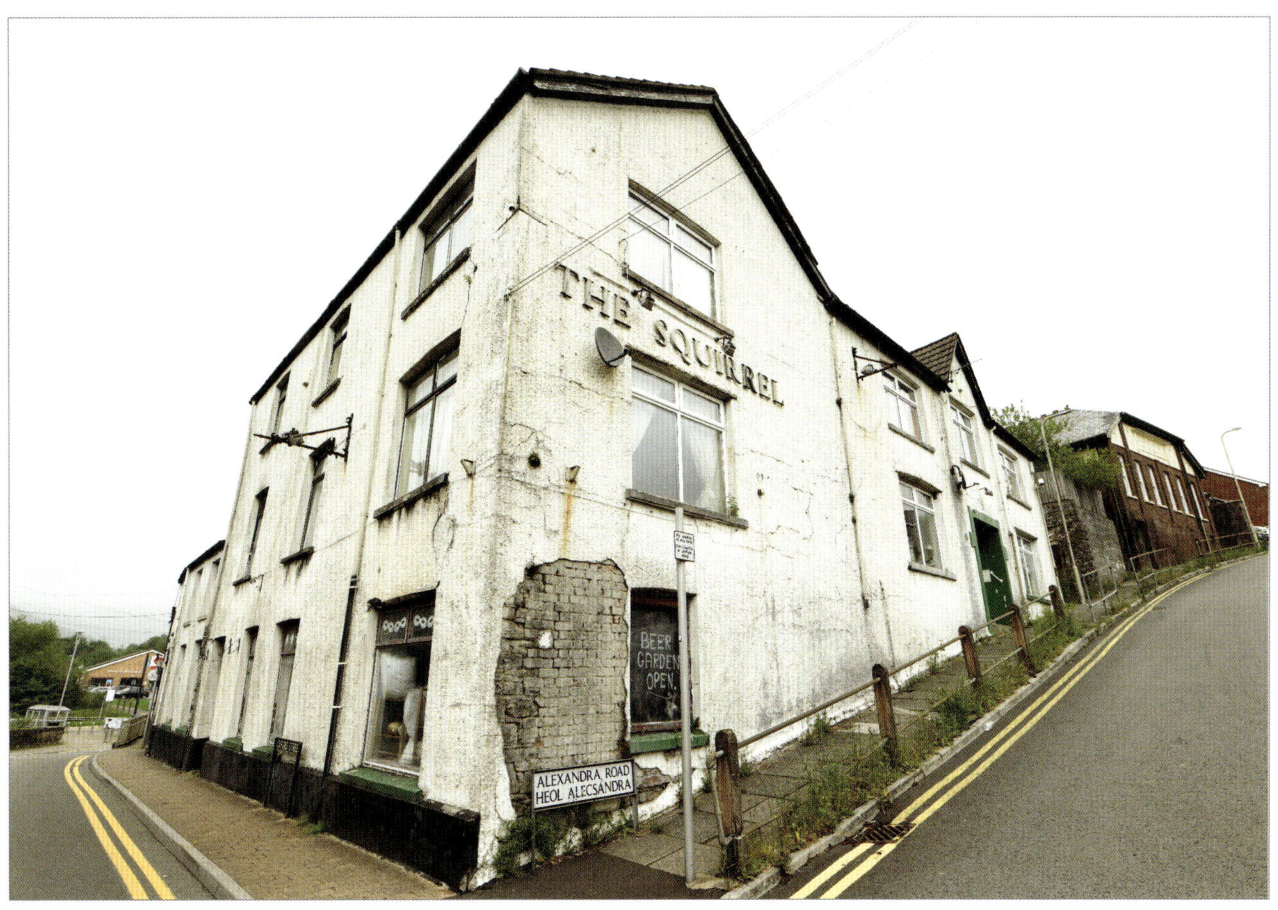

The Squirrel Hotel, Ffaldau Square, Pontycymer:

Workers stayed here in the 1870s, during the early years of coalmining.

My grandfather kept The Squirrel ... [so] they weren't allowed to take communion ... the minister would, after church, come around the pub and they'd have communion in the house, and then the minister would take home a bottle with him. People used to go around ... and sit in a place in the back ... deacons and various people who were supposed to be non-drinkers.

Merlin Madog from *The Valleys Autobiography 2: a people's history of the Garw, Llynfi and Ogmore valleys*, Valley & Vale, 1997

opposite, clockwise from top left:

This plaque is all that is left of a chapel which once stood in Katie Street, Blaengarw;
Salem Mount Zion chapel, New Street, Pontycymer, currently being renovated as a private dwelling;
eroded plaque, Bethania Welsh Baptist Church;
memorial plaque, the Tabernacle, Blaengarw, also now being renovated as housing

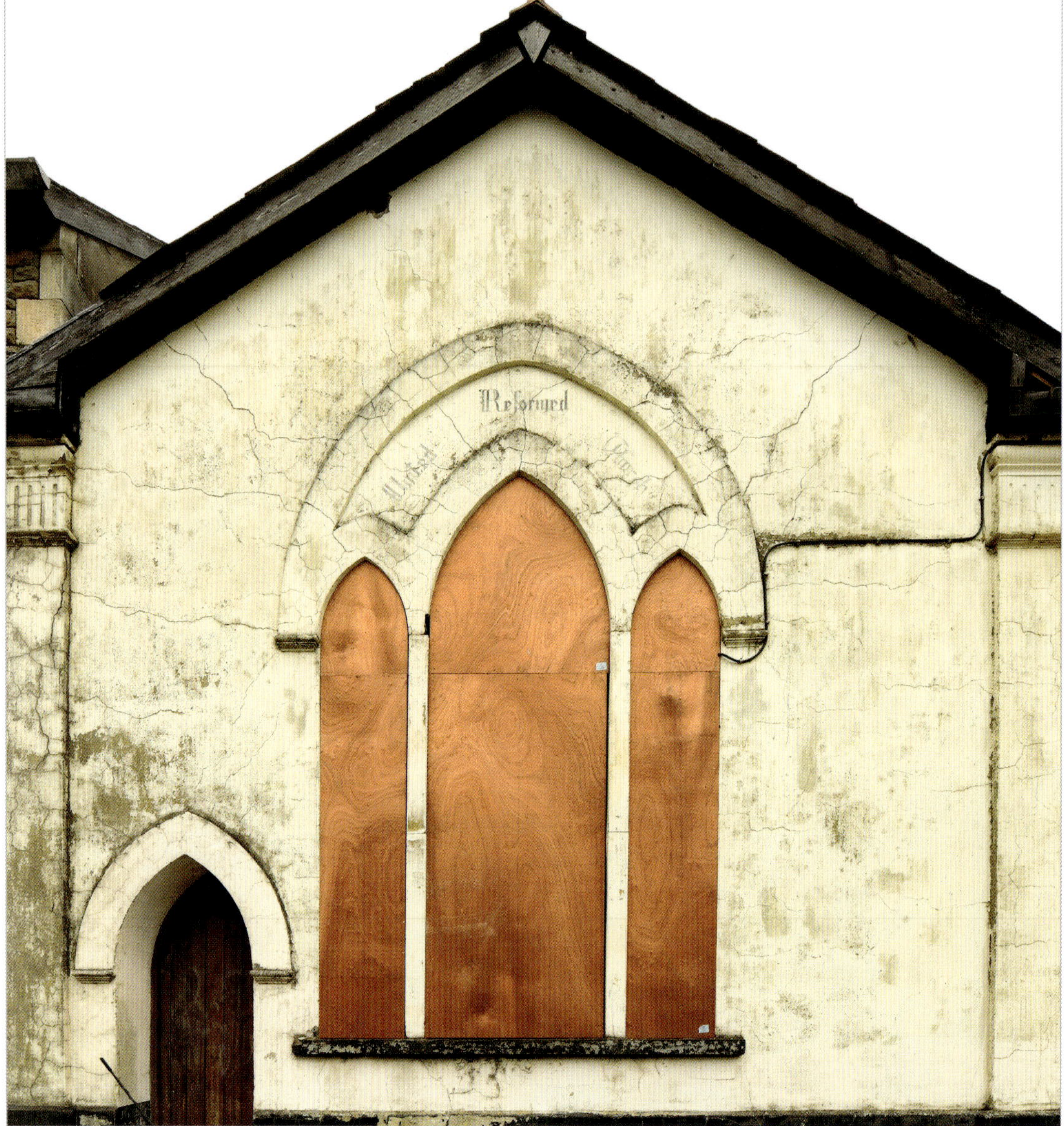

United Reformed Church, Meadow Street, Pontycymer:

Years before the chapels were built, worshippers met in the front rooms of their own homes.

When faith was in coal, churches and chapels flourished, though now we are mostly agnostic to both the 'black gold' as well as to the god we once worshipped, with many of his buildings boarded up or converted into homes or workshops.

It was the life, and sometimes death, experiences that coalmining presented that helped forge – alongside the distinctive snaking ribbons of houses, the pithead baths, the winding gear silhouetted against a night sky, the male voice choirs and the miners' blackened faces – another of the South Wales Valleys' identifying marks: the solidarity of its people.

Oppression can create a dog-eat-dog mentality; in the Garw, as in the other Valleys, it generated a unity of effort to help each to survive, as well as to imagine and to build, in microcosm at least, an alternative reality to raise one's community above the always-inequitable, often-inhuman realities of daily life.

Dr Wyn Price has described the Valley during the coalmining years as "a battlefield for unionism versus capitalism", and introduced to me important, though largely-forgotten leaders such as Llewellyn Jones who ran the Garw Medical Aid Society; and Frank Hodges, a one-time Methodist preacher who became the Miners' Agent for the Garw at the age of 24 before being elected to lead the Miners Federation of Great Britain in 1919.

A pioneer of the early suffrage movement, trade unionist and Labour Party activist, Fanny Margaret Thomas was the headteacher of Ffaldau Girls' School in Pontycymer between 1908 and 1931.

Thought to have been the first woman in South Wales to ride a motor-cycle and the first in the Garw to wear breeches (for which she earned the nickname 'Fanny Bloomers'), she's

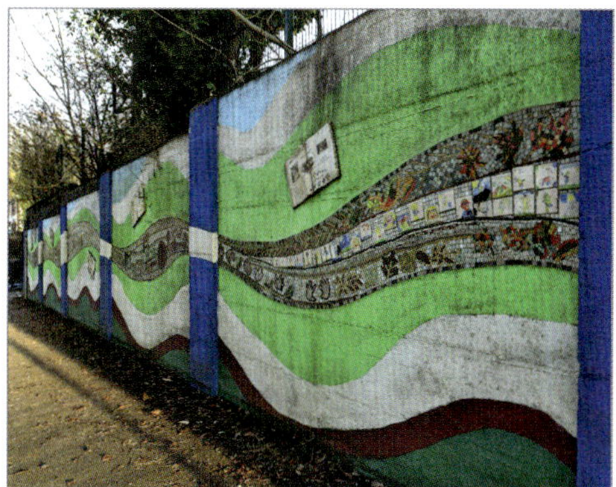

also remembered for drinking pints of beer and refusing to sit in the 'Ladies' lounge of the Royal Hotel in Pontycymer, preferring the public bar.

In 1912, she became the first Welsh woman to be elected as president of the National Federation of Women Teachers, and in 1919 the first woman to serve on the Ogmore and Garw Urban District Council, making her the first female councillor in the whole of Wales.

Re-elected on five occasions (until her retirement in 1937) and also the first Labour woman to chair a Council in Wales, Fanny campaigned through-out her life for equal pay and opportunities for female teachers, and for women's suffrage, as well as for maternity and child welfare services, public health and decent housing.

Fanny was instrumental in invitations to Emmeline Pankhurst (in 1906) and her daughter Adela Pankhurst (in 1907) to come and visit the Garw Valley to speak, as well as to some of the pioneers of the Labour movement, including Keir Hardie, George Lansbury and Ethel Snowdon.

children's mural,
Tynyrheol Primary School,
Llangeinor

There were theatres built here, like the Hippodrome in Pontycymer, later known as 'The Rink', famous for its roller skating and the visit once of Stan Laurel of Laurel and Hardy fame. This was one of four theatres in our tiny Valley, and there were four cinemas, too. The world famous Buffalo Bill's Wild West Show once performed on Blandy Park, complete with 'Red Indians', a dancing bear and an elephant kitted out in the regalia of the Indian Raj.

Blaengarw Dramatic Society was one of the best in the country, touring widely throughout South Wales and beyond. Annual Drama Weeks saw a different play every night with adjudication on the Saturday; and mini-*eisteddfodau*, or 'Penny Readings' (where children recited verses in competition for a penny coin) were always popular.

Male and female voice choirs and silver bands flourished, and Pontycymer had its Amateur Operatic Society, and Pantygog its Tynton Players. The National Eisteddfod-winning Pontycymer Male Choir was established in 1886, followed with even greater success by the Garw Male Voice Party.

The first Ladies Choir was formed here in 1915 and Children's Choirs were a particular feature of the 1925 Depression.

But the most significant of the Garw's humanising tendencies was the construction of the Workmen's Hall in Blaengarw and the Institute in Pontycymer, paid for by contributions from miners' wages. These provided places to celebrate local and national culture, for political education, and for the exploration of different ways to live:

… half of them had had no schooling, half of them had to go and earn to keep bread and cheese in the house .. few of them had seen very little daylight, but their education was wonderful. And it all went back to the privilege of reading in the library of Blaengarw Hall that the miners had provided for the workmen and the little boys like myself … to better ourselves in the world.
Bryn Williams
from *The Valleys Autobiography*

Ivor Novello [1893-1951], the Welsh actor, singer and composer, appeared as a boy soprano at Blaengarw Workmen's Hall, and there was a regular diet of Shakespeare and Bernard Shaw plays, as well as the latest musicals.

This is an account of Jack Jones [1884-1970], the miner, playwright and novelist (author of *Rhondda Roundabout, Off to Philadelphia in the Morning, Black Parade*, etc.) who was Secretary of both the International Miners' Lodge and Blaengarw Workmen's Hall, recalled here by Grafton Radcliffe (and printed in *The Valleys Autobiography*):

Jack didn't do things by halves, wanted the Edward Dunstan Shakespearian Company at the Hall … a top company, ranking with the RSC and the Old Vic of today … They quoted him a fee of eight hundred pounds for one week. A man's wage in the colliery in those days was two pounds, so eight hundred pounds represented the wages of four hundred men for one week … an unheard of sum. Jack accepted.

They did a performance in the morning at half-past-ten for the afternoon shift, one in the afternoon at two or two-thirty for the night shift, and another in the evening at seven o'clock for the day shift. The price of the seats was just 3d, 6d and 9d … but they made money … they showed a profit.

They packed the theatre out to see Shakespeare … Shakespeare made money!

Large libraries and virtually every daily newspaper and journal published in Britain were available in these innovative centres, based upon the self-education and Enlightenment principles of Llangeinor's Richard Price and those that followed him.

Classes were held in subjects as varied as philosophy,   religion, art, political history, and   musical appreciation:

In the Pontycymmer Institute … the room that was opposite the library was Politics … and if you went and opened the door, you could swear that you were in the House of Commons.
Berwyn Price,
from *The Valleys Autobiography*

And out of the values which under-pinned the workmen's hall and institute movement also arose the Medical Aid Society, similarly paid for by contributions from miners' wages. Collected in order to provide access to a doctor, medicines, an ambulance to and from hospital, and a bed at Cardiff Royal Infirmary, these ideas were eventually to crystallise in the establishment of the National Health Service in July 1948.

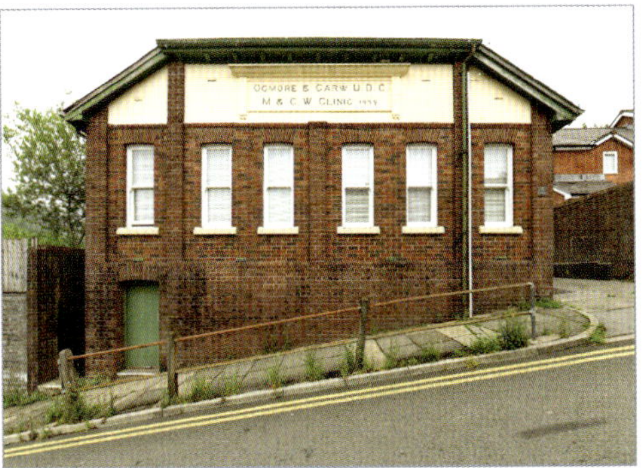

the 1939
clinic building,
Alexandra Street,
Pontycymer

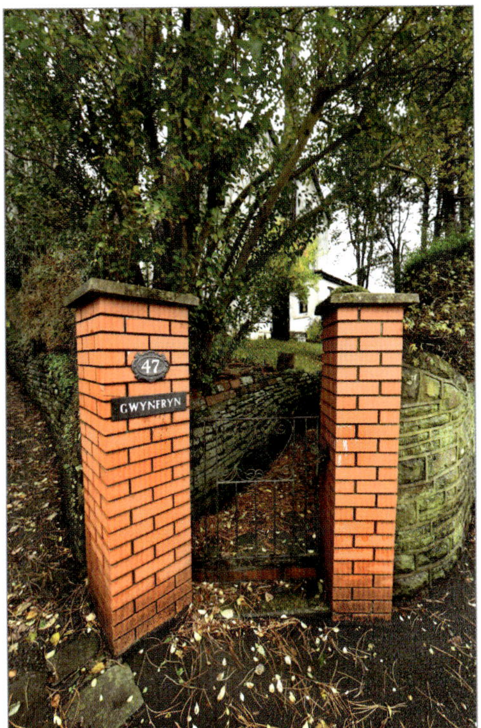

In the days of mining, Gwynfryn on Victoria Street in Pontycymer, was the doctor's house and surgery.

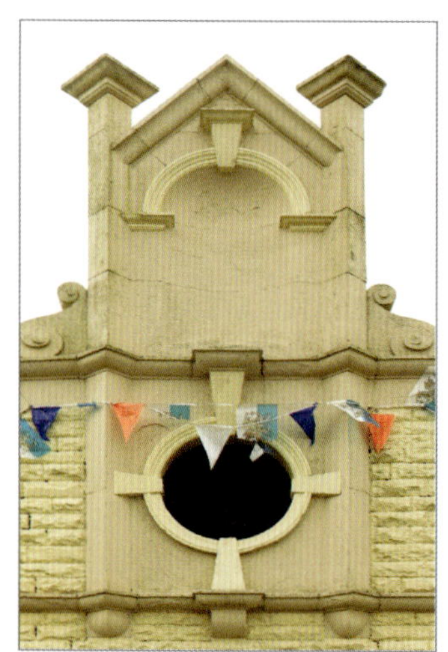

Opened in 1901,
the Ffaldau Workmen's
Institute in Meadow Street,
Pontycymer contained
a public hall (capacity 350),
a lending library and
reading room, committee
rooms, a five-table snooker
/ billiards and games room
(added in 1905, part of its
exterior pictured above),
as well as a sometimes
centre for the
Christadelphians.
Behind the Institute
was the office of the
Medical Aid Society.

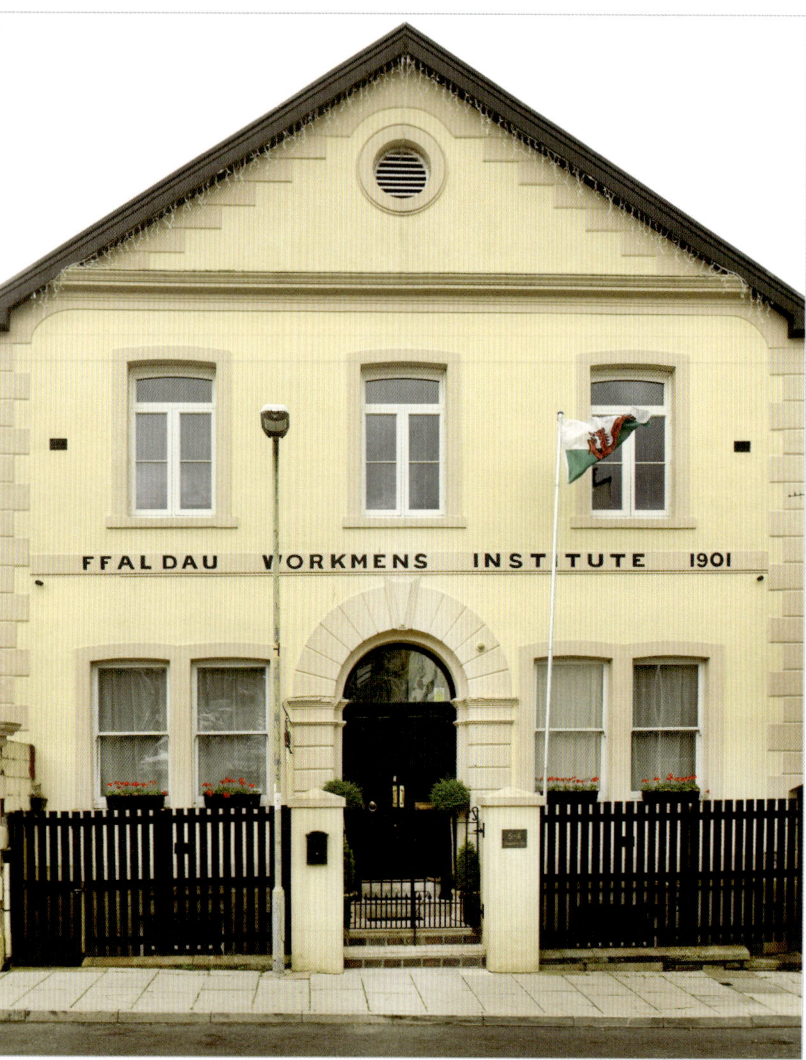

opposite:

*Blaengarw Workmen's Hall
ran university extra-mural
classes in the Lesser Hall.
On Saturday afternoons,
the building was always
crammed with youngsters
all eager to learn.*

Grafton Radcliffe, from
The Valleys Autobiography 2,
Valley & Vale, 1997

As one of the Garw's
principal political,
educational and cultural
focuses for more than a
century (and, today, the only
ex-miners' hall not to have
been sold or demolished),
the retention and
ongoing development of
Blaengarw Workmen's Hall
should be seen as a priority
for the future development
of the Valley.

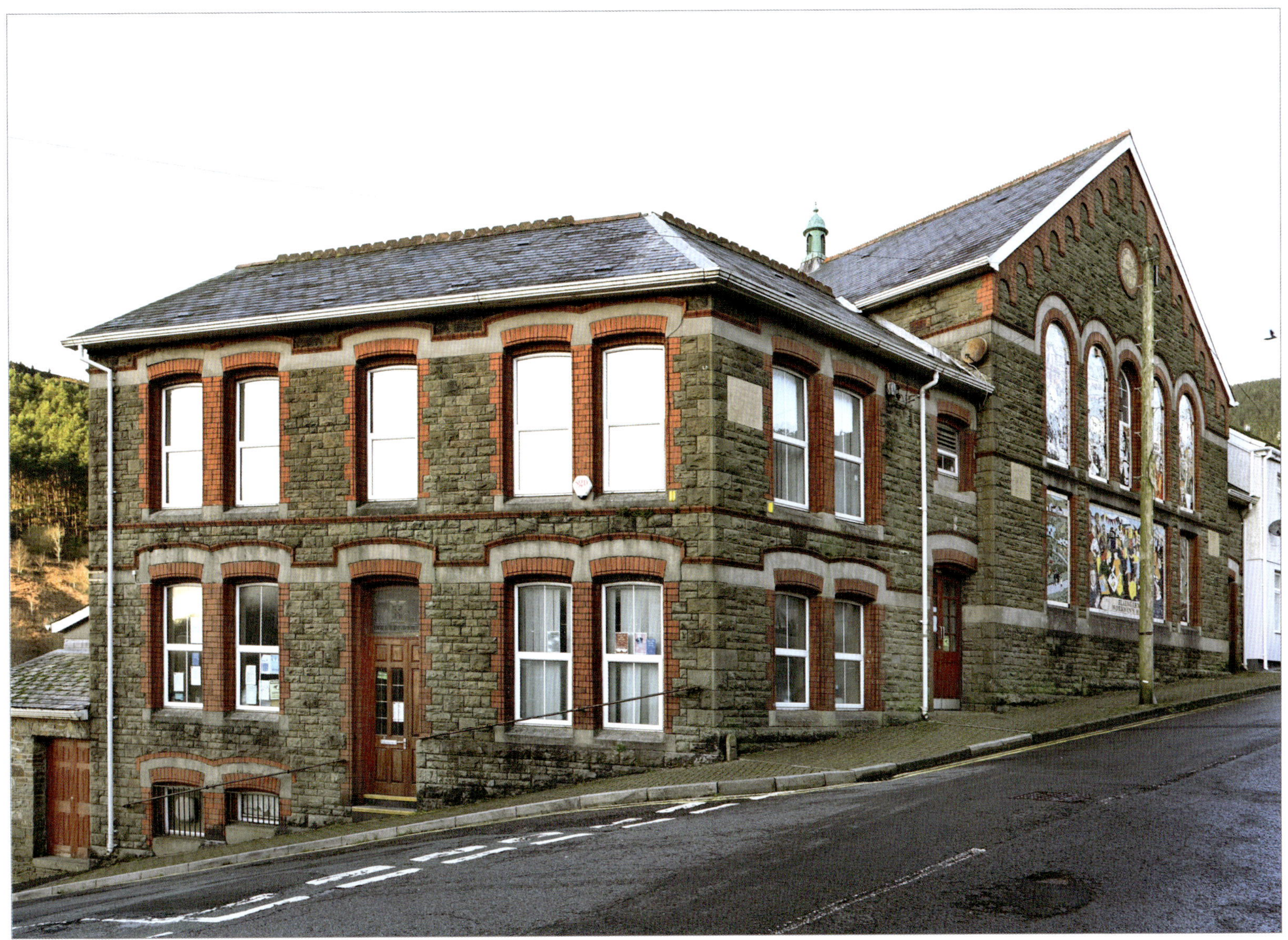

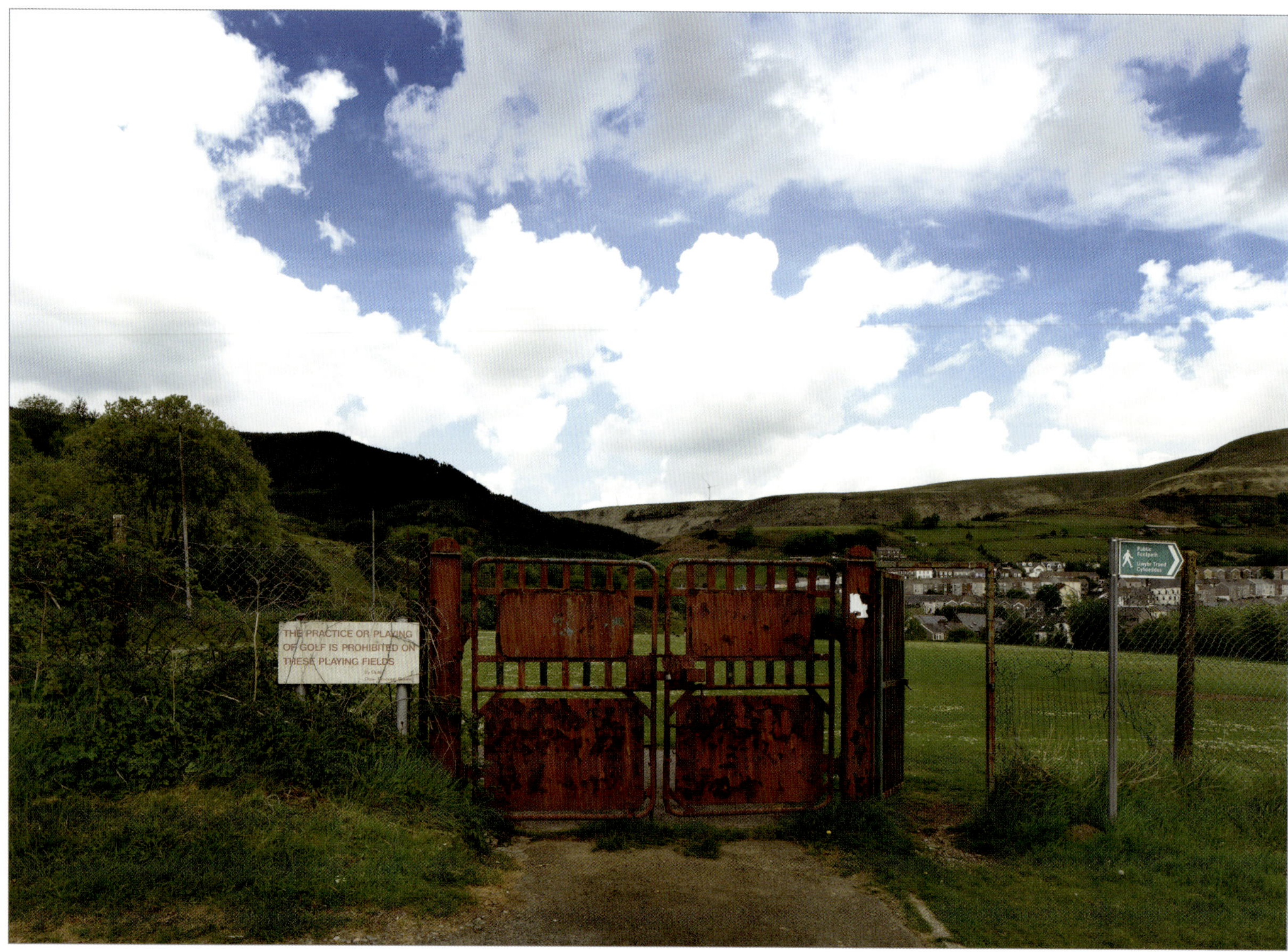
THE PRACTICE OR PLAYING
OF GOLF IS PROHIBITED ON
THESE PLAYING FIELDS
Public
Footpath
Llwybr Troed
Cyhoeddus

"There is not sufficient level land available ... to play a decent game of marbles."
Glamorgan Gazette, 1914

Pontycymer Rugby Club was formed in 1887. For many years, games had to be played on top of the mountain, called the 'Cow's Back' because of its irregular shape. It wasn't until 1967 that Lawrence Park – named for one of its capped players – was built on top of an old refuse tip.
Blaengarw Rugby Club was formed in 1897 but it only had to wait 30 years before its Recreation Ground was opened. The first football game was played on Christmas Day 1885, on some waste land in Blaengarw; a cricket team existing as early as 1902; and there is even a report of horse racing in the Garw in 1905.
(from information supplied by Dr Wyn Price)

opposite:

Carn Park

right, clockwise from top left:

Blaengarw Rugby Club;
Carn Rovers changing rooms;
Blandy Park,
home of Garw FC (x2);
Carn Rovers FC
changing rooms;
Carn Rovers FC ground

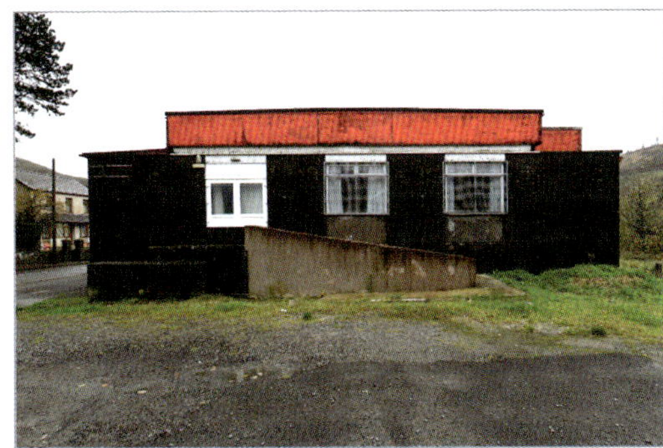

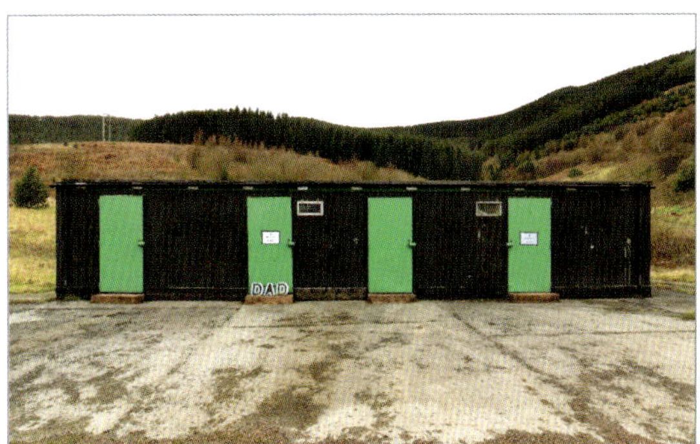

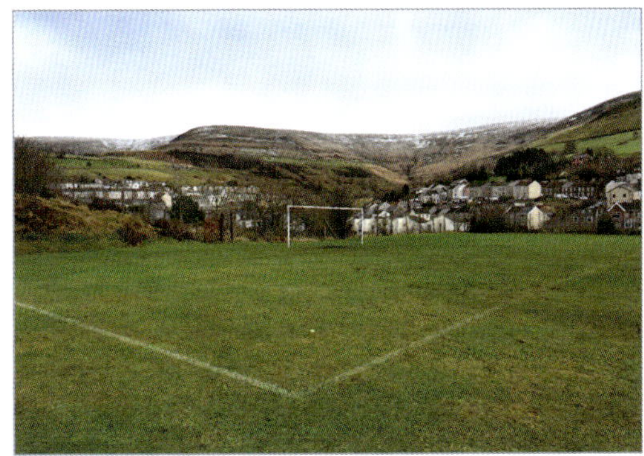

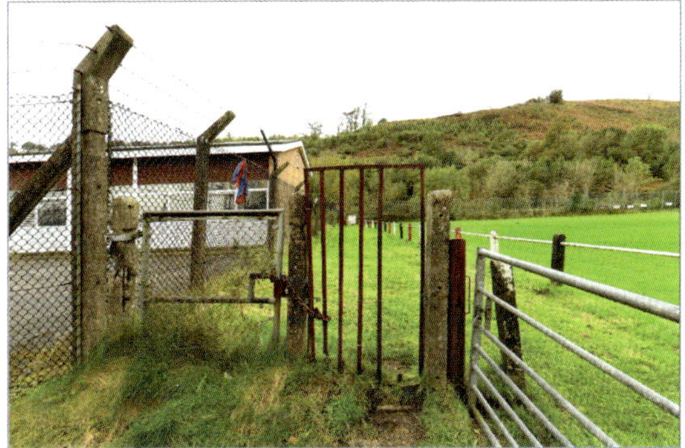

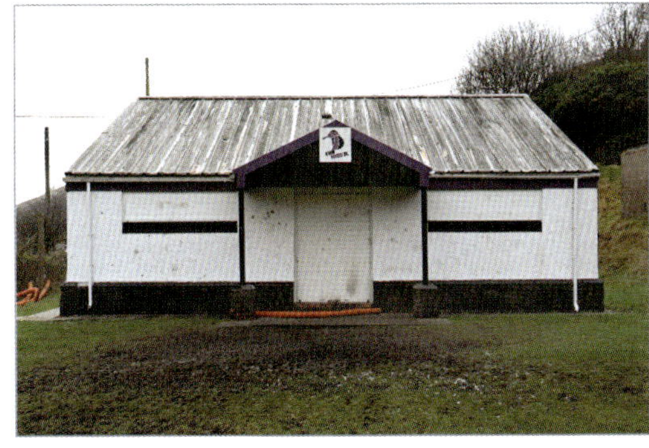

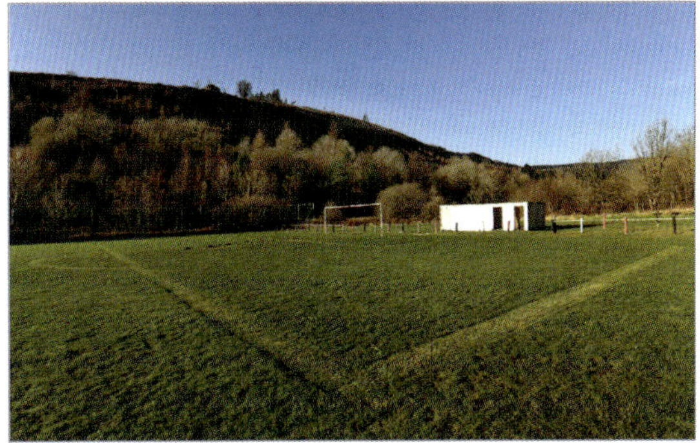

Blaengarw Cricket Ground (and its well);
and (centre) Lawrence Park, home of Pontycymer RFC and the Valley Ravens

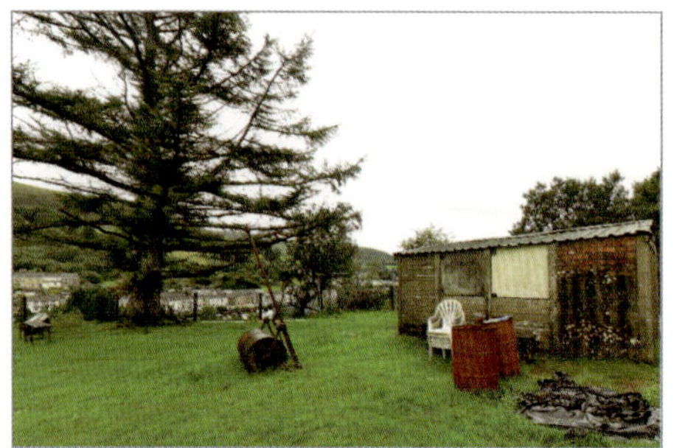

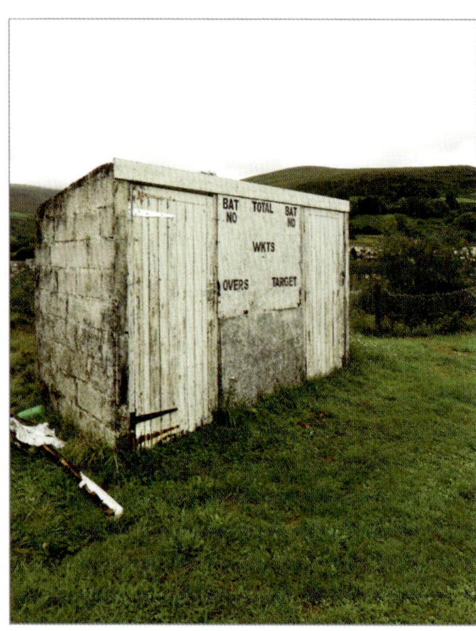

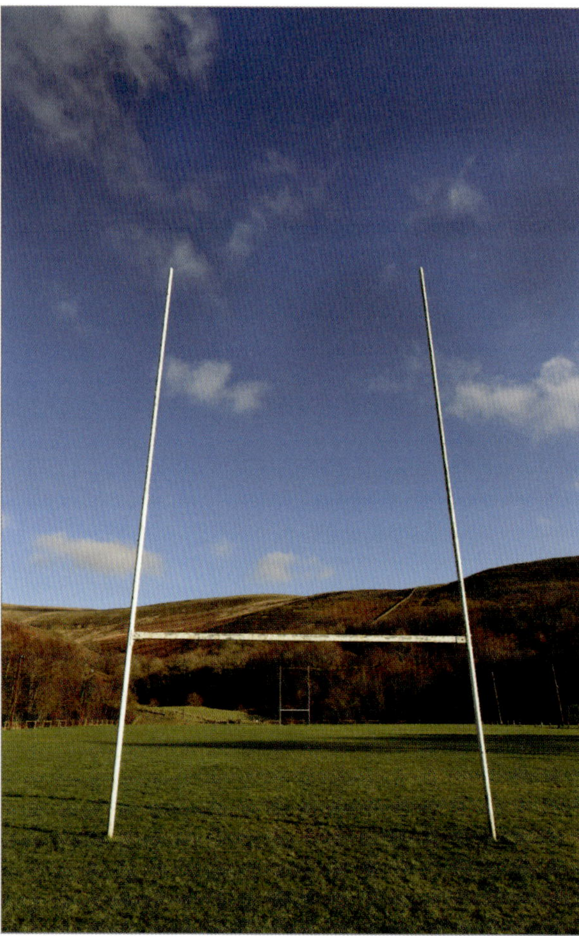

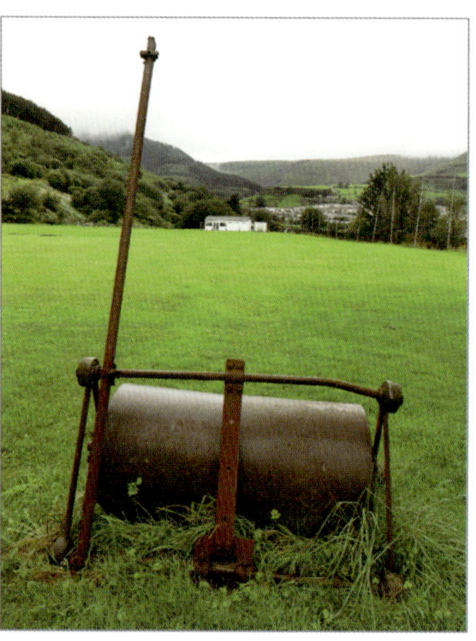

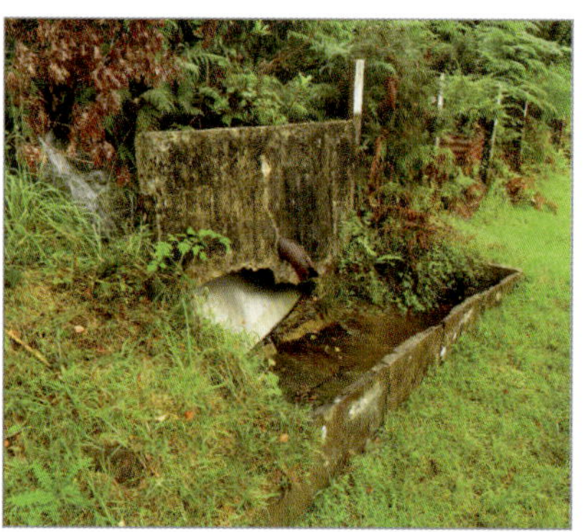

opposite:

Blandy Park, Pontycymer

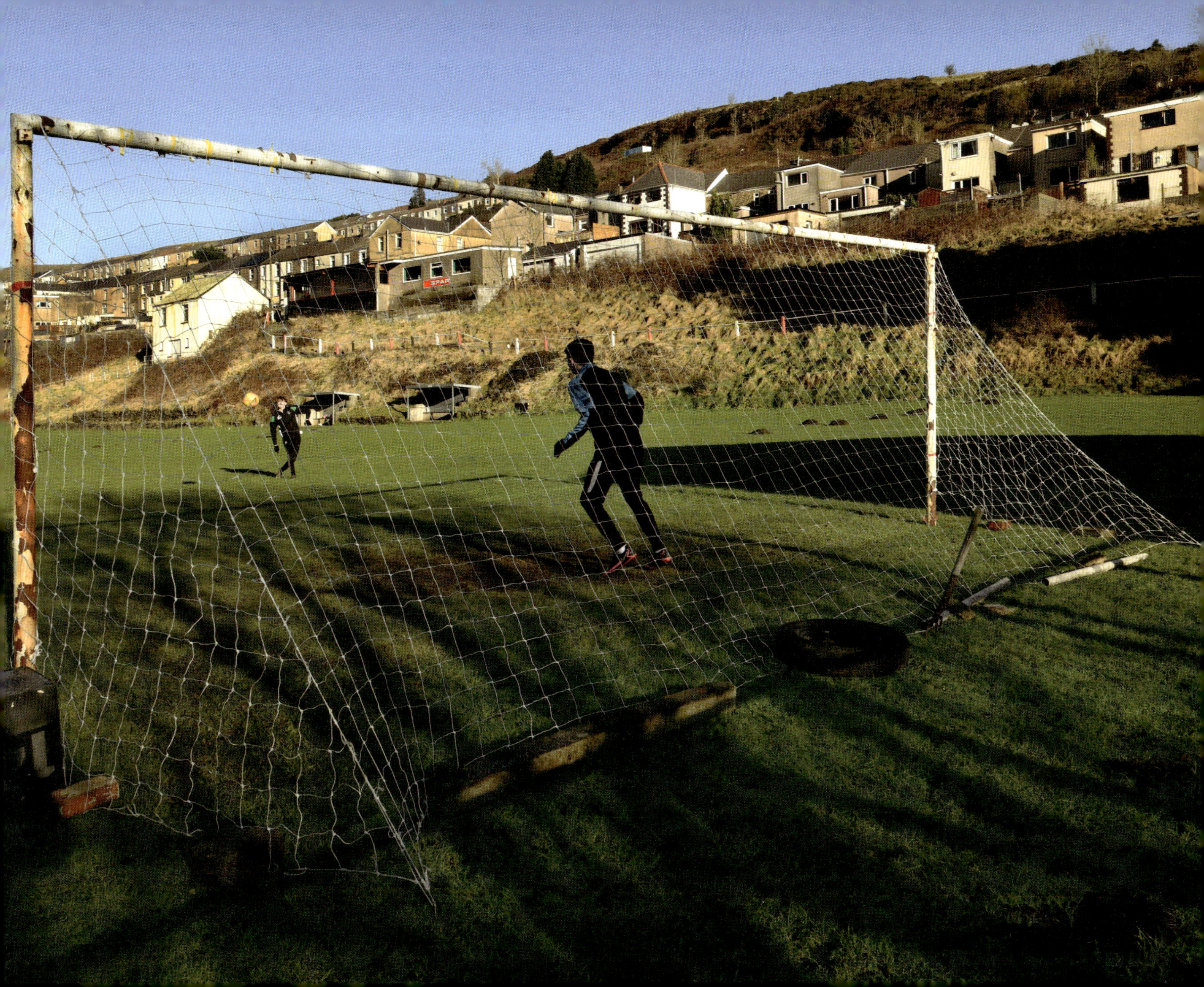

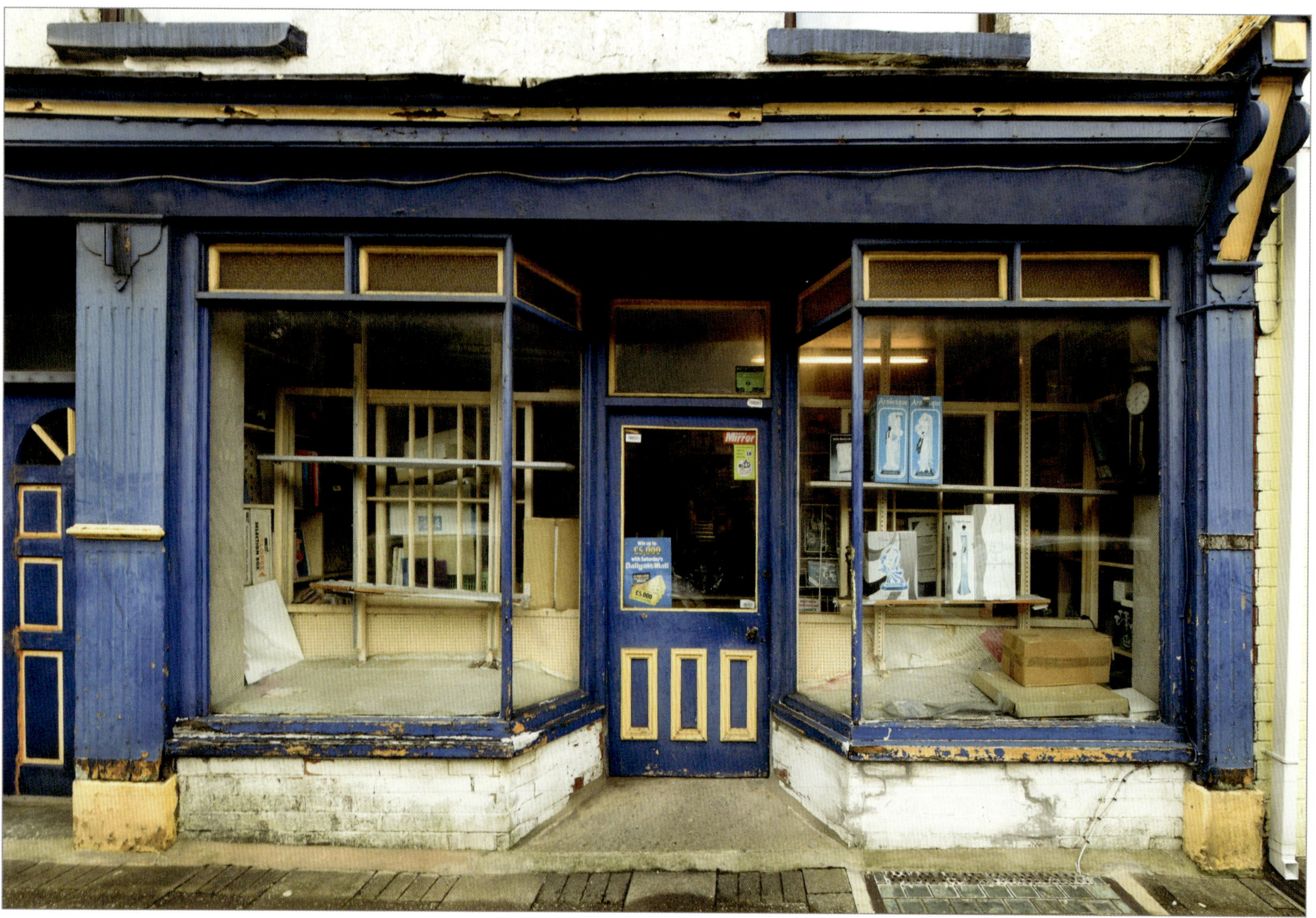

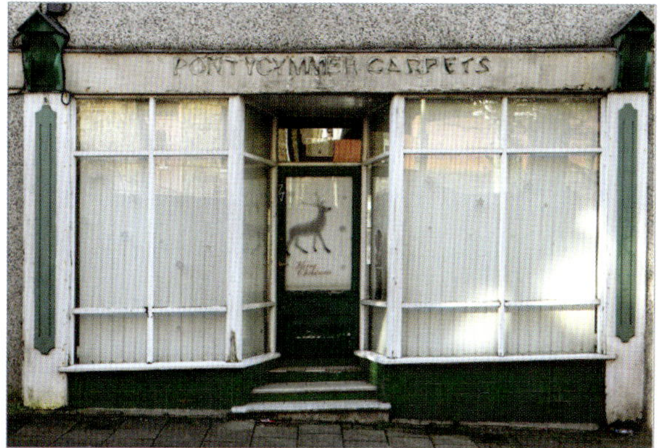
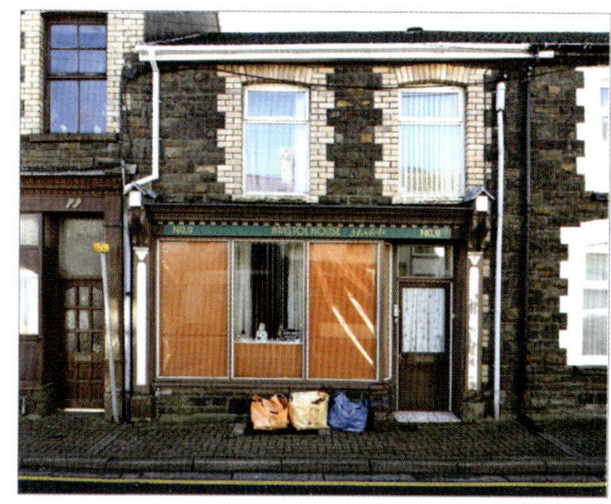
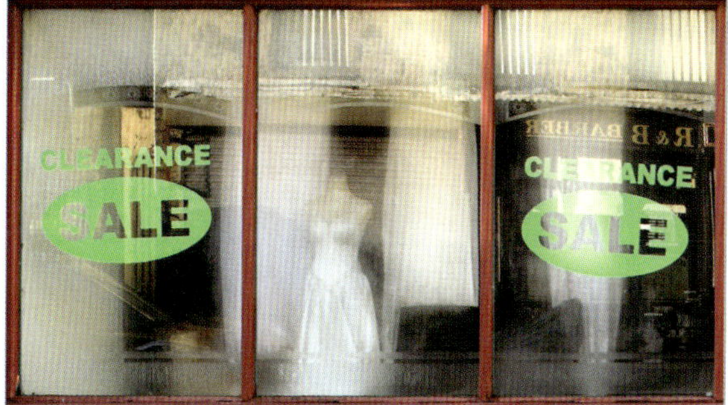

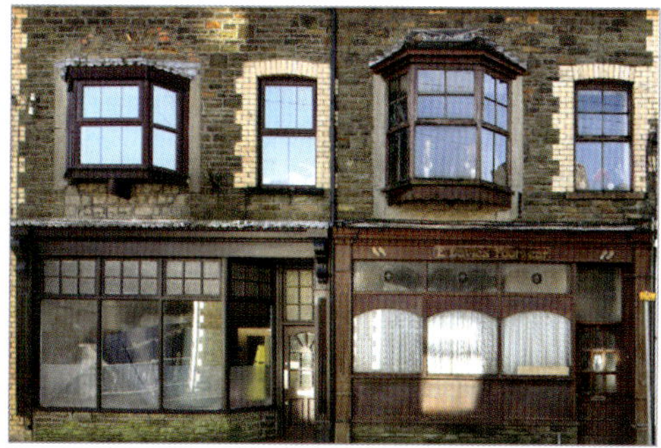

Although there are today a small number of fully-functioning clothing and food shops in the Valley, these are a few of Blaengarw and Pontycymer's other surviving and evocative shop fronts, many of which have been boarded up, or look like their last window-dressing was in the 1950s.

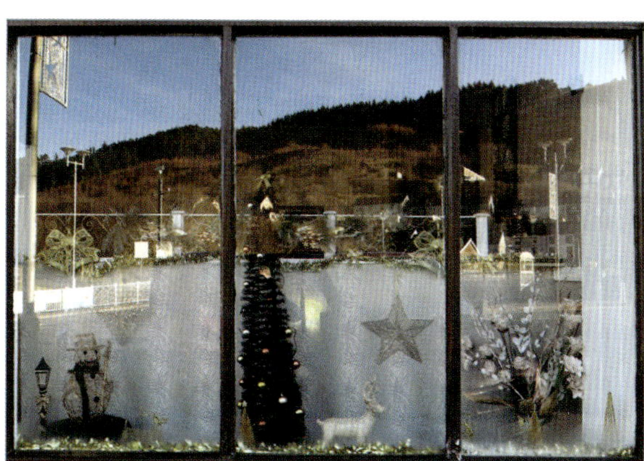
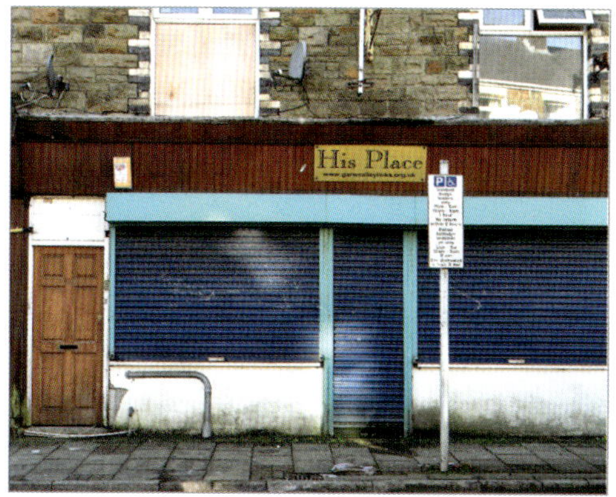

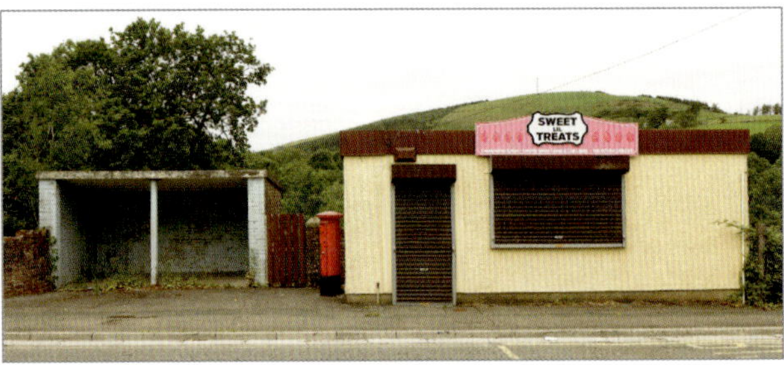

Sweet lil Treats, freshly-made cakes, Lluest

Blaengarw bakehouse:

… we used to take it up to the bakehouse to be cooked … a penny a tin. Then you'd fetch your tins back … and sometimes the bread used to rise up and it would be like one large crust. You'd snap it off and eat it then. There's nothing you can have today to taste like it …

Will Trigg
from *The Valleys Autobiography*,
Valley & Vale, 1992

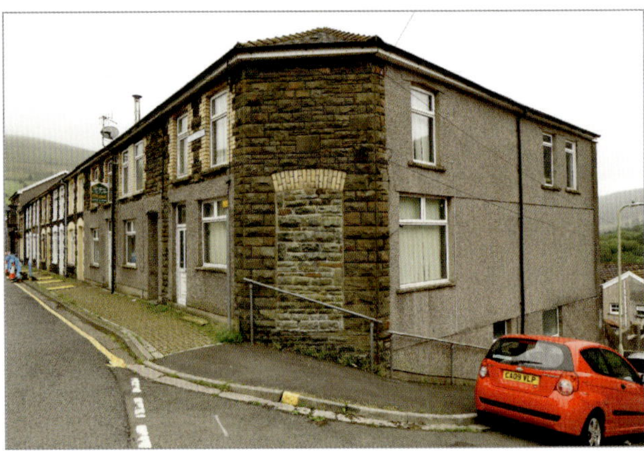

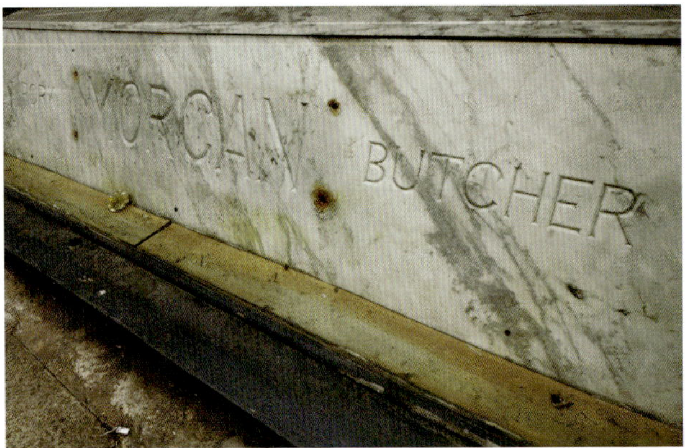

a reminder of Morgan's Pork Butchers, Oxford Street, Pontycymer

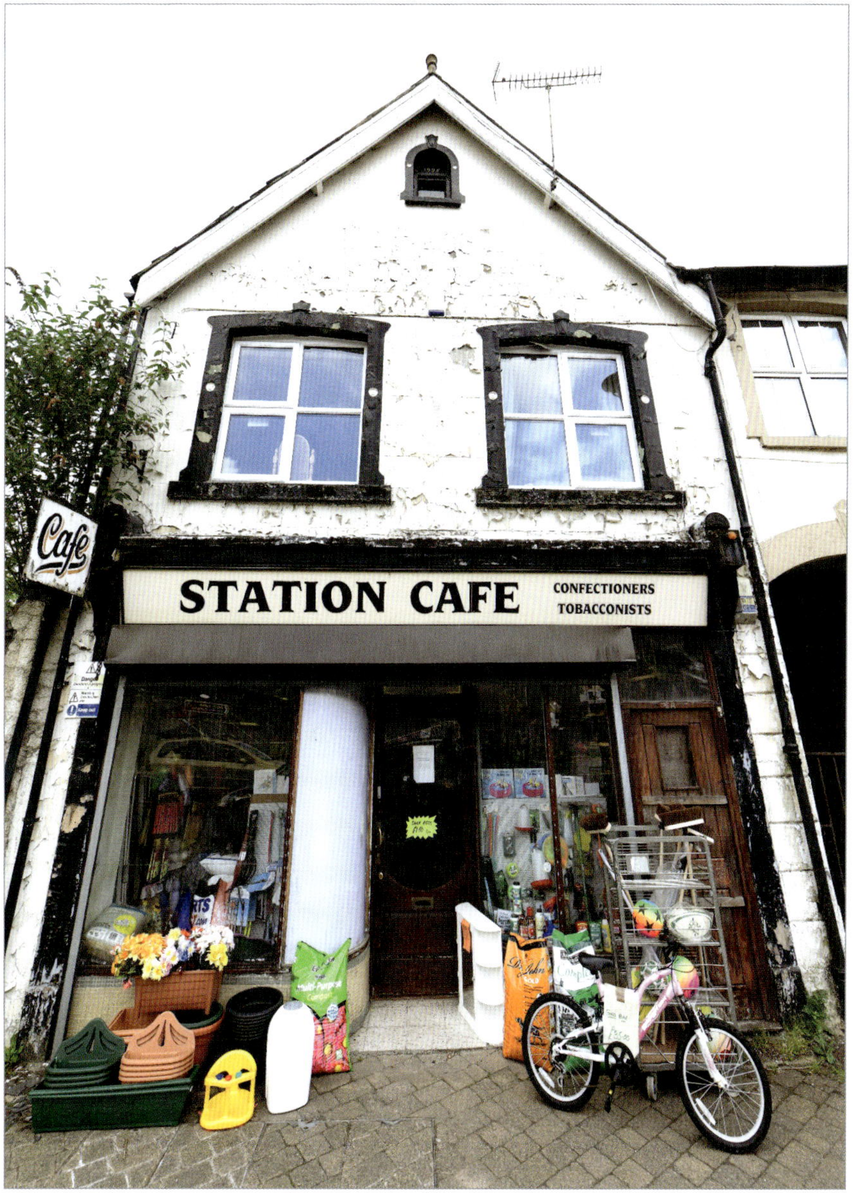

The Station Café on Ffaldau Square in Pontycymer was owned and run (from 1932 until 2007) by Giuseppe Assirati and his wife, Teresa. They came to the Valley from Bardi in Italy.

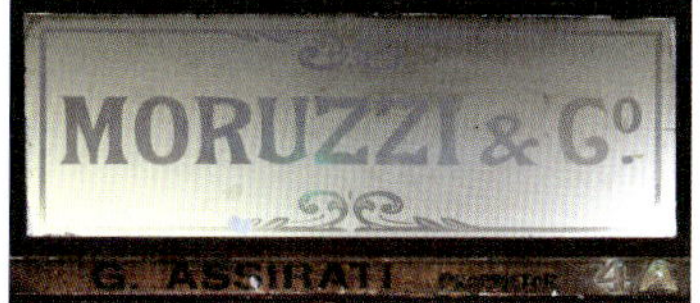

A well-known landmark for many years, the Station was strongly featured in Sara Sugarman's film *Very Annie Mary*, starring Jonathan Pryce, Rachel Griffiths, Ioan Gruffudd and Matthew Rhys.

Small screen productions which also used the Garw as a backdrop have included the ten hour 2001 ITV series, *Fallen Hero* with its fine footage of the collieries and pubs in full operation; and the 2010 post-mining made-for-TV movie, *Framed*, based on a book by Frank Cottrell Boyce, and starring Eve Myles and Trevor Eve.

Today, the Station Café survives as a wool and novelty goods store.

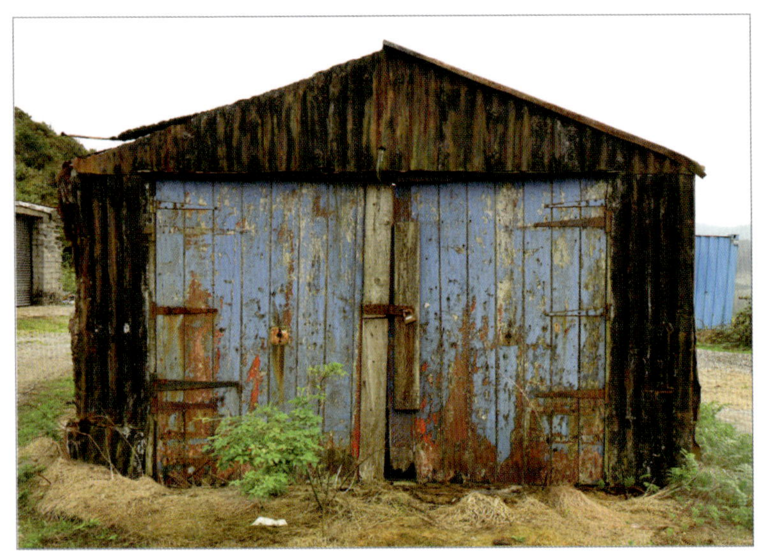

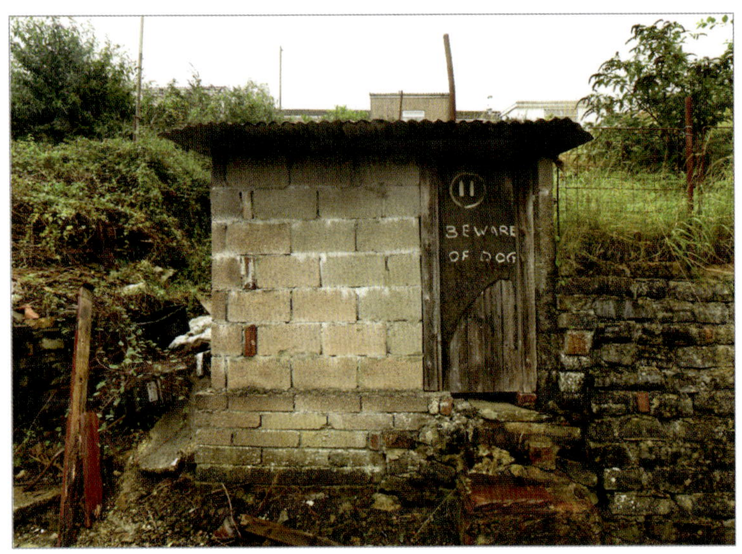

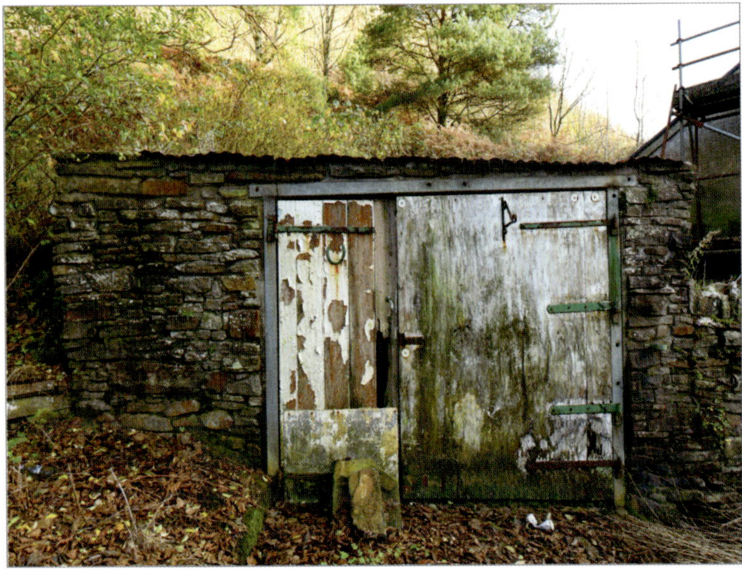

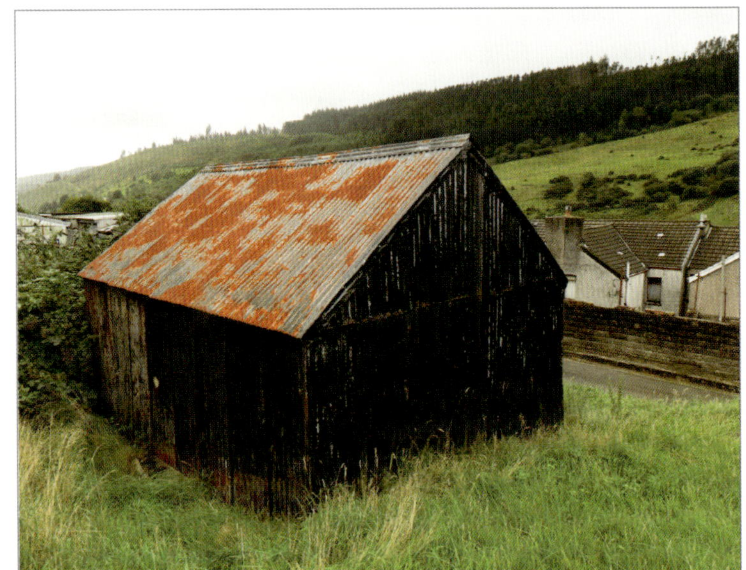

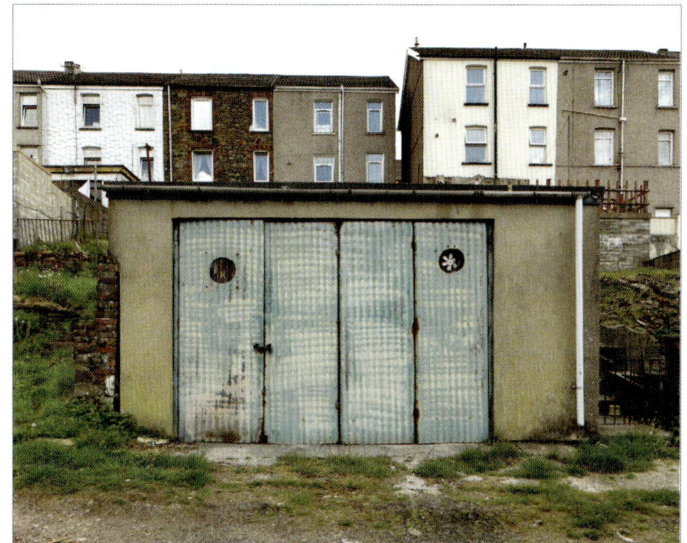

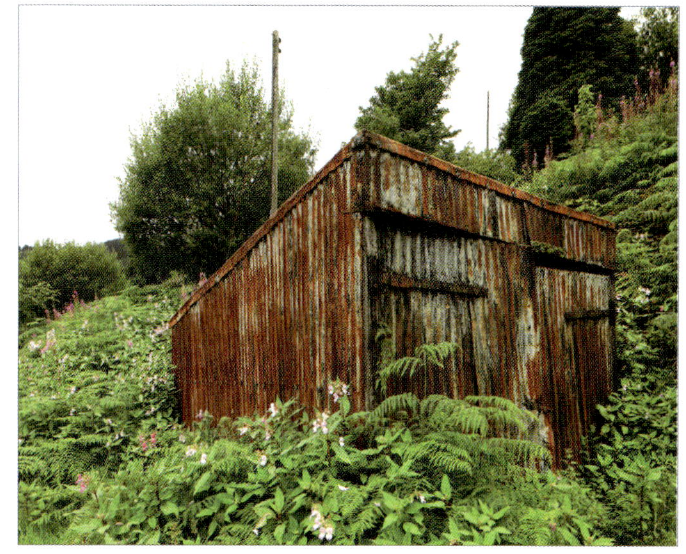

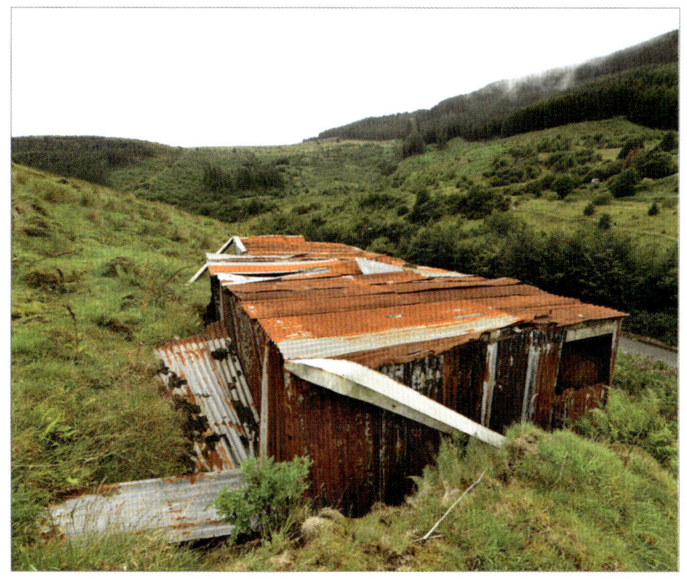

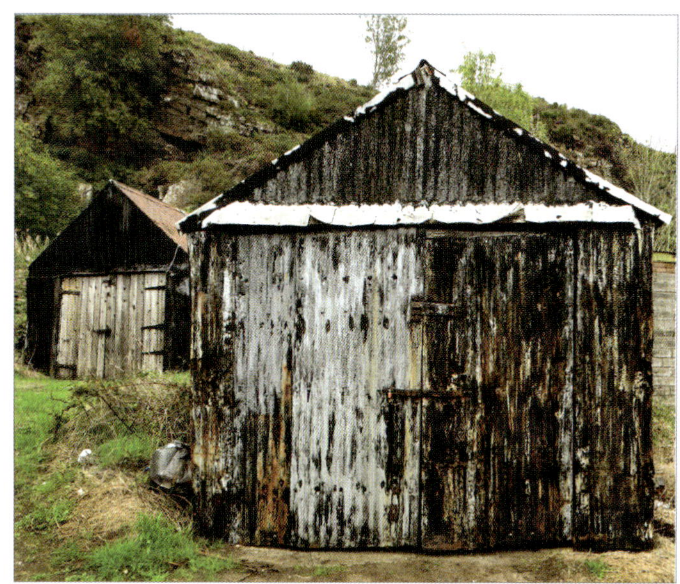

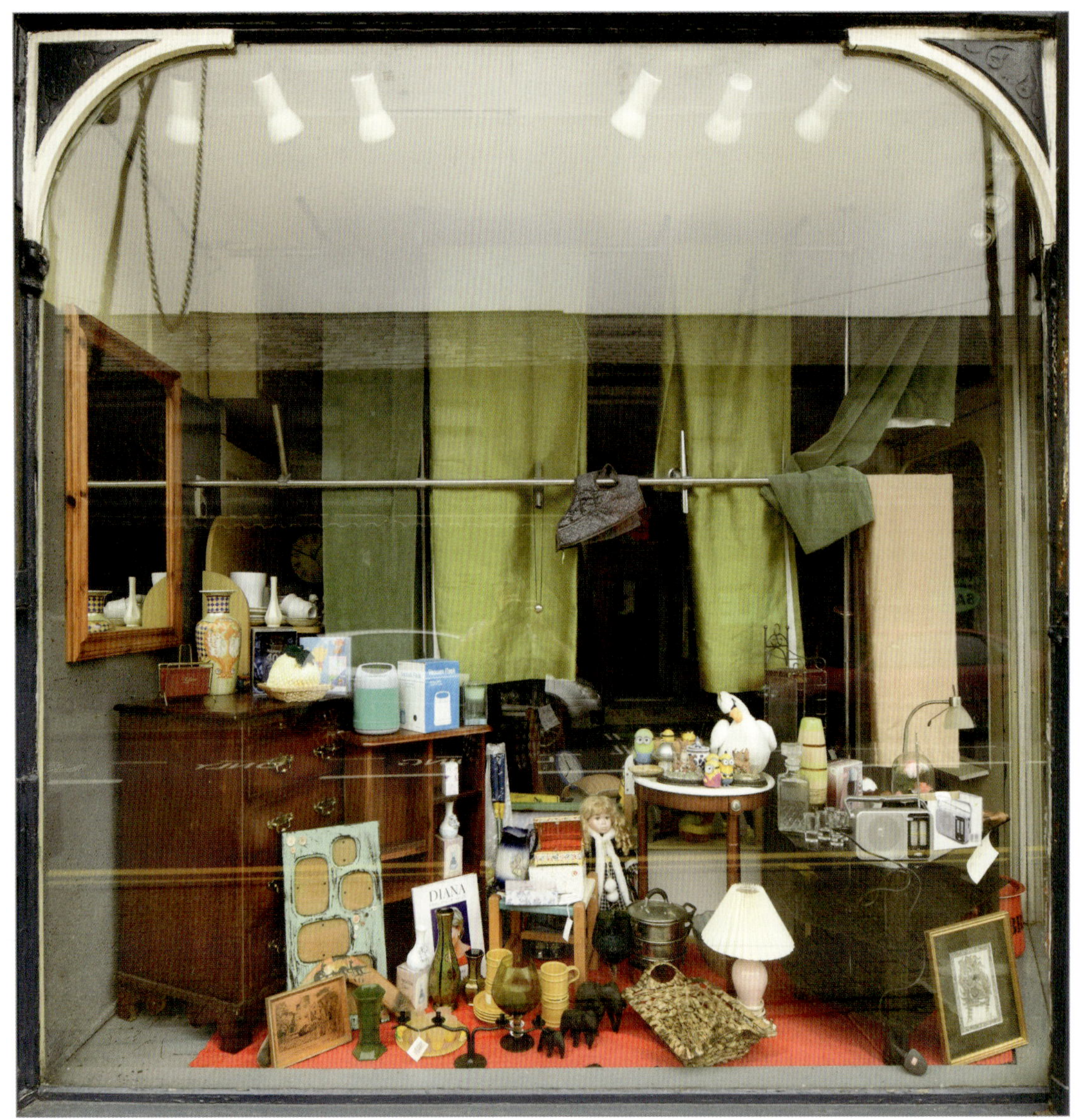

shopfront,
Oxford Street,
Pontycymer

opposite:

view across the
river to Pontyrhyl,
from the Bridgend
Road

Dannie Abse (in his poem 'A Heritage') described the miners' experience as "A heritage of comradeship and suffocation", and mining as a "black-robed god of fossils and funerals".

In the early days, coalmining provided plentiful (though perilous) work and good pay, but this was not to last. The recessions, the strikes and the lock-outs of the 1920s and '30s were responses to the industry's steady decline following an increasing substitution of oil as the principal fuel and a rise in overseas competition:

"The recession of the early 1920s was felt more severely in South Wales because there was a high dependence on exports.

It became difficult selling the coal on the international market and the only way the coal-owners believed this could be rectified was to reduce the cost of their coal.

To do this, they set out to reduce the wages of the miners and make them work extra hours for less money."
Dr Wyn Price

Between 1921 and '31, the Garw's population fell by 23%, and it was

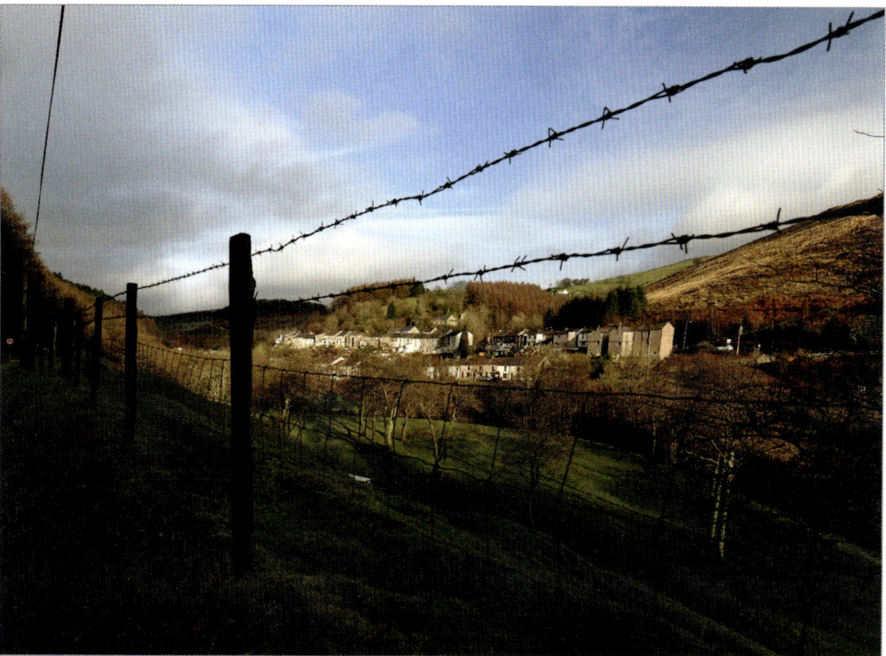

often the youngest and strongest who left, a continuing story to this day.

Though briefly revived by a new demand for steam coal during the Second World War, the last pit, the Ocean / Ffaldau was closed in an act of political vengeance by the Thatcher government in December 1985, after a final bitter strike. Its workers and their families were severely punished for their offence of solidarity against all of the odds, and a brief though momentous era in the life of the Garw came to an end.

The world of the miner was a world of darkness, often having to walk to work before sunrise, labouring below ground in low artificial light, and returning to a world pillaged of colour.

Coal was created through compression and this weight was directly transferred onto the shoulders of the men and their families who moved here to dig it out. But in their struggles to stay alive both above and below ground, a unique sense of solidarity was created, strengths which are still recalled ... though perhaps too rarely practised today.

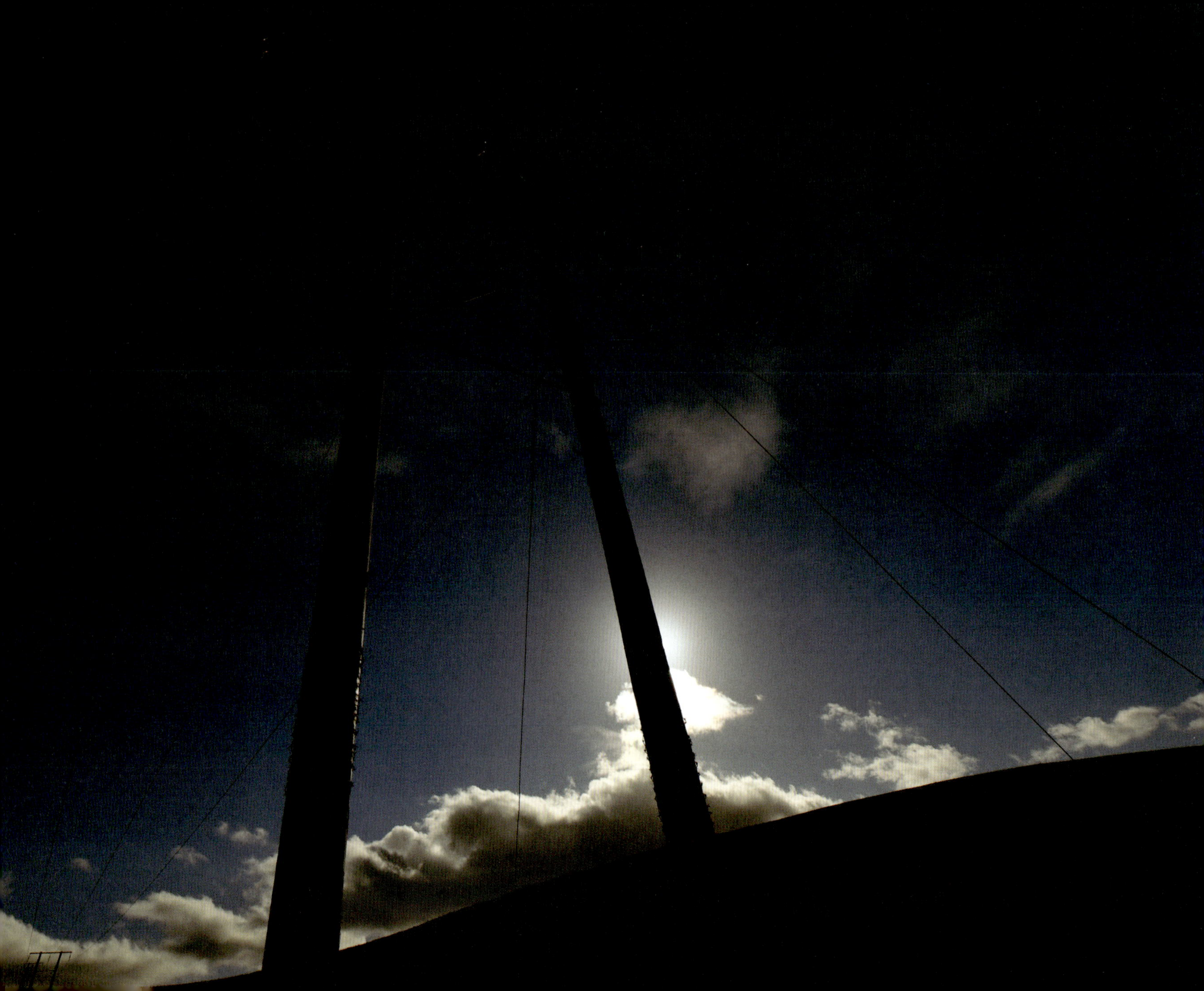

AFTER COAL:
you cannot hold the world in darkness *

The composer Gustav Mahler [1860-1911] – borrowing perhaps an idea first floated by Sir Thomas More in the early sixteenth century – wrote that "Tradition is not the worship of ashes but the preservation of the flame" … but I think they both probably meant 'should be' not 'is', as so often we are clearly blinded at least by the embers.

Although the period when coalmining dominated was little more than a hundred year blip, little less than a chronological flicker, today these relatively few moments have so often become the whole of the tale.

The Garw's name – alongside those of all of the other South Wales coalfield valleys – is almost always preceded by the epithet 'ex-mining', a denomination set as deep within our psyches as the coal measures themselves.

Within the vast sweep of our history, this Valley could just as well be known today as the home of Silurian tribes, the birthplace of Richard Price, the stamping-ground of 'Fanny Bloomers' and the inspiration for Calon Lân, or even as the land of waterfalls, lakes and sculptures.

above
Nant
Fforchwen

Despite this dominating narrative stasis, there is surprisingly little here that remains to proclaim the Valley's coalmining past. But, while the usual clichés of coalfield life have mostly gone, mining's legacy is everywhere, though you have to look a little deeper nowadays to find it.

It's in the often-artificial contours of the land; in the streetscapes, jam-packed with terraces of houses pressed into the Valley's sides, many three-storied when facing down to the river, but only two- up to the hills. It's in the half-buried detritus of metal rods, of bolts and cables, the bits of rubber ripped from conveyor belts, the discarded bricks stamped 'Brynmenyn' or 'Tondu'; and it's in the scattered survivals of small nuggets of coal you will find at your feet if you walk in the hills.

The cuts, the scars and the blemishes all still remain, but with few real memorials to acknowledge the difficult history which inflicted them: there's the odd half-buried colliery wheel here; and there, the coal-filled dram to remind of the most serious of the Valley mines' losses of life, at the site of the Lluest colliery explosion which we speed past on the main road above its well-hidden location within undergrowth beside the river. It's in the miner's lamp beside the memorial to Richard Price in Llangeinor, and in the grassed-over remains of the tramway routes to transport coal to the waiting railway below and slag to the mountain tops. And there's the lonely sign at the entrance to the Ocean / Ffaldau Colliery beside the track which, once walked by miners, leads today to two of our reclamation

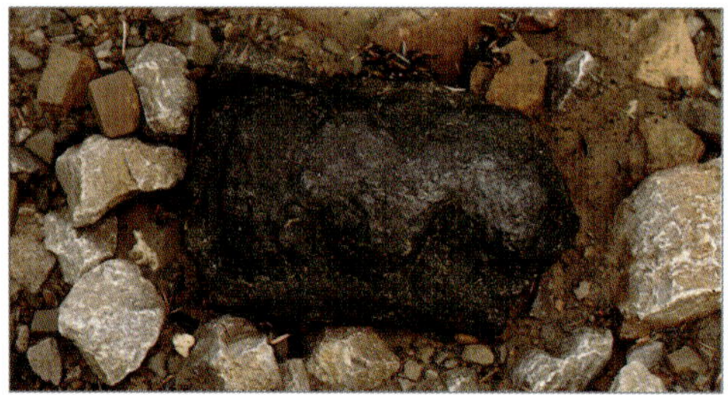

scheme's deep lakes which sit directly above the pits' even deeper tales of union and of pain.

The Garw's vanishing memories of coal are also held within the faded rainbow mural to block entry to a drift mine off one of the modern forestry roads, high above Carn; in the fine new ceramic sculptures dotted around the upper Valley; and it's in the lungs of older silicotic men.

And there's the Blaengarw Workmen's Hall mural which positions the mining experience in its wider context, looking both pre and post its disruptive arrival and demise.

In April 1976, the Hall's cinema was forced to close when a gas leak poisoned a packed house of more than one hundred people, most of whom were children. Carbon monoxide seeping from a blocked chimney was pumped into the audience during the showing of *Peter Pan*, the boy who would never grow old:

I was walking down Blaengarw Road and I could see a child sitting on the kerb outside, vomiting. I thought, 'more pop and crisps', but then another came out, and then another … they were passing out … It never opened tidy after that.

Will Trigg
from *The Valleys Autobiography: a people's history of the Garw, Llynfi and Ogmore valleys*, Valley & Vale, 1992

a solitary
lump of coal

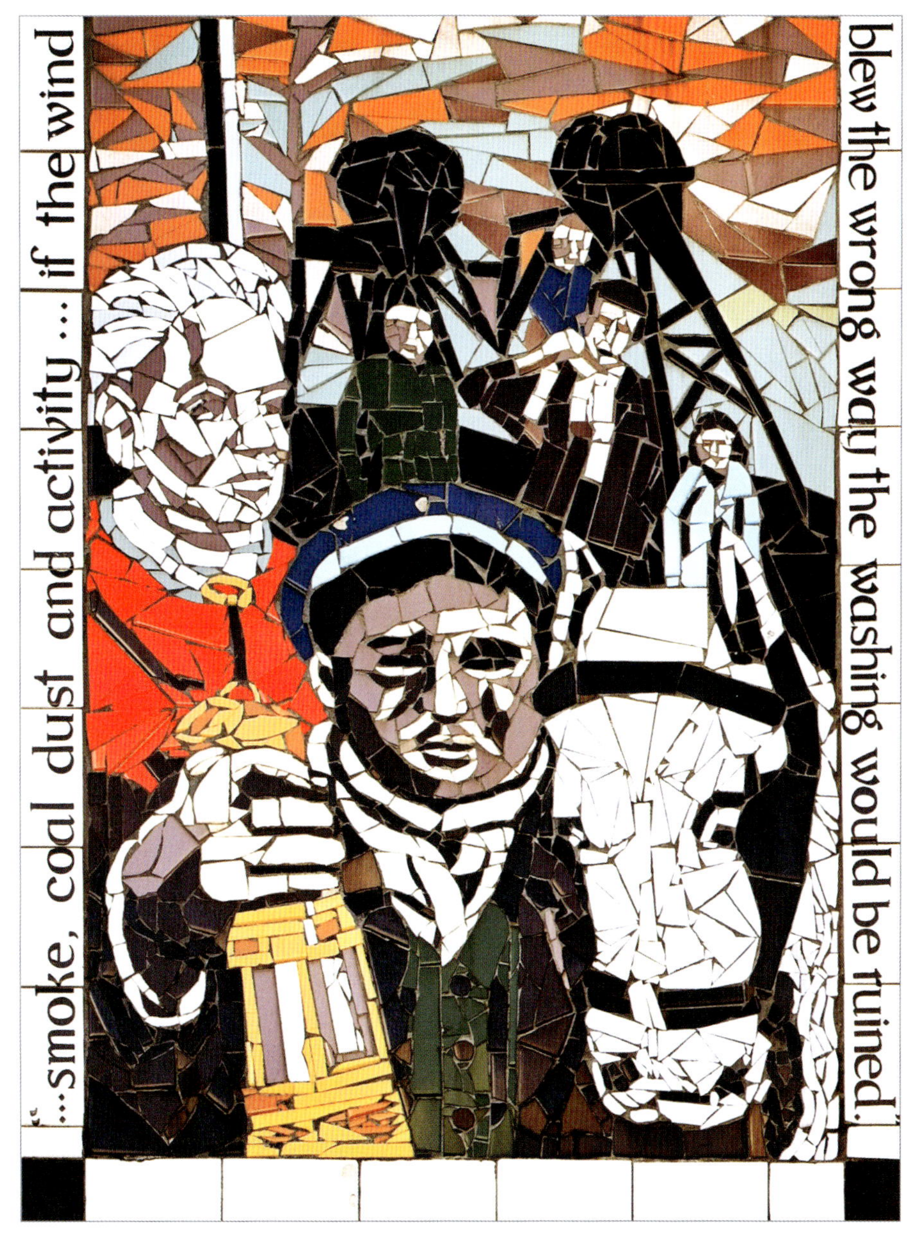

the mining panel
on the Blaengarw
Workmen's Hall
mural:

*"smoke, coal dust
and activity ...
if the wind blew
the wrong way
the washing would
be ruined"*

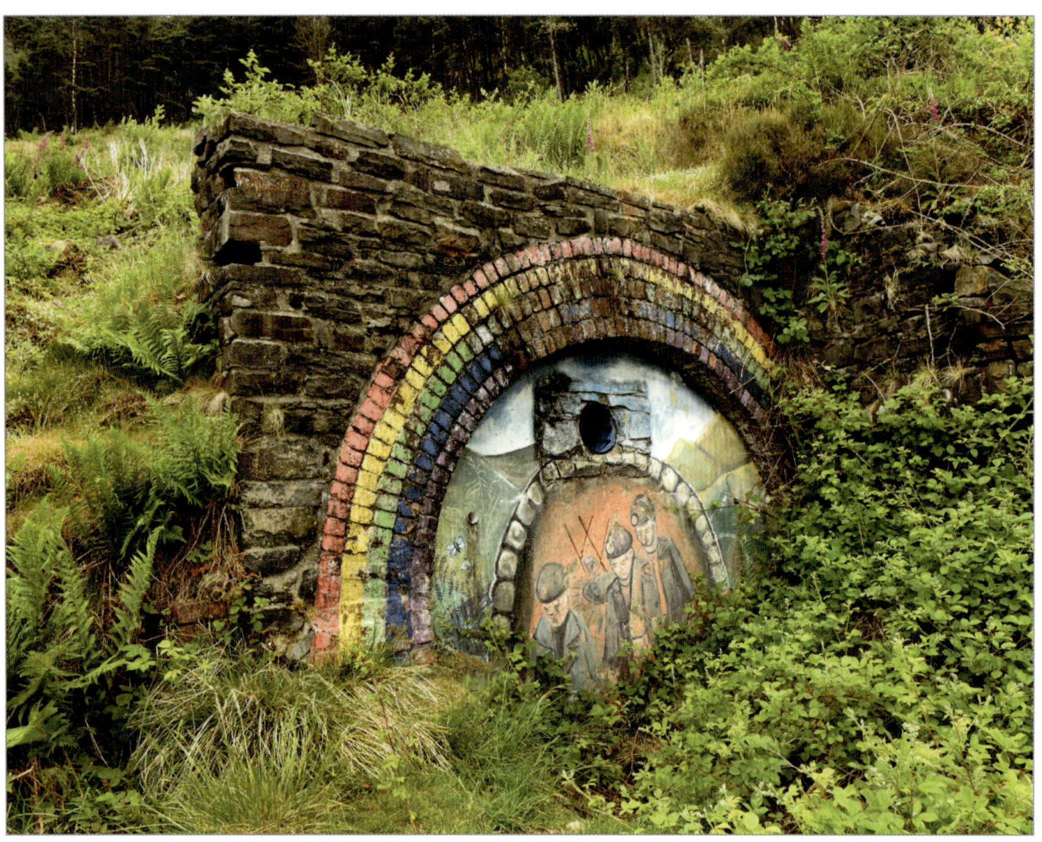

the miners' rainbow mural, painted by local young people on the bricked-up entrance to an old drift mine, above Blaengarw

opposite:

some of the panels from the Blaengarw Workmen's Hall mural, designed and constructed by local people and Valley & Vale (with the help of The Pioneers), including the four Garw history panels: Richard Price, the railway, music, strike and protest; and, below, the Valley's traditional and contemporary culture

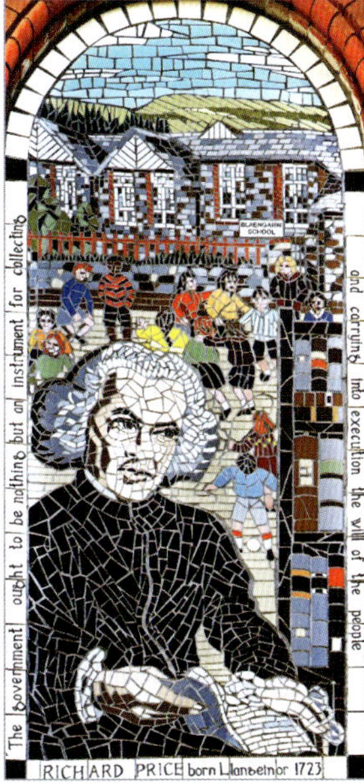

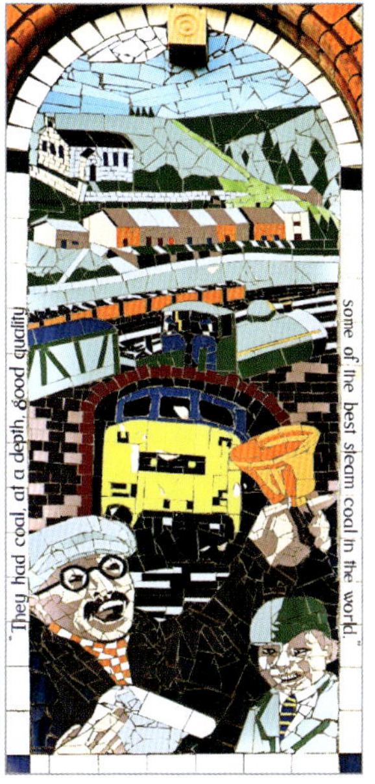

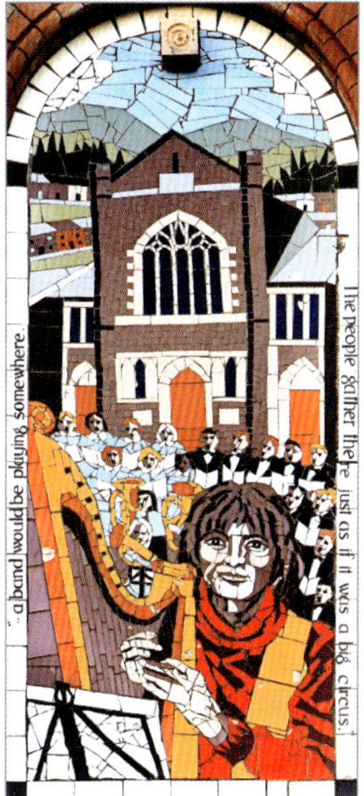

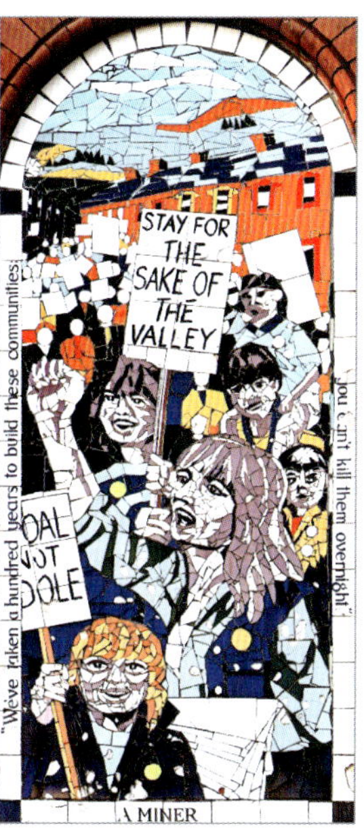

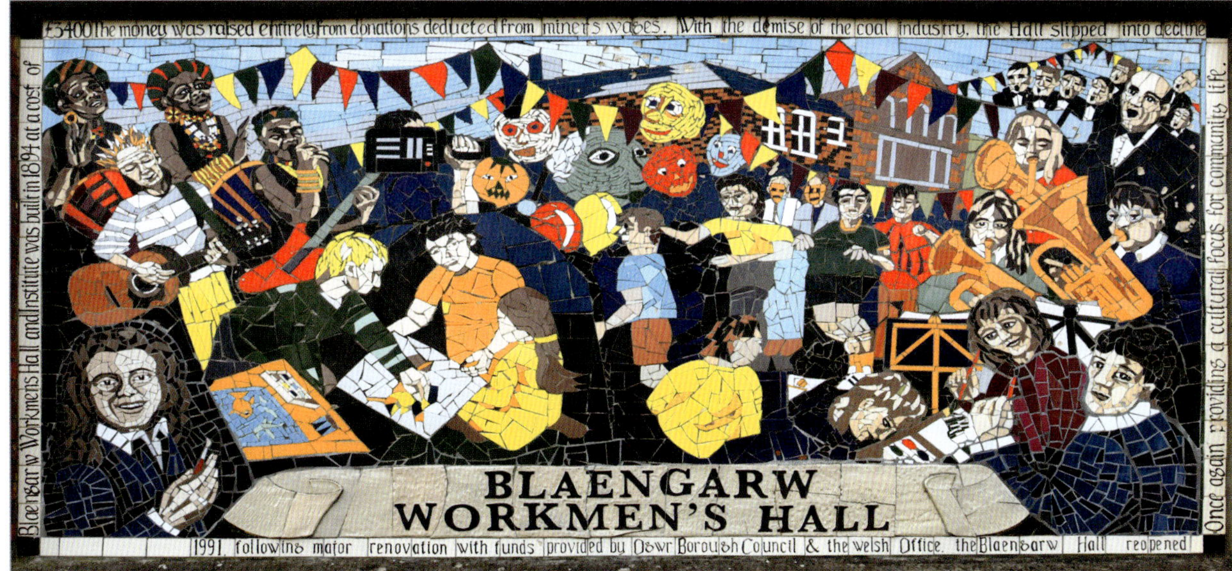

Blaengarw Workmen's Hall is currently operated by the Awen Cultural Trust. Established in 2015, Awen is a charitable organisation with objectives to "enhance cultural opportunities in Bridgend and the wider region".

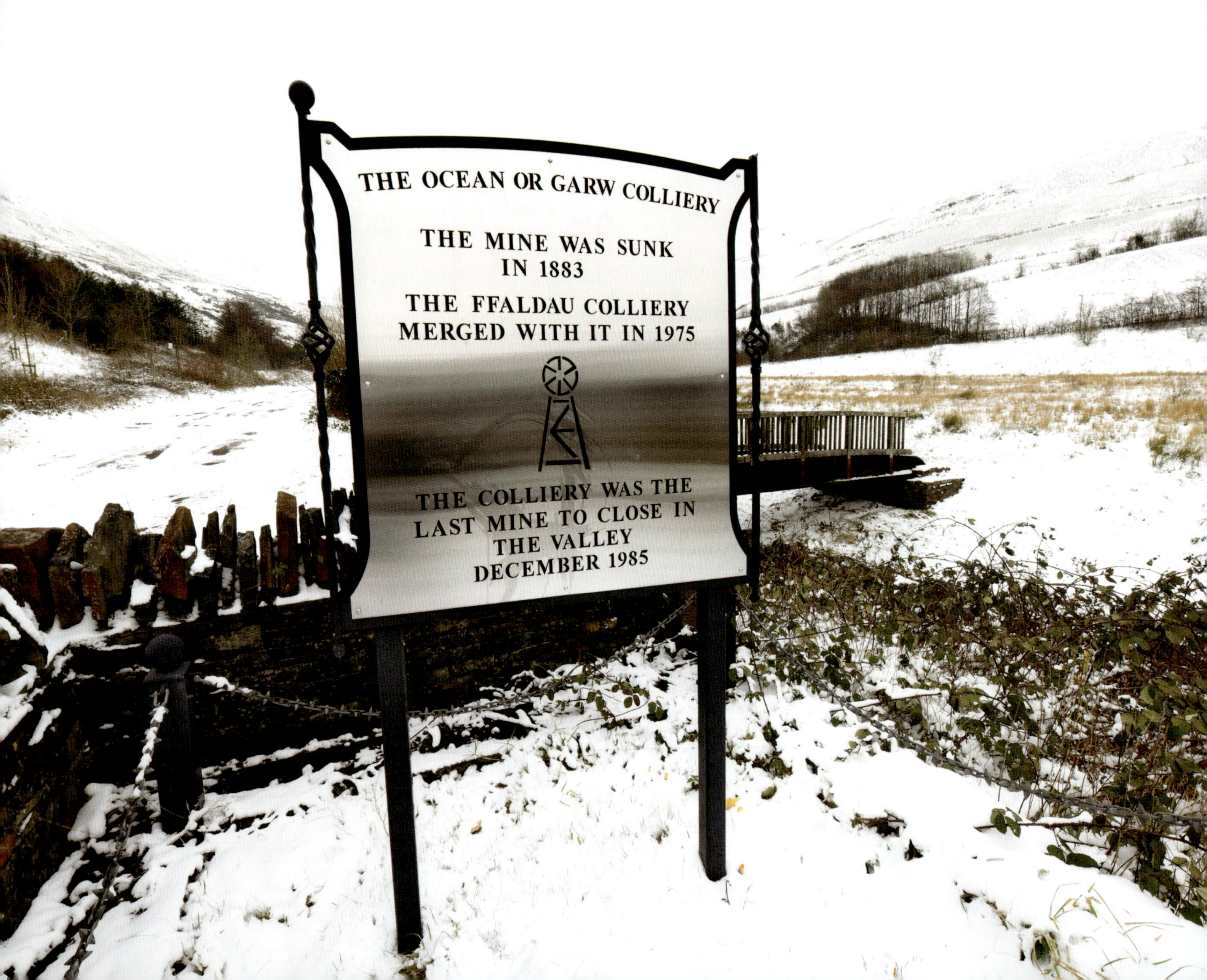

THE OCEAN OR GARW COLLIERY

THE MINE WAS SUNK
IN 1883

THE FFALDAU COLLIERY
MERGED WITH IT IN 1975

THE COLLIERY WAS THE
LAST MINE TO CLOSE IN
THE VALLEY
DECEMBER 1985

In December 1985, less than ten years after Blaengarw Workmen's Hall's carbon monoxide poisonings – and following the Valley's continued decline – the last pit in the Garw was to close. To mark the end of coal-mining here, more than 2,000 men, women and children marched from the pit gates through the streets of Blaengarw. And, despite nationalisation being regarded as a victory for the workers back in 1947, the planned burning of the National Coal Board flag had to be abandoned because it rained so hard on our parade. Instead, angry feet trampled it into the ground. Even the weather, it seemed, was on the side of the Tories, robbing the miners and their families of a last, defiant gesture in a day full of anger and of hopelessness.

But just eight months later, another march took place from the pit gates and through the streets of the village, but this time with a very different mood. *Staying for the Sake of the Valley* was a major street event devised by young people of the Garw, the culmination of Easter and Summer playscheme projects run by Valley & Vale Community Arts.

The initiative began with question-naires and discussions to establish a theme for the proposed event. Central to the young people's experiences of living in the Valley was, of course, the recent pit closure and its effects on their families and the wider commu-nity. Most were clear that they wanted to remain here rather than join the increasing numbers moving away in the search for 'better opportunities'. Strong feelings emerged about the kind of environment and facilities they wanted, the things that would best enable them to stay:

> *The last train is going*
> *And it's never coming back.*
> *The buses are being privatised*
> *And my dad's got the sack.*
> *We're staying in this Valley,*
> *You can hear us shout.*
> *We're staying 'cos we want to,*
> *Not 'cos we can't get out!*

Following this street parade – which was also performed in the rain – a video of the same name was produced by what was to become the Garw Valley Youth Video Group (later to be featured in *The Waste Game*, a major BBC documentary, directed and produced by Phil George and John Geraint, and broadcast in 1987):

> *We want work with decent pay,*
> *We want somewhere for the kids to play.*
> *You can wash coal dust off with soap,*
> *But you can't wash away our hope.*

The future of the then near-derelict Blaengarw Workmen's Hall emerged as a key concern, which resulted (to cut a very long and difficult story short) in its comprehensive renova-tion before re-opening on 3 October 1992, complete with the re-instate-ment of its theatre and 35mm projec-tion, a new sound recording work-shop, dance studio, video edit suite, computer design facilities and photo-graphic darkroom, as well as general purpose rooms. The community once again had a focus for its survival, but this time while staring into a much more uncertain future, devoid of the always-questionable security of coal.

A third march, in January 1996, entitled *Ten Years Without Coal*, celebrated the imagination and resilience of those who had stayed. Huge colourful banners were created and specially-commissioned music performed about both the history of the Garw as well as our prospects and hopes for the future. This march was, once again, dominated by young people … but, this time, it didn't rain!

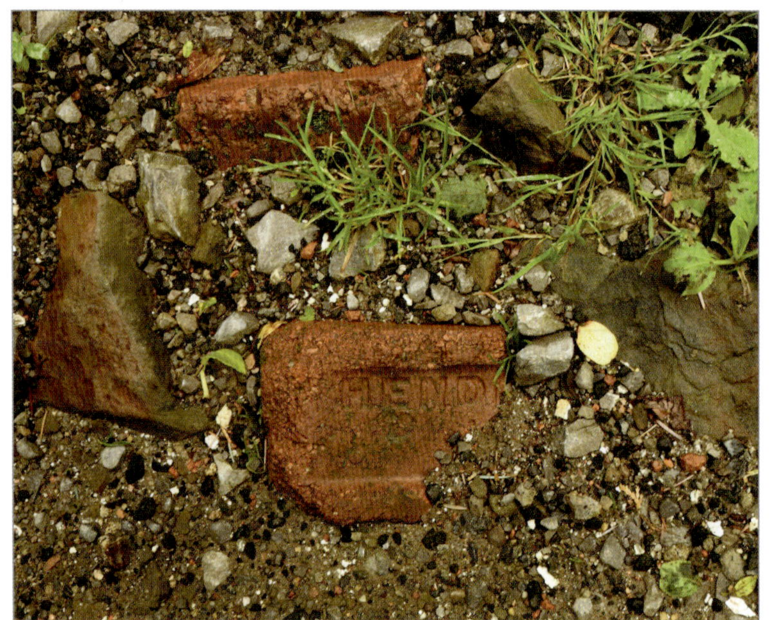

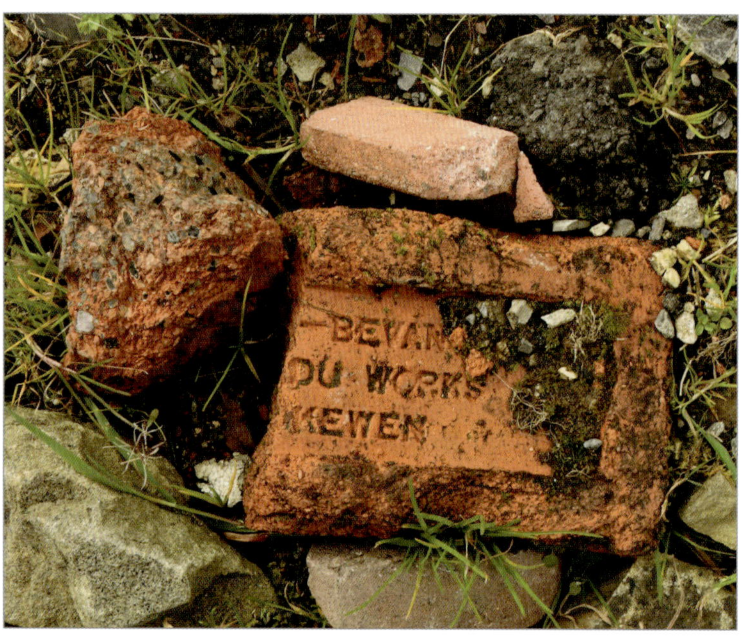

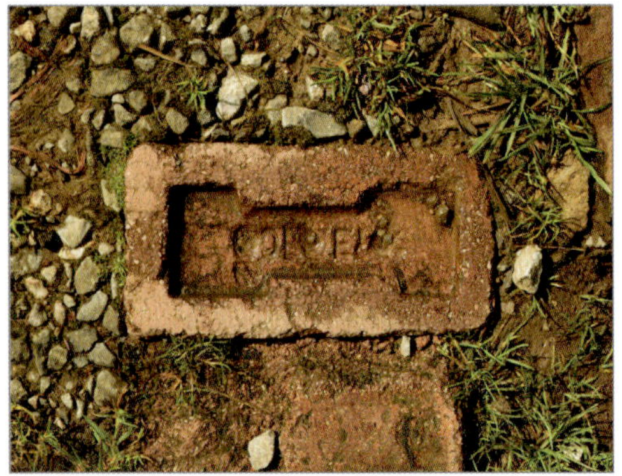

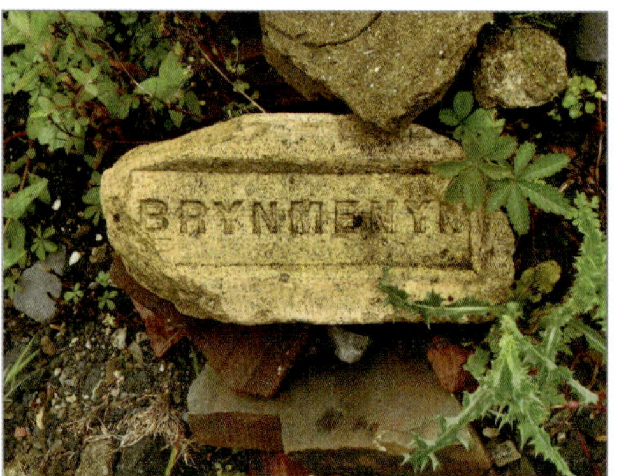

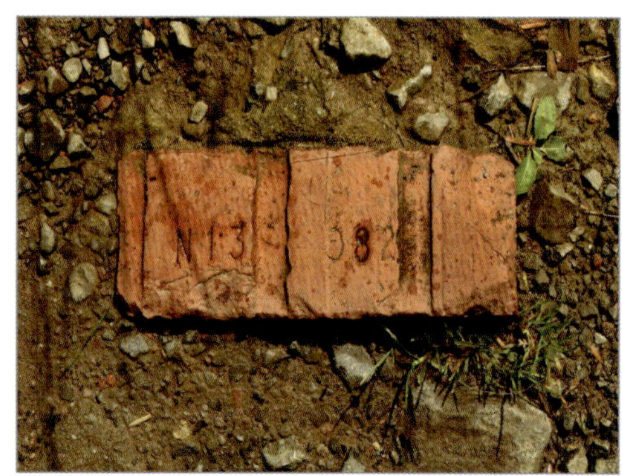

locally-made bricks and mining detritus

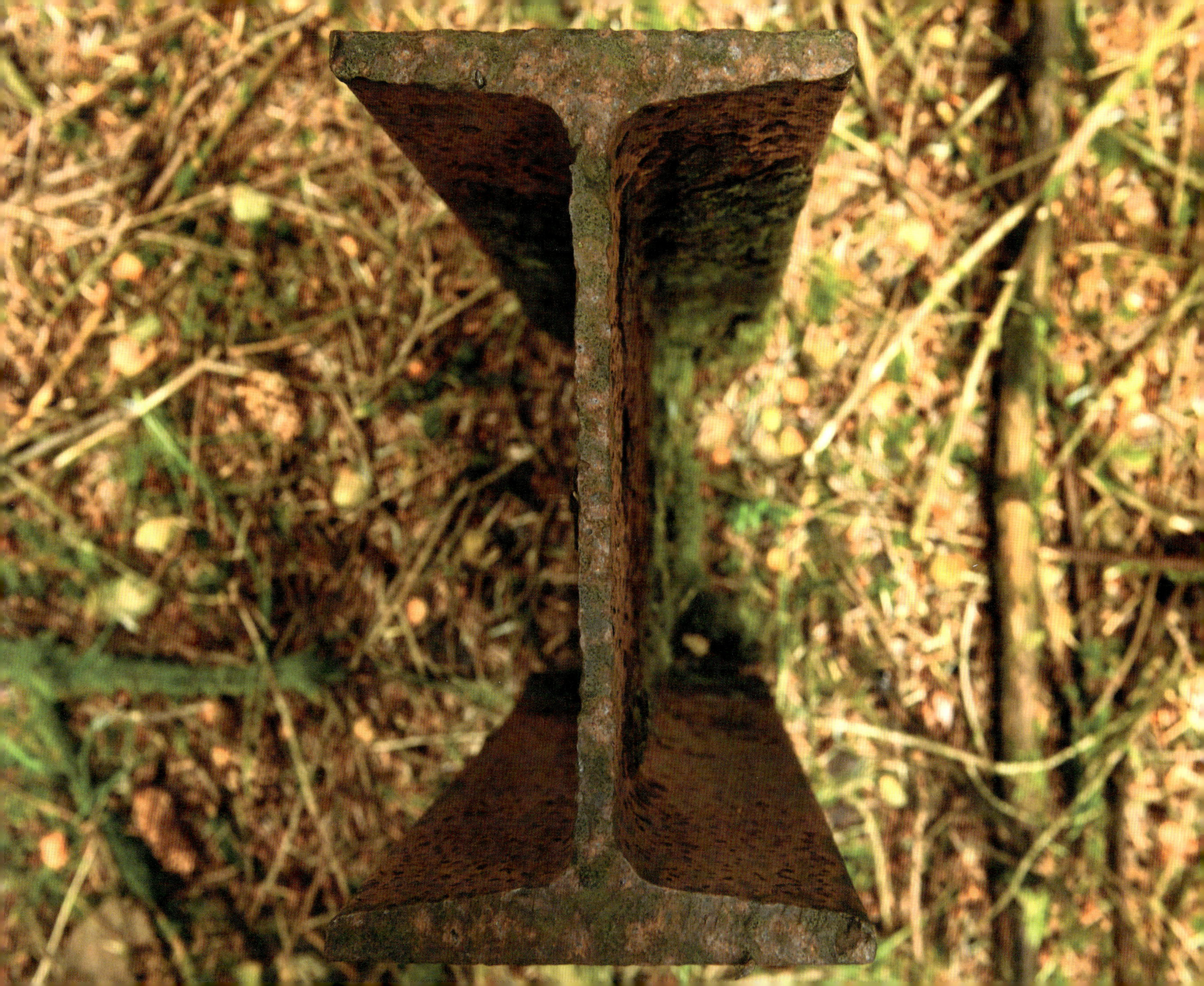

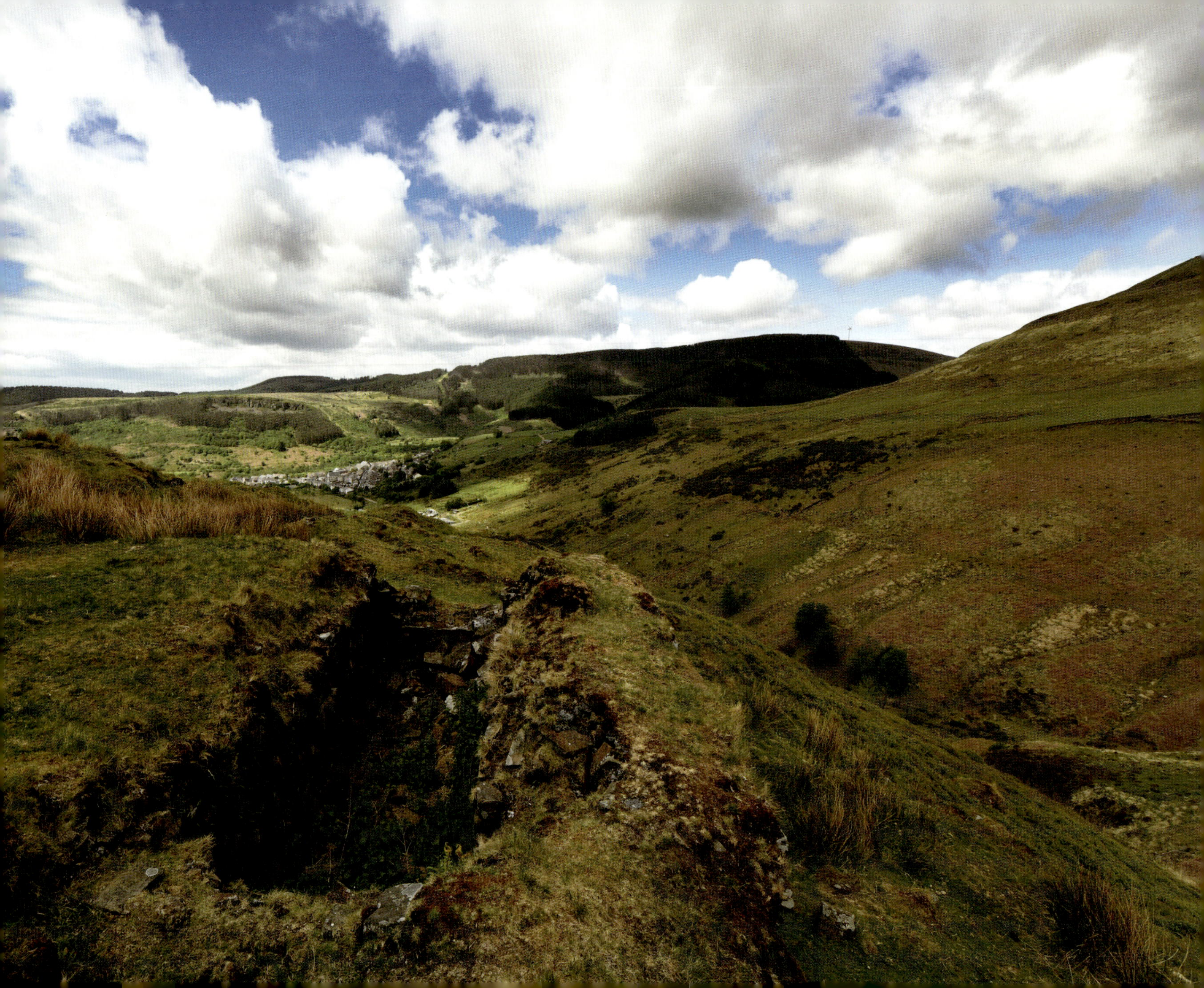

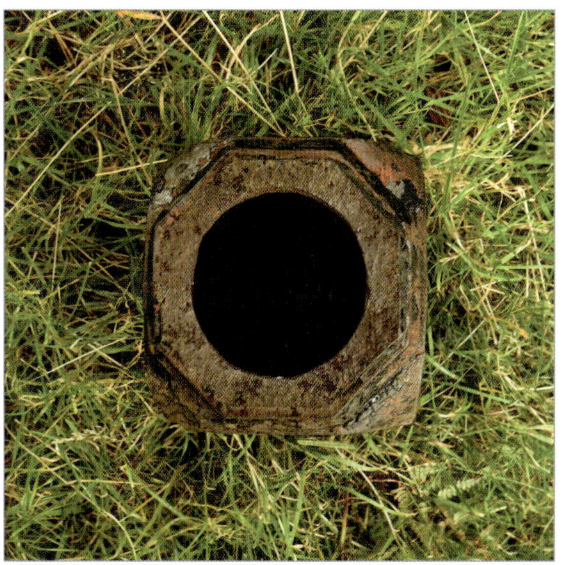

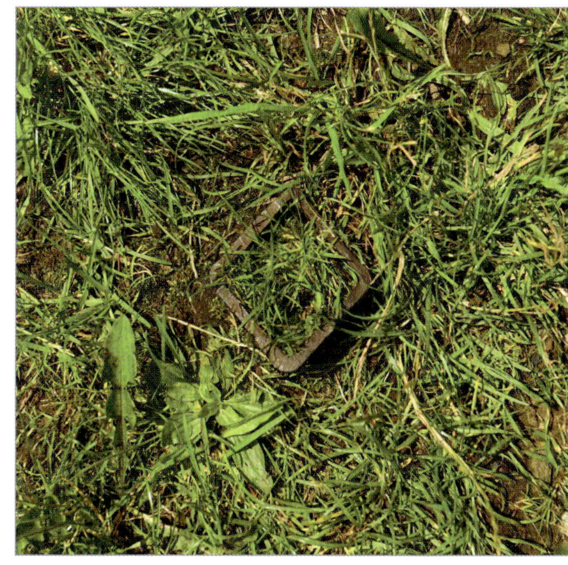

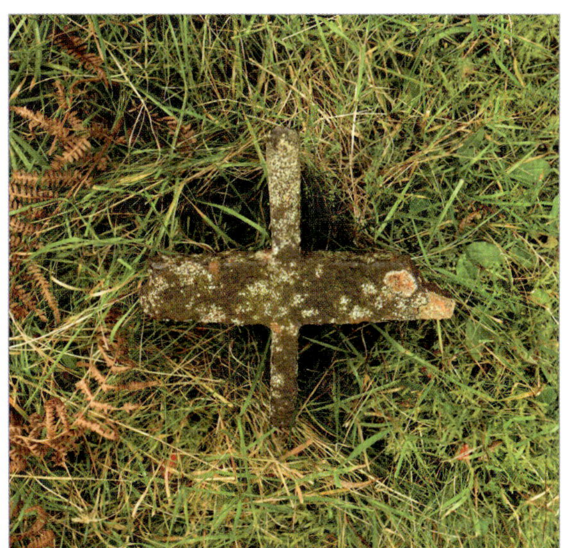

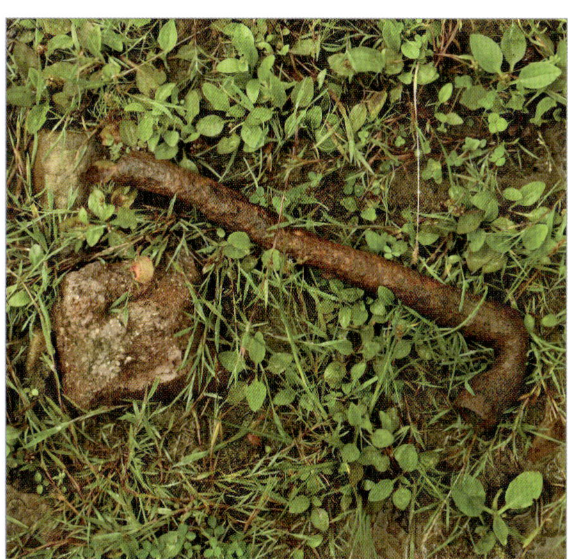

opposite:

early workings
(which were
probably part of
the tramway system),
Nant Hir,
above Blaengarw

mining
detritus

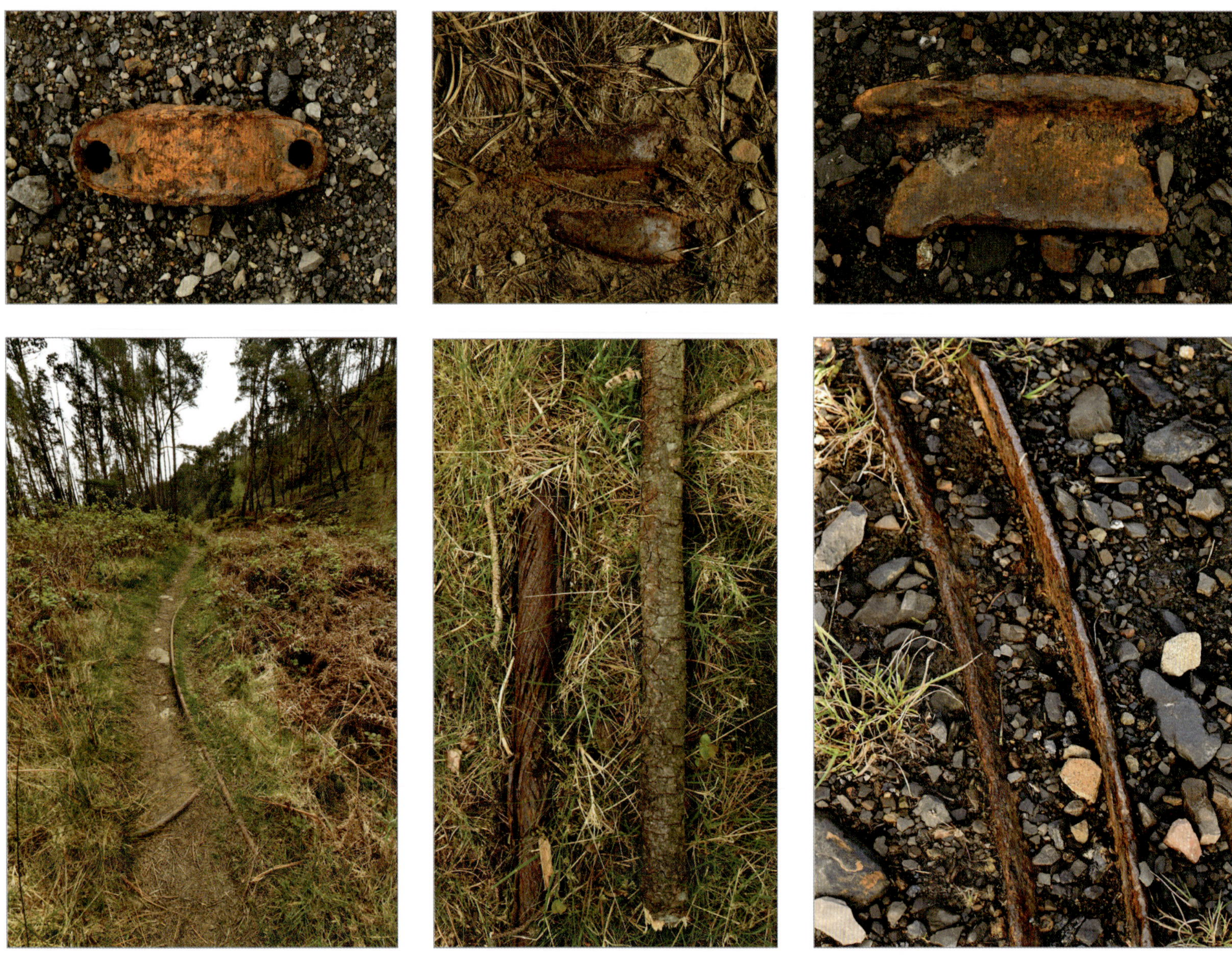

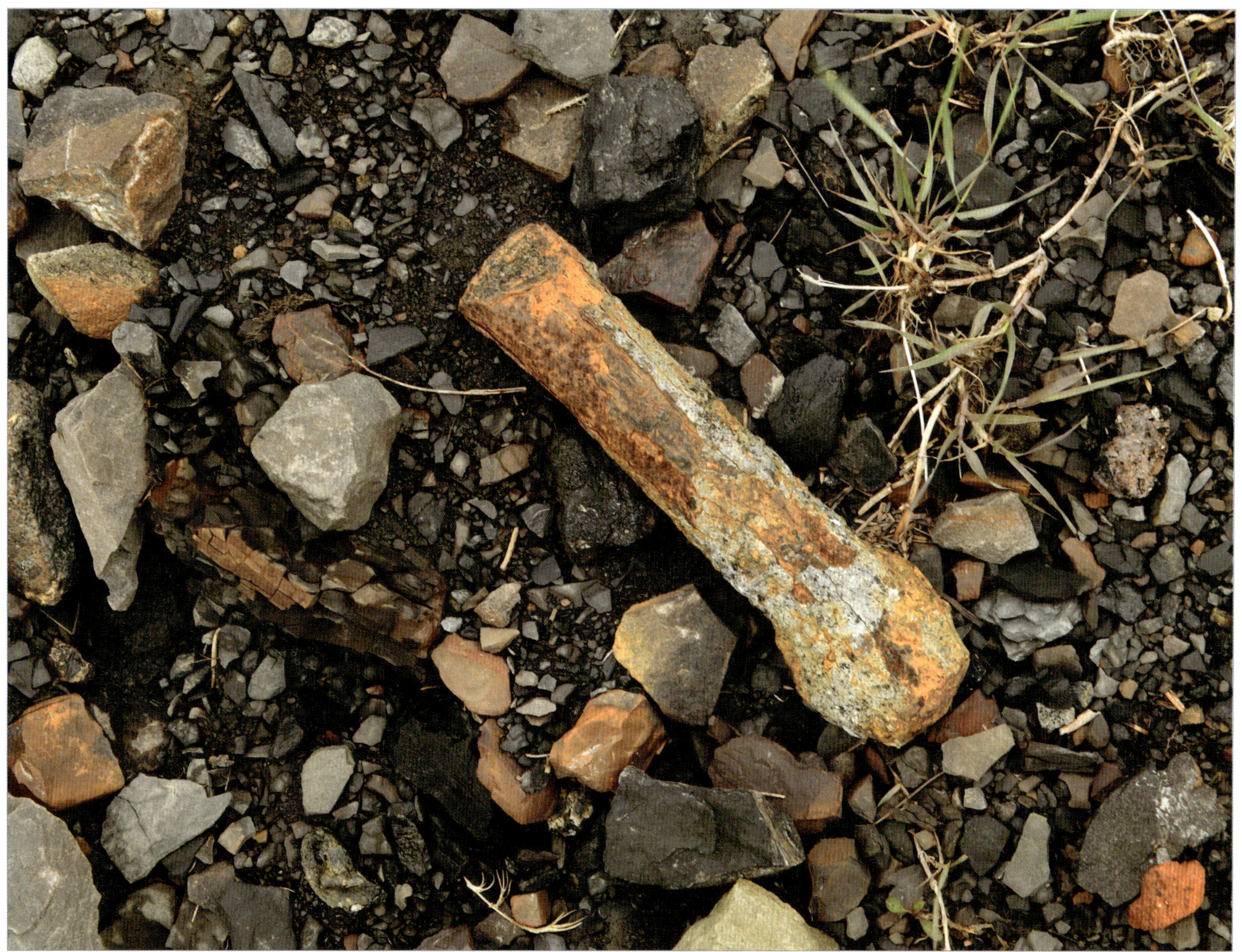

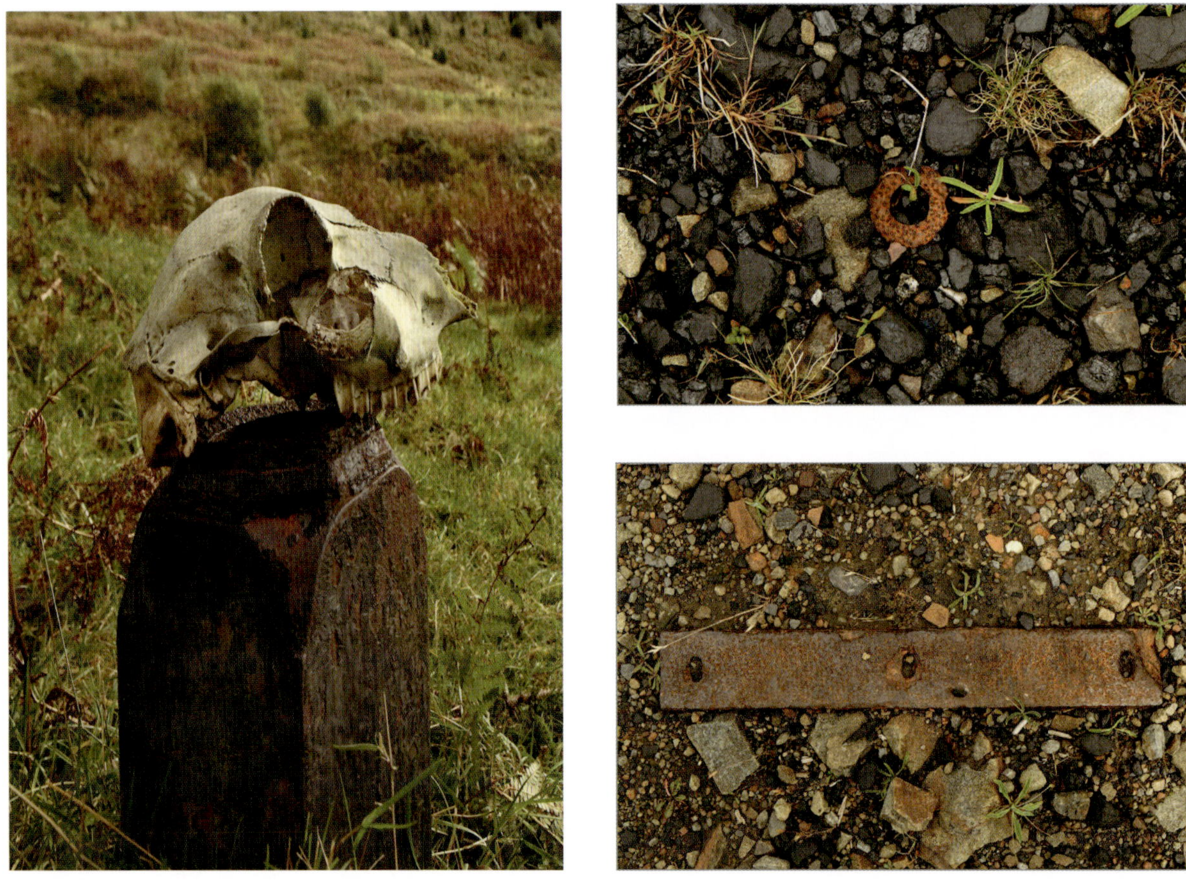

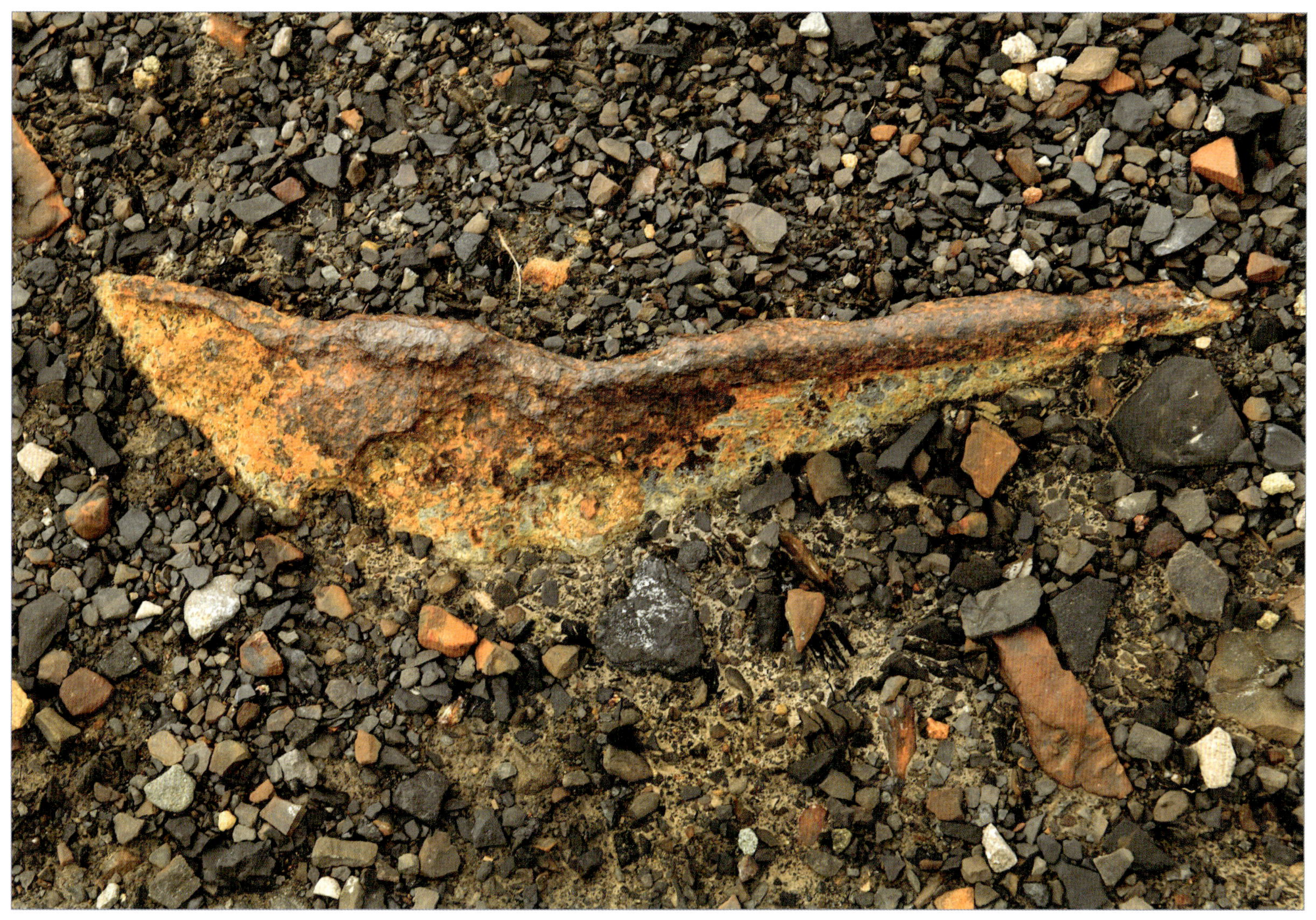

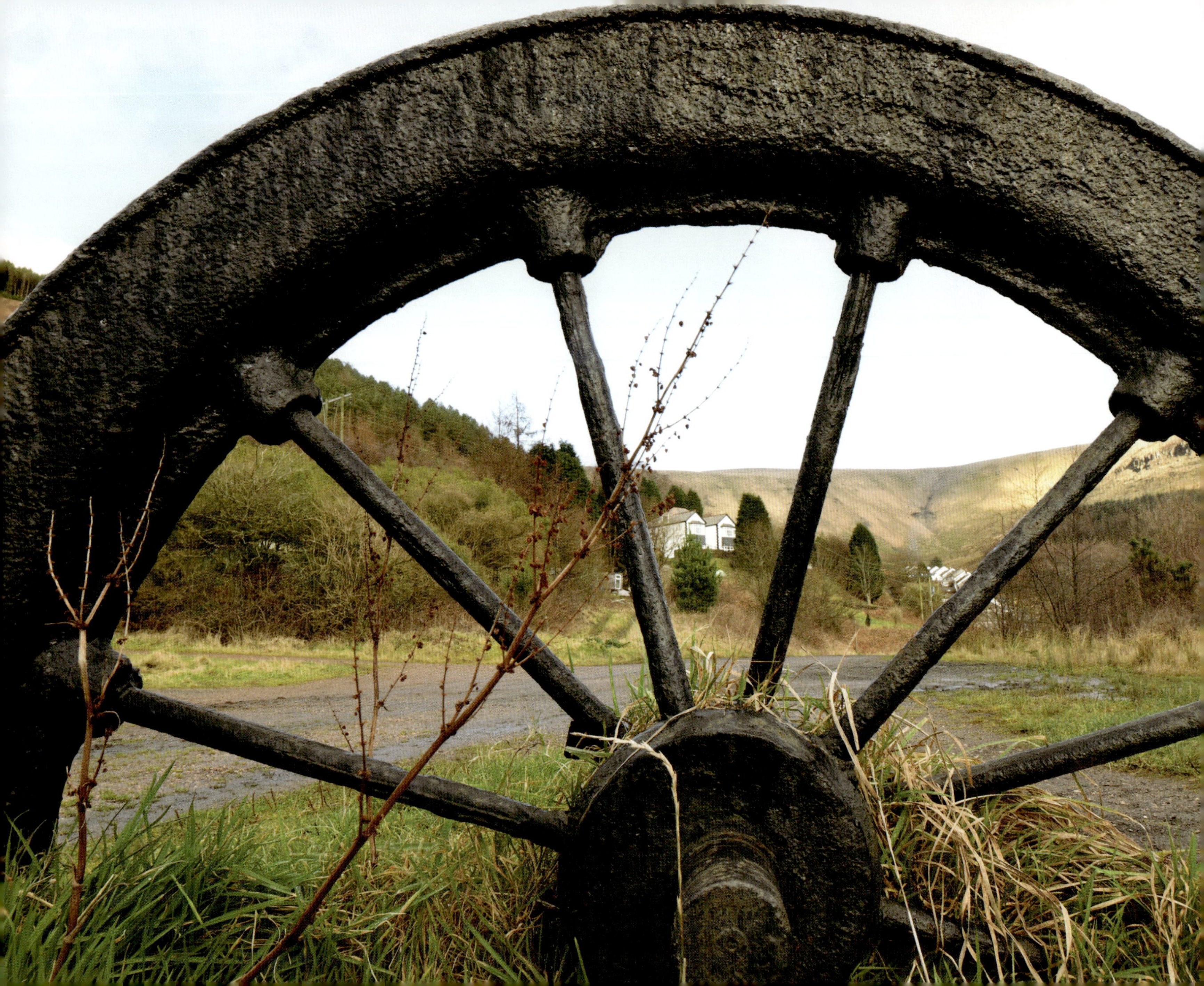

pit wheel,
with the pit
manager's
elevated house
in the distance,
Carn

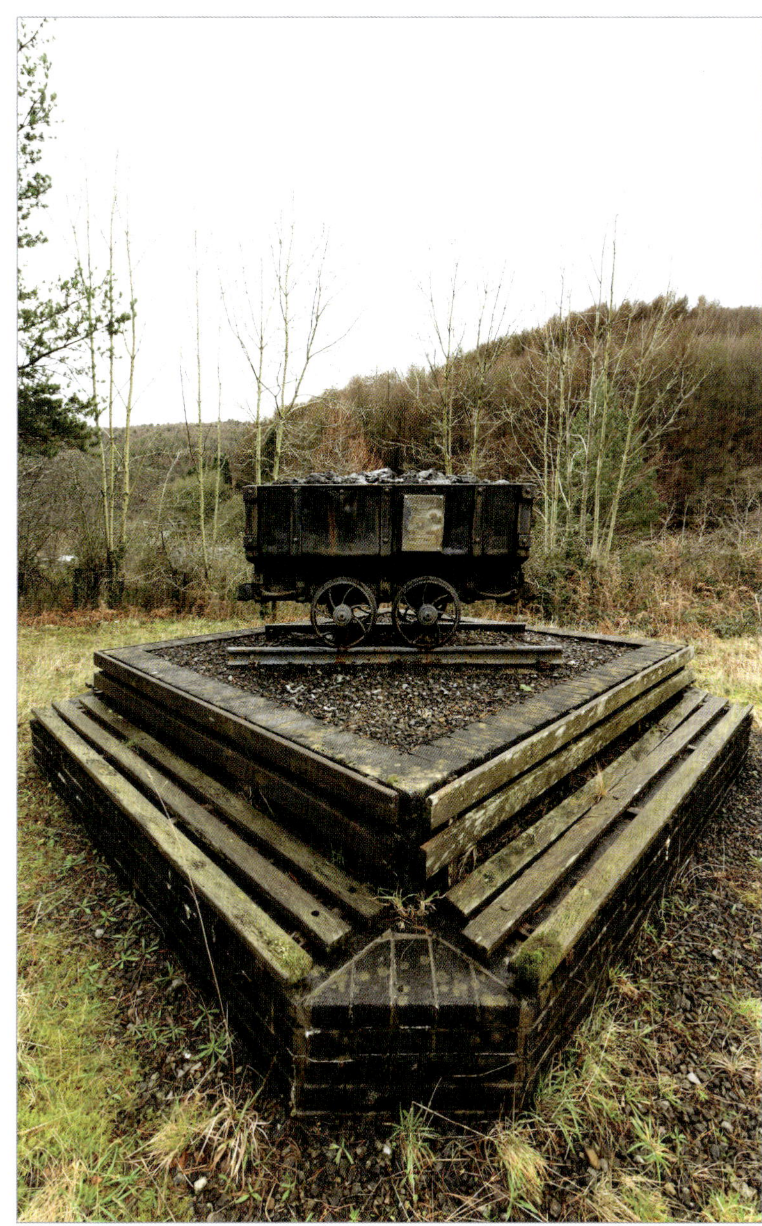

Lluest
Colliery
disaster
memorial,
Lluest

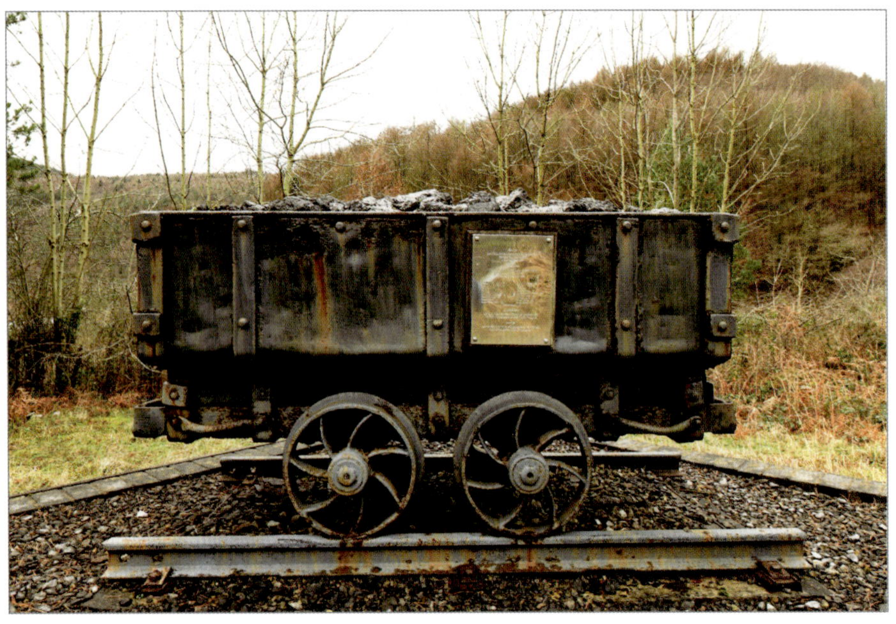

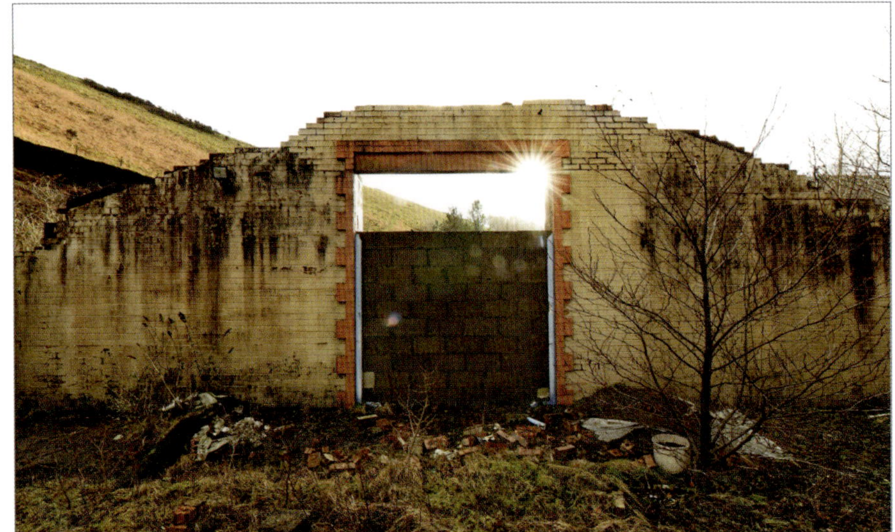

Once a tin soldier then a kite factory, the now-derelict building at the place where the Lluest memorial is to be found, sits directly above the fateful colliery.

opposite:
The impressive wall art, telling the first-hand stories of coal-mining, runs for much of the length of the upper Garw.

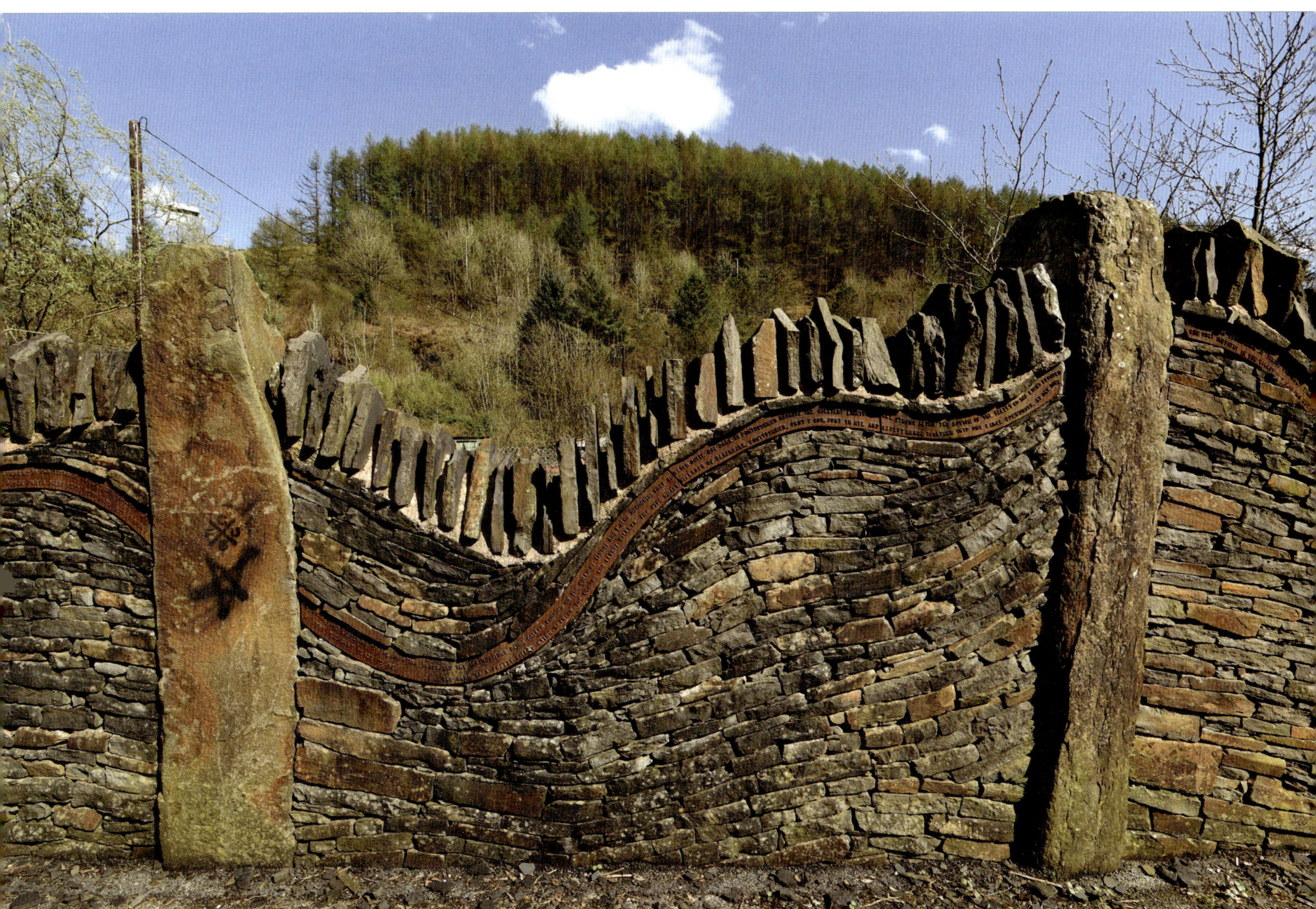

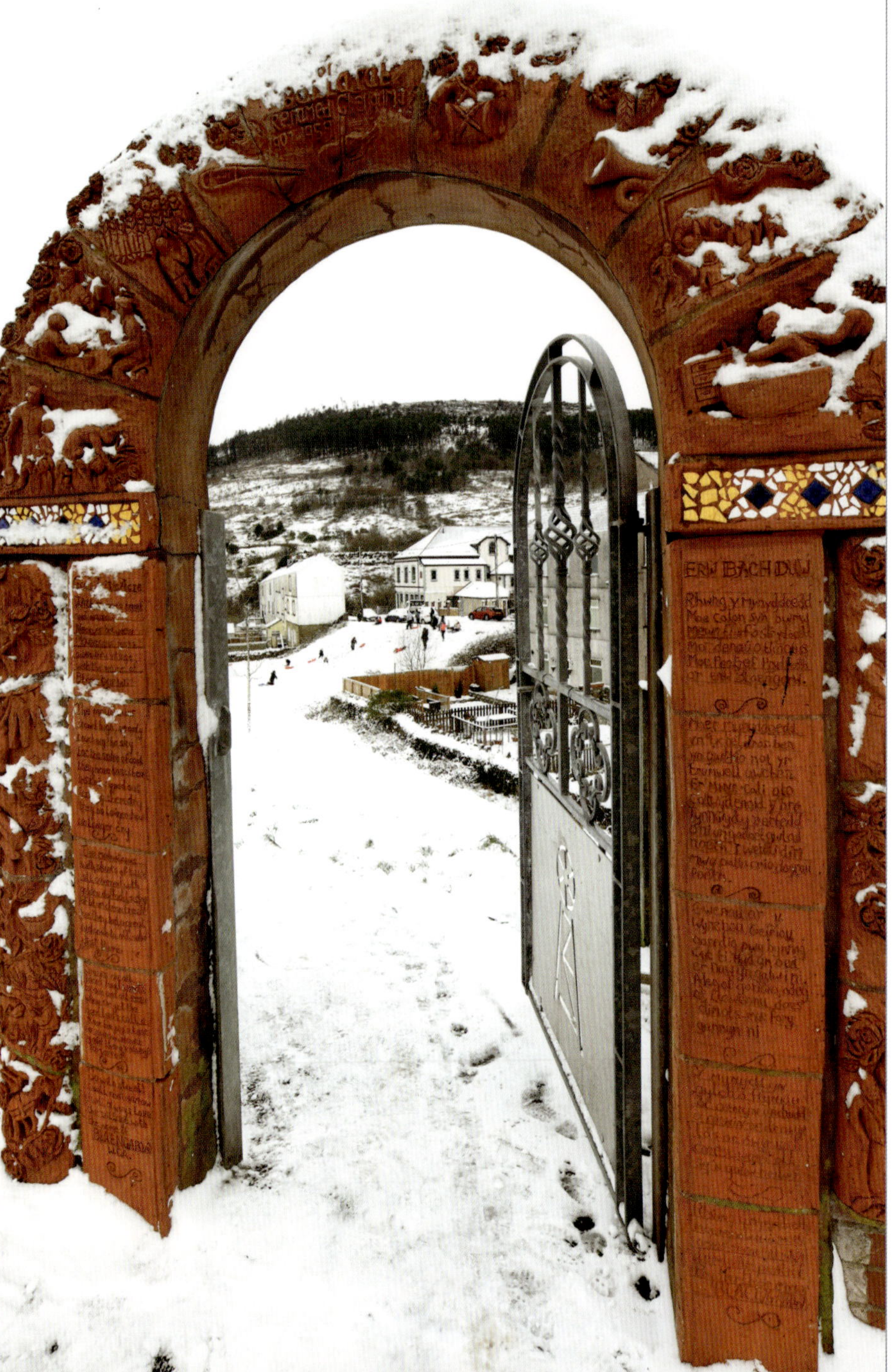

The 'Balarat Pit Marker Gateway' (on the site of the Glengarw Colliery) is one of the impressive ceramic sculptures made by Rebecca Buck of Osprey Studios, Ynyswen in the Upper Tawe Valley, working alongside local volunteers from a make-shift studio in an abandoned shop front in Blaengarw.

Scattered within the parks of the upper Garw, the sculptures explore and celebrate the struggles of the mining experience.

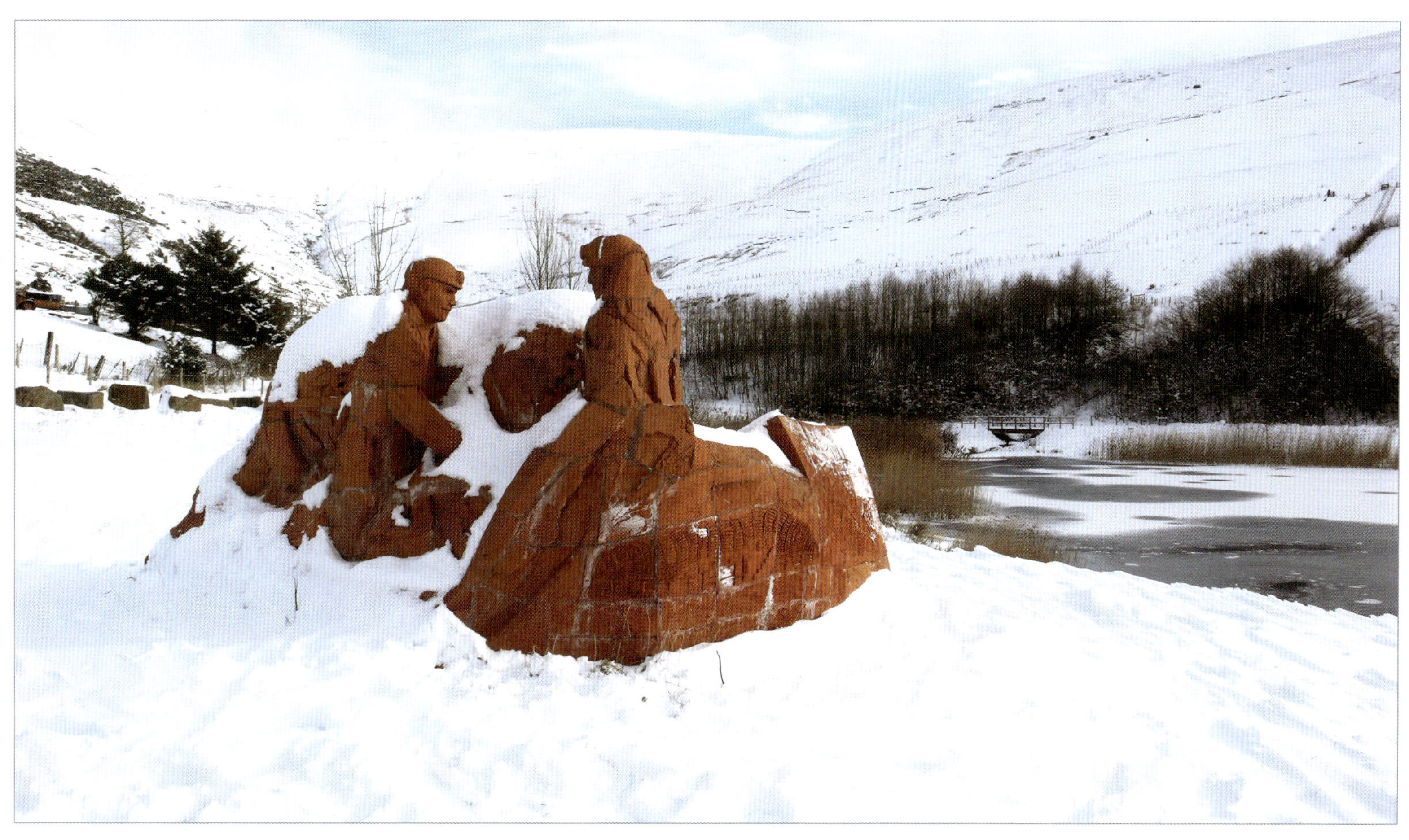

the Ocean Colliery Pit Marker sculpture:

Some of the volunteers who helped create
this powerful piece themselves worked underground.

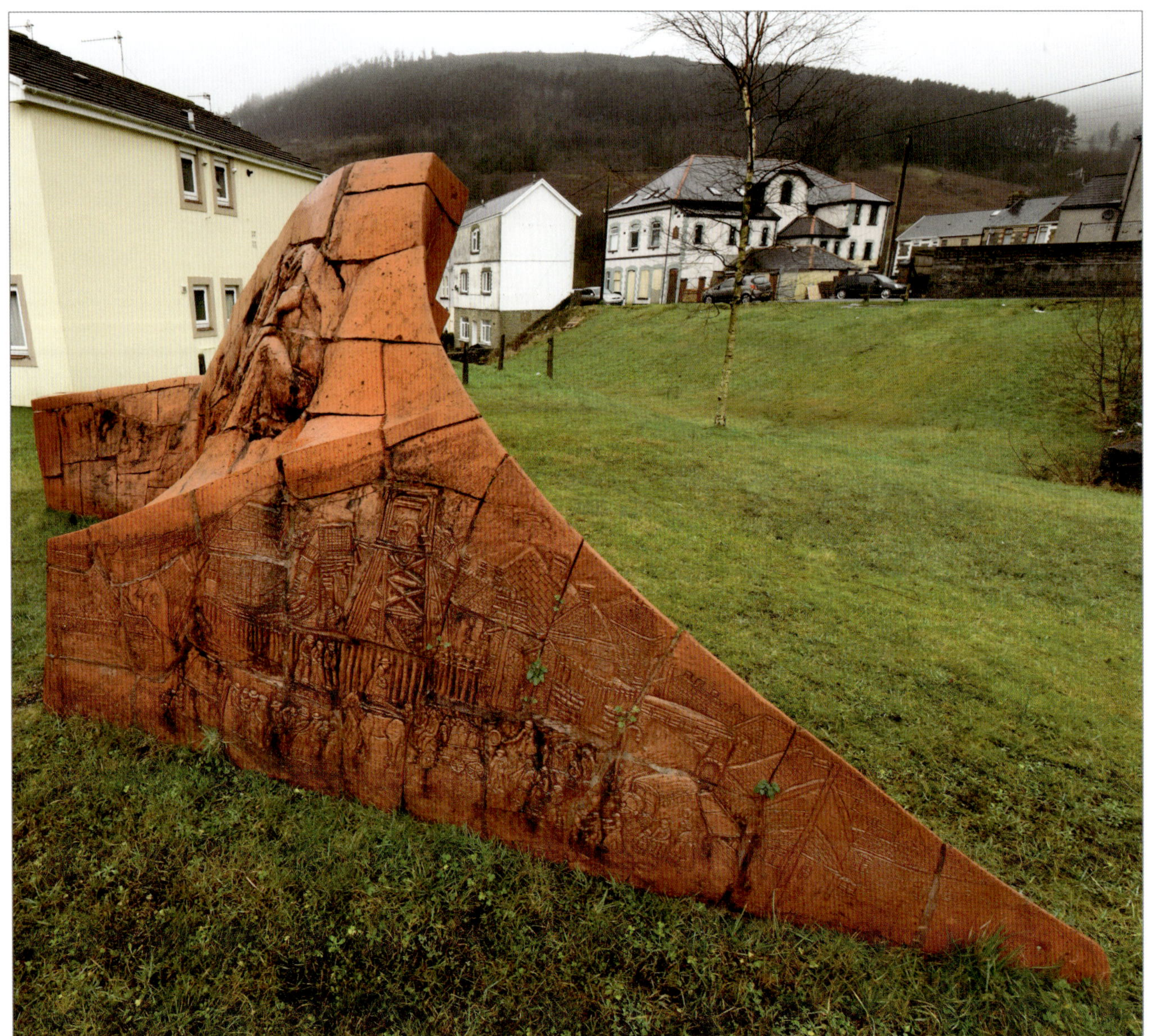

the 'Balarat Pit Marker' sculpture, Glengarw Colliery, Blaengarw (with the Charter Club in the background, now converted to flats)

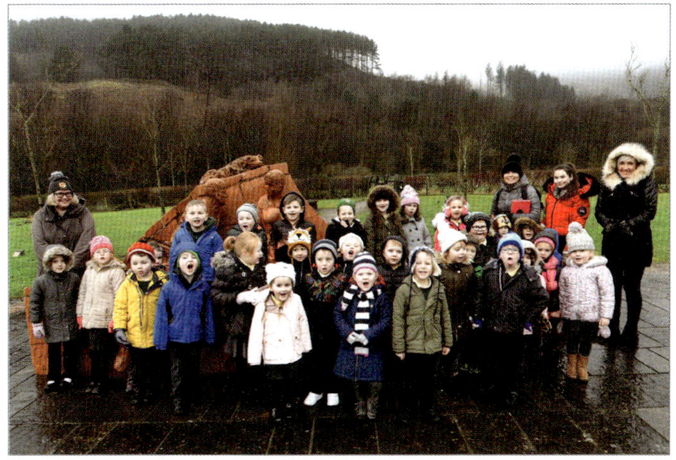

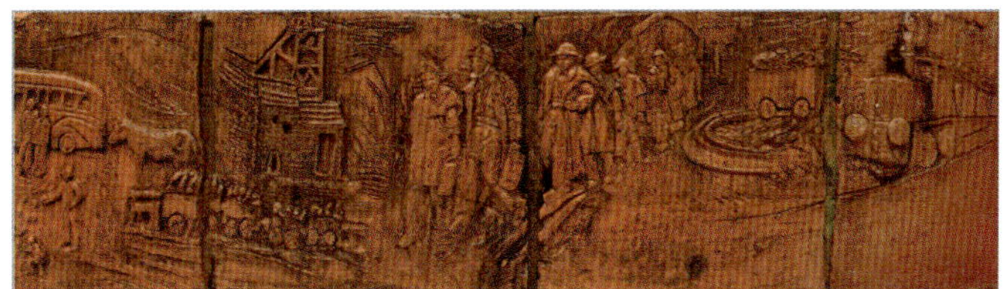

children from Blaengarw Junior School visiting Parc Calon Lân, and its sculpture celebrating the life of the reformed-alcoholic Daniel James [*Gwyrosydd*] and his famous hymn, the words of which he penned while working under-ground in the Ocean Colliery and living at 8 Herbert Street, Blaengarw

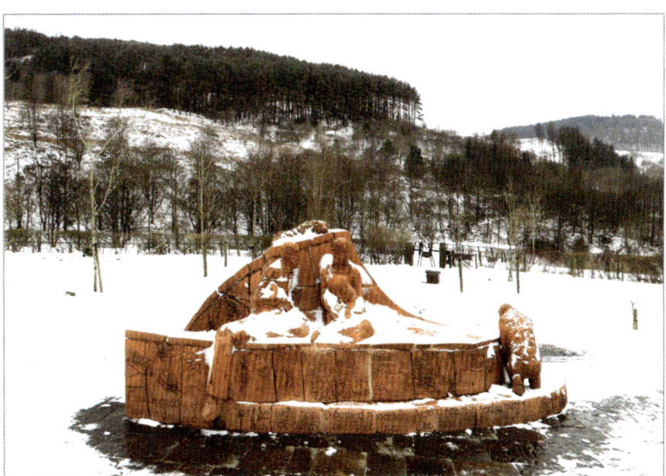

During the post-coal years, many efforts at reviving the Garw's fortunes have been proposed.

In addition to the renaissance of Blaengarw Workmen's Hall, the land reclamation schemes of the late 1980s and early '90s have successfully managed to return parts of the land to something approaching its original appeal.

One of the most recent to see its coal exploited on an industrial scale and one of the last to be afforded a land reclamation scheme, the Garw has emerged from the savagery of its abuse less scathed, perhaps, than many of its neighbours, at least in physical terms.

The work of reclamation recovered the then-profitable shale through a brief period of opencast mining, followed by the securing and/or contouring of the slag and small coal tips into rolling hills (to avoid, amongst other things, another Aberfan).

Flattening, grassing and fertilising the slopes, this was both a physical salvage as well as a symbolic act of societal redemption for a community, quite literally, left on the rubbish heap.

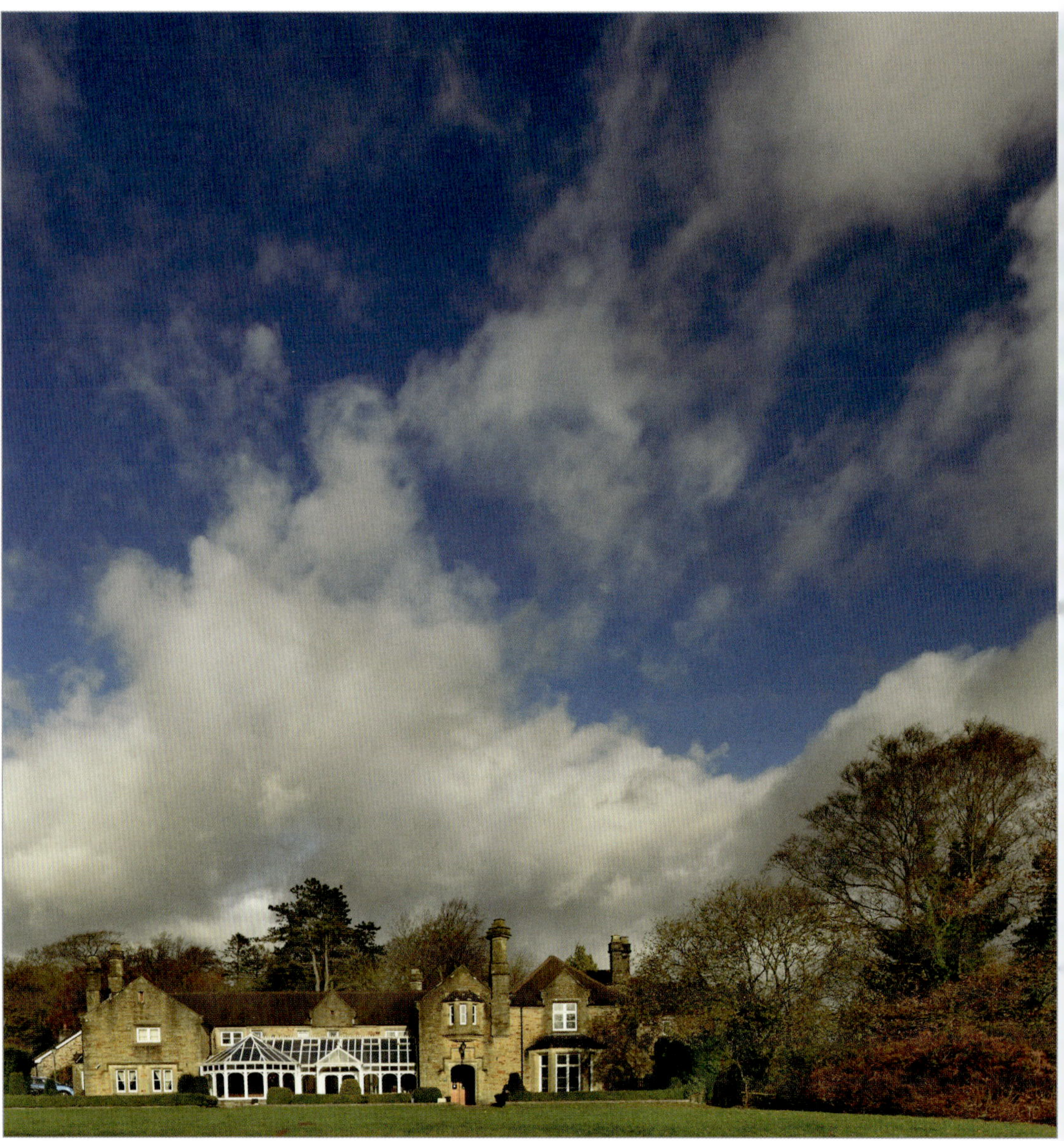

With our four new lakes, our walking and leisure and (much more challenging) mountain bike trails beside and above the old railway line, and the new more democratic uses of the mid eighteenth-century Bryngarw House and Park (once the residence of the coal-owning Traherne family), a new identity is being explored.

Huge sums of money were made by the great landowning families who had once leased their lands to farmers, but who now recognised the much greater sums that could be made from the new coal barons.

In addition to the rental fee for access to their land, they were also able to charge royalties per ton of coal raised, as well as for its conveyance.

This was a time when these un-worked-for profits were used to build luxurious houses on large estates, like that (opposite) at Bryngarw.

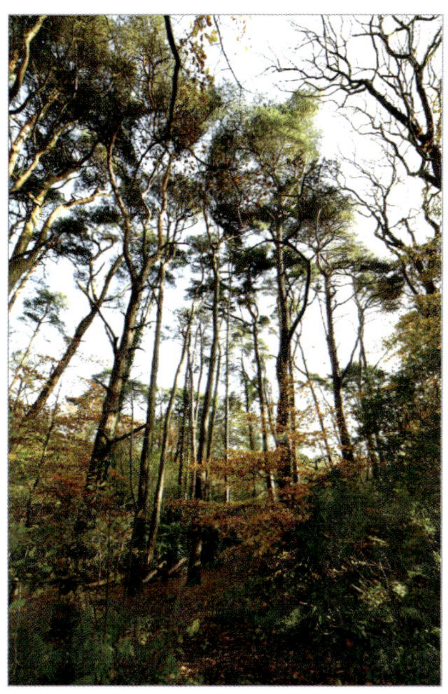

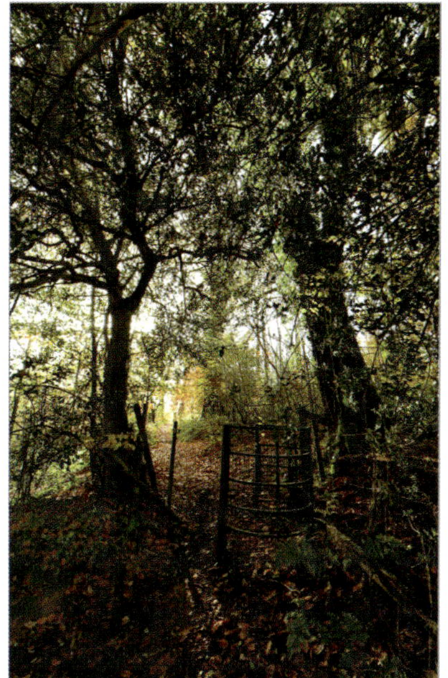

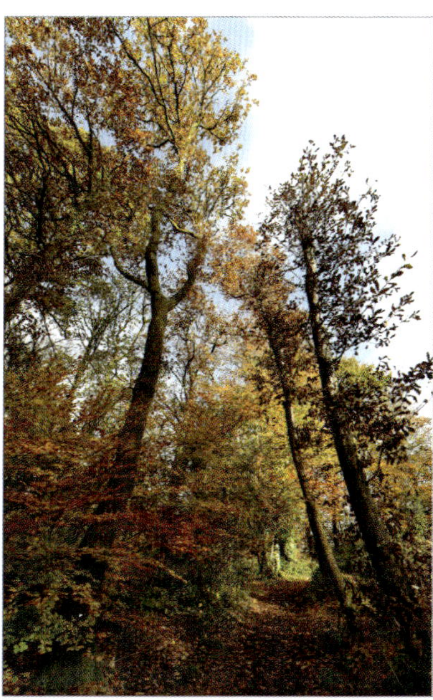

above:

some of the fine walks within Bryngarw Park ...open now not just to the land-owning, super-rich

Bought by the local council and open to the public since 1986, Bryngarw, set beside the last runnings of the Garw river, offers a partial metaphor, perhaps, for an alternative approach to the use of this land's significant riches.

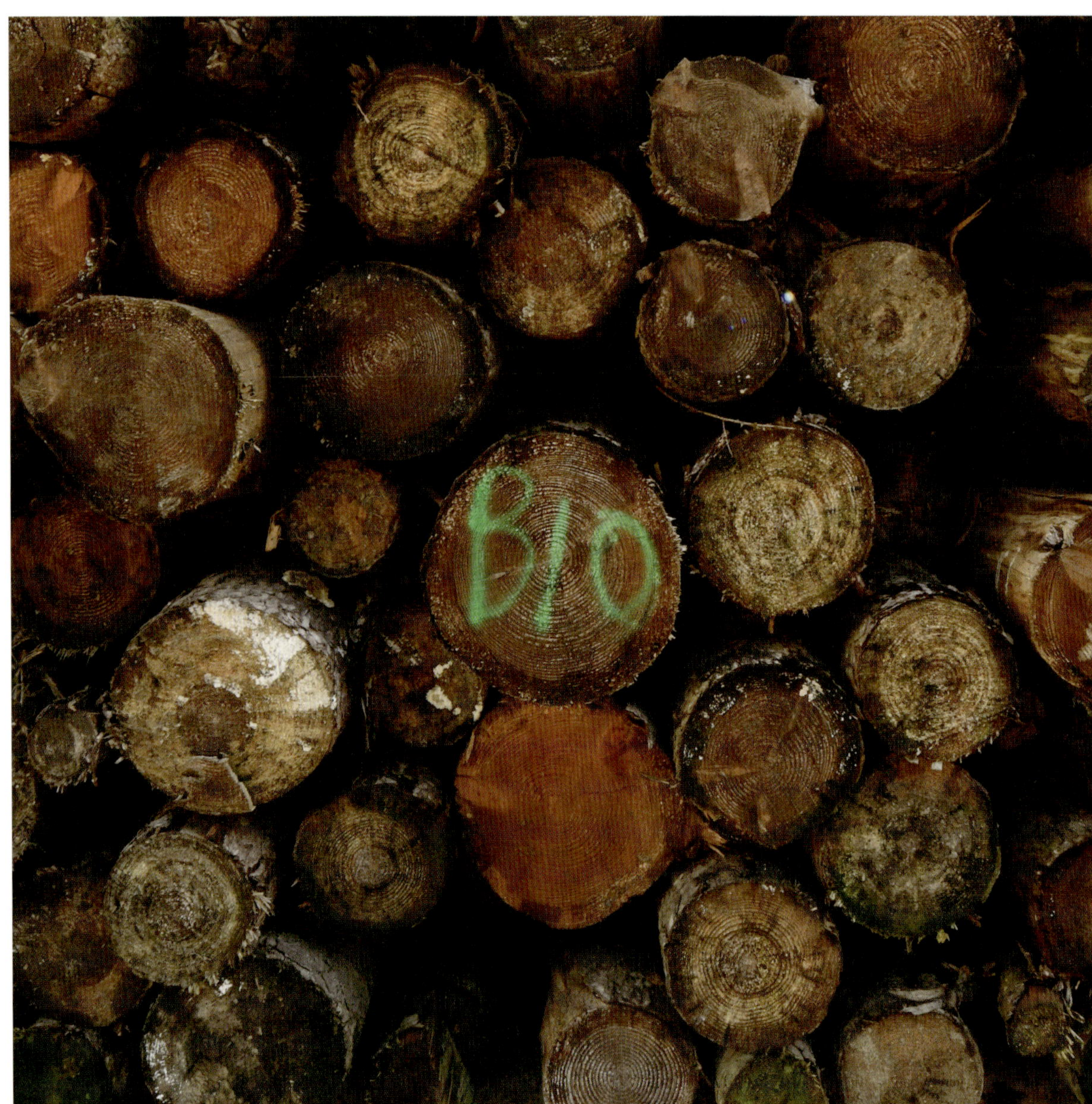

from the forestry
above
Pontyrhyl

During the mining century, the trees and plants that managed to survive were dusted with a coating of coal; the air was often foul; and mountains of slag grew higher daily on people's limited horizon. The Valley's waters were heavily polluted, earning them the local nickname of Afon Ddu ('the black river'). Meic Stephens in his poem *Eels*, recalled that "At school we used to paint our rivers black, / blue was for the sky and sea".

Today, the rivers and streams – the greatest barometers of nature's renewal – run clear and wild (though often within artificial channels constructed as part of the reclamation efforts).

And the Valley's hillsides are once again clothed in trees, albeit now of a more regulated variety, in what Robert Minhinnick described as "black sitka on their needlebeds / beloved of arsonists and speedway boys" (from *At the Cairns above Blaengarw*, 2020).

These alien ubiquitous tree-farmed conifers discourage the co-habitation of most bird and animal life, and only tell you what season it is when clothed in snow.

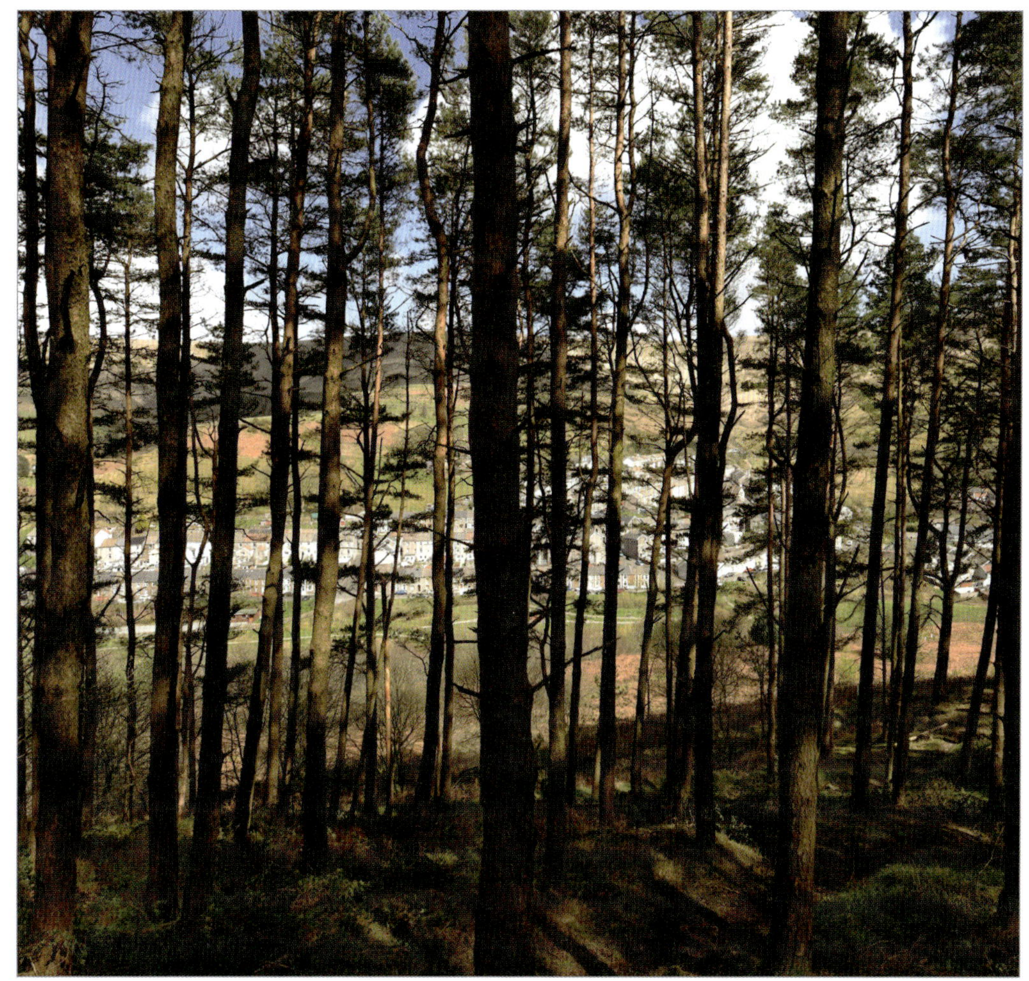

the forestry
above Blaengarw

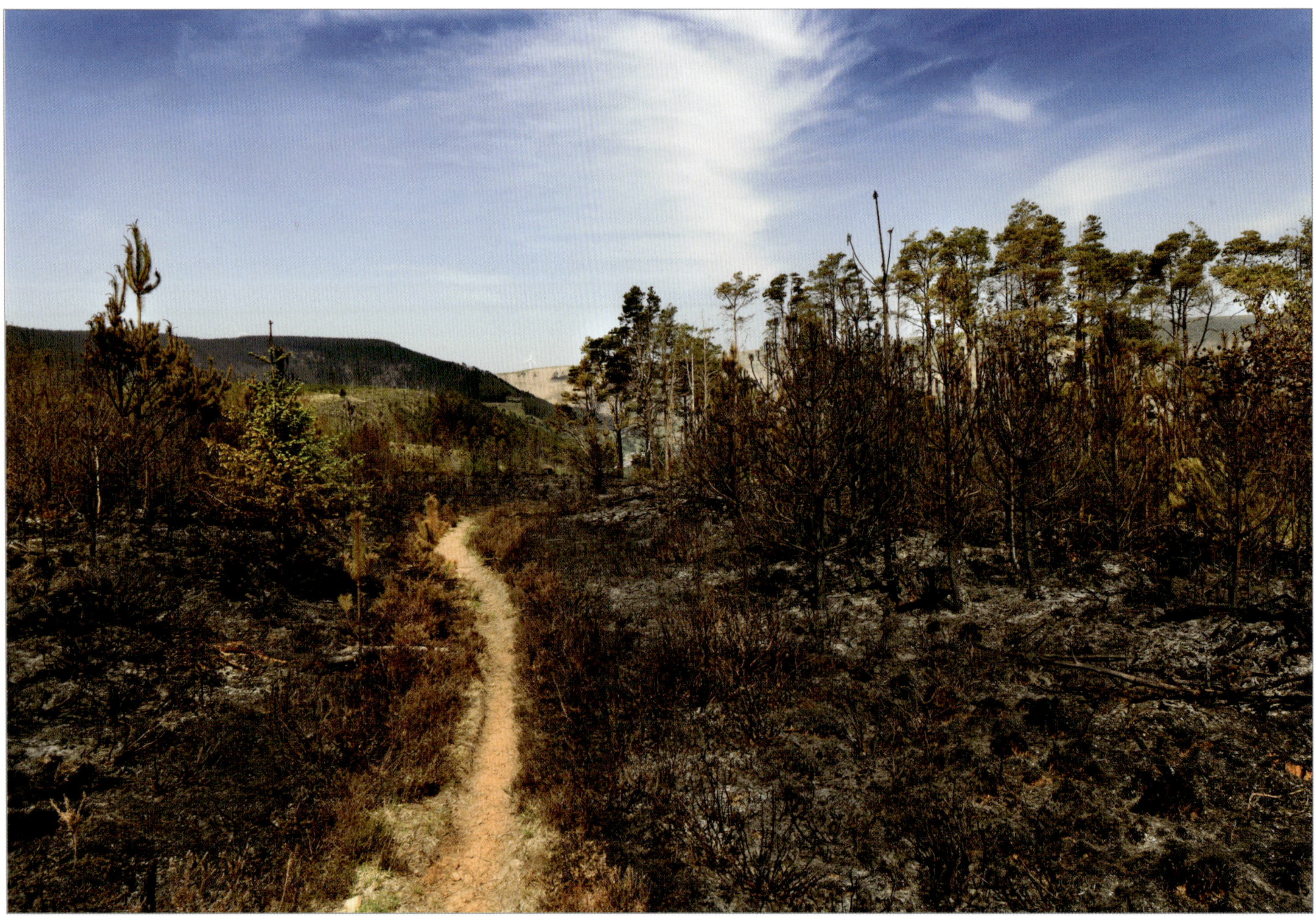

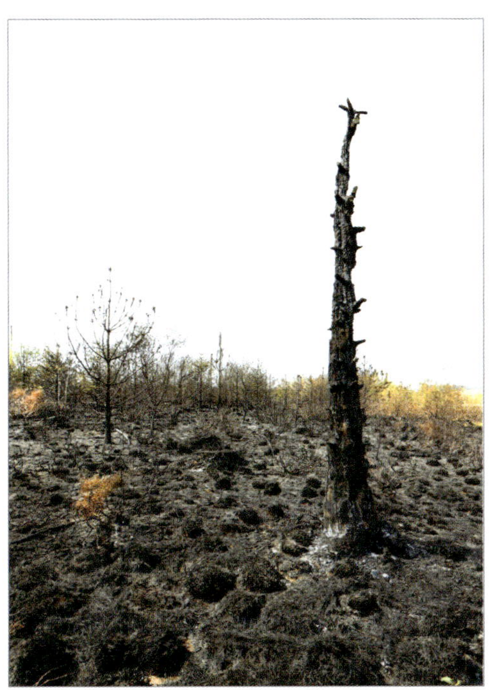

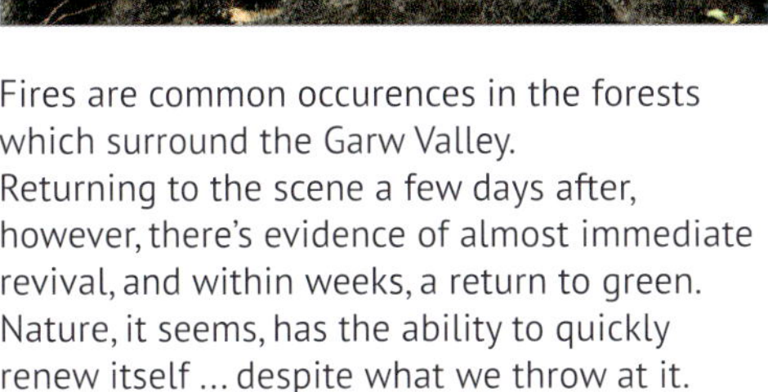

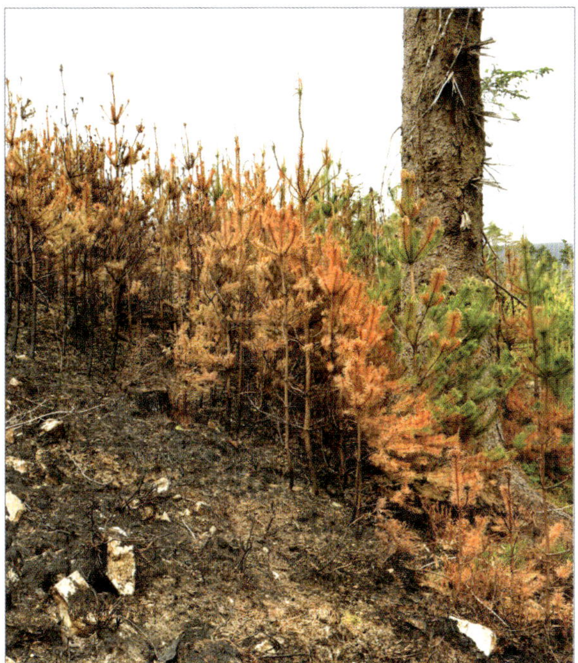

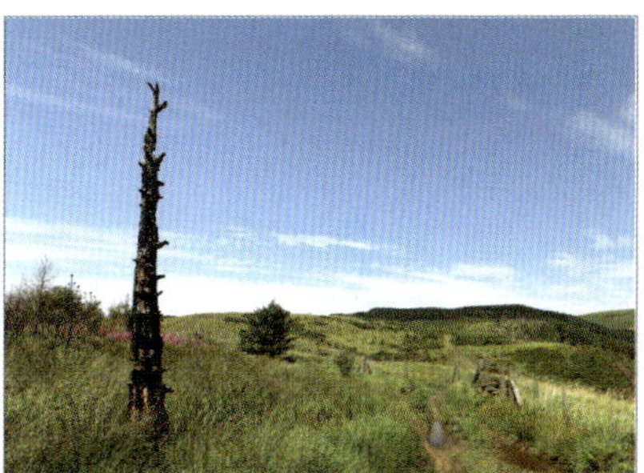

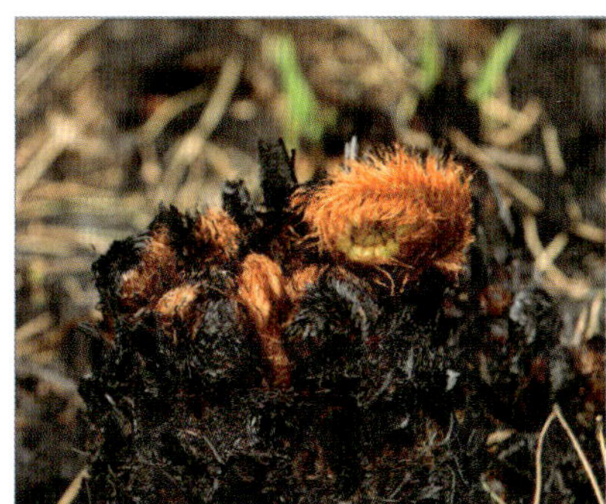

Fires are common occurences in the forests
which surround the Garw Valley.
Returning to the scene a few days after,
however, there's evidence of almost immediate
revival, and within weeks, a return to green.
Nature, it seems, has the ability to quickly
renew itself … despite what we throw at it.

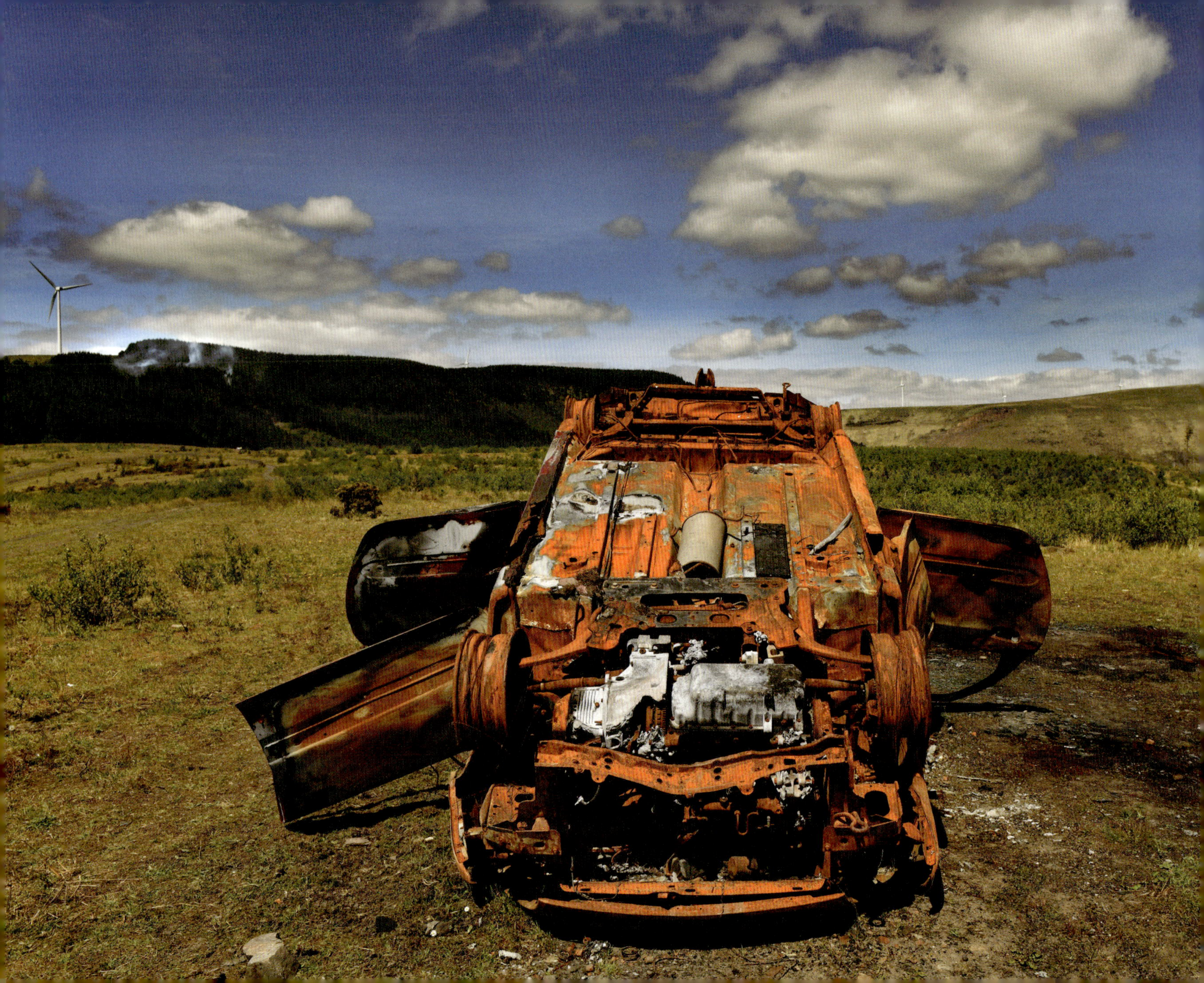

a burnt-out car
on the hilltop
above Blaengarw
(and note the
wind turbine and
forestry fire in
the left distance)

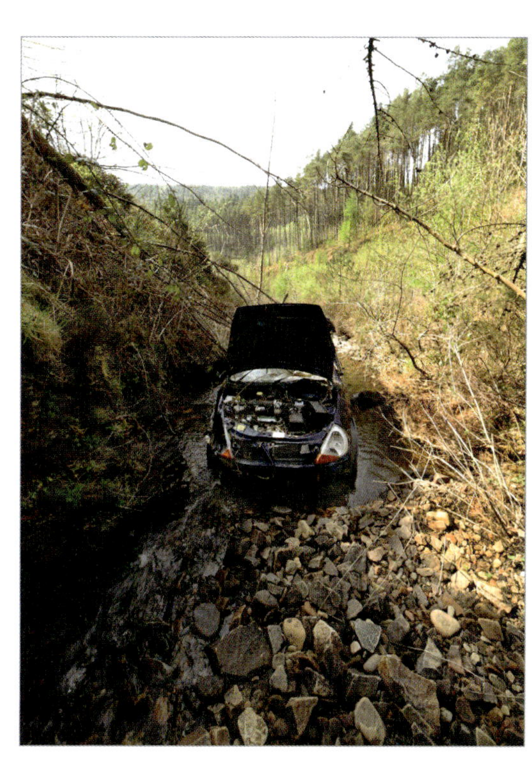

another
abandoned,
probably stolen,
car, this one
in the Garw
Fechan river
gorge

The river contains a large proportion of human excrement, stable and pigsty manure, congealed blood, offal and entrails from the slaughterhouses, the rotten carcases of animals … old cast-off articles of clothing and bedding, and boots, bottles, ashes, street refuse and a host of other articles … In dry weather the stench becomes unbearable.

from the 1893 Report of the Medical Officer for Health for Rhondda Urban District Council

This was the condition, it seems, of most of the mining valleys during this period, Garw included. While it was perhaps understandable that such disrespect for the land might be shown at a time when little of nature was still visible and its very heart was being ripped out for profit, it is difficult to comprehend why such an attitude remains to this day in the constant streams of litter discarded throughout the Valley, whether fast food containers thrown out of car windows on the main roads, the discarded crisp packets and soft drinks cans decorating every path or, as at Sweetwells, the unwanted gifts of garbage bags, fridge freezers, burnt-out cars and, even, a discarded cannabis factory! Our littering, perhaps, is symbolic of a loss in some of hope, a sad act of pessimism in our futures.

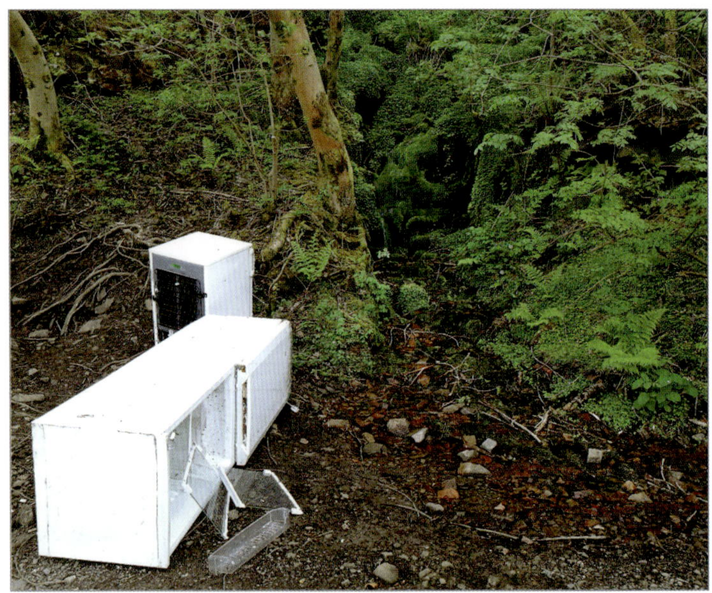

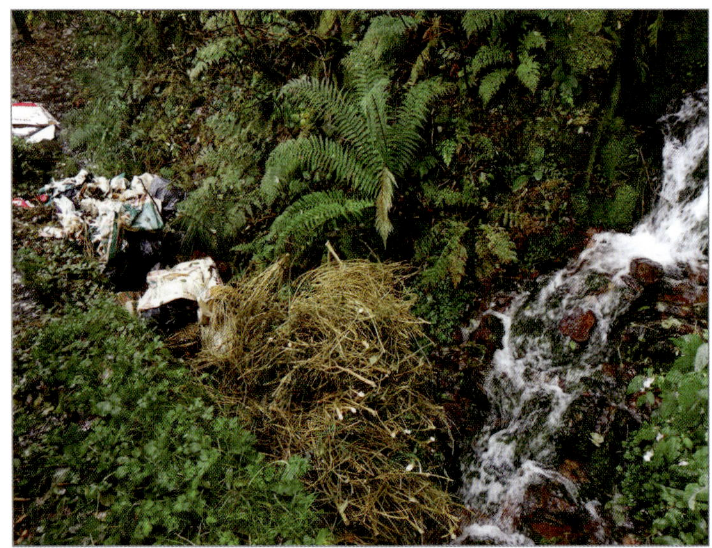

I could fill a whole
book with the images
of Garw littering I've
recorded over the
years … but I've
limited this section
to just one place:

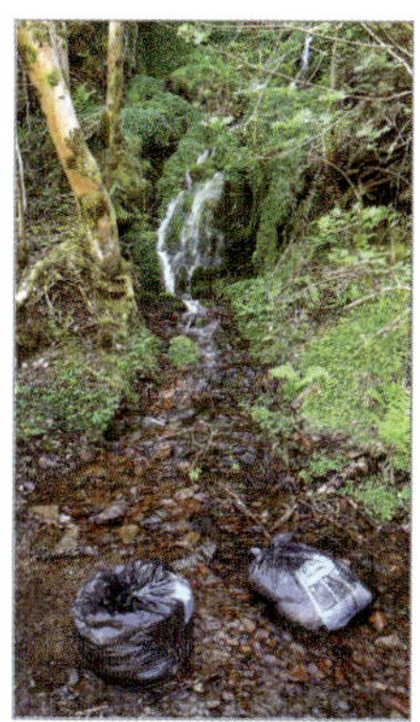

the Sweetwells
waterfalls near
Pontyrhyl –
one of my favourite
spots in the Valley –
but one which,
for some reason,
acts as a magnet for
our thoughtlessness.

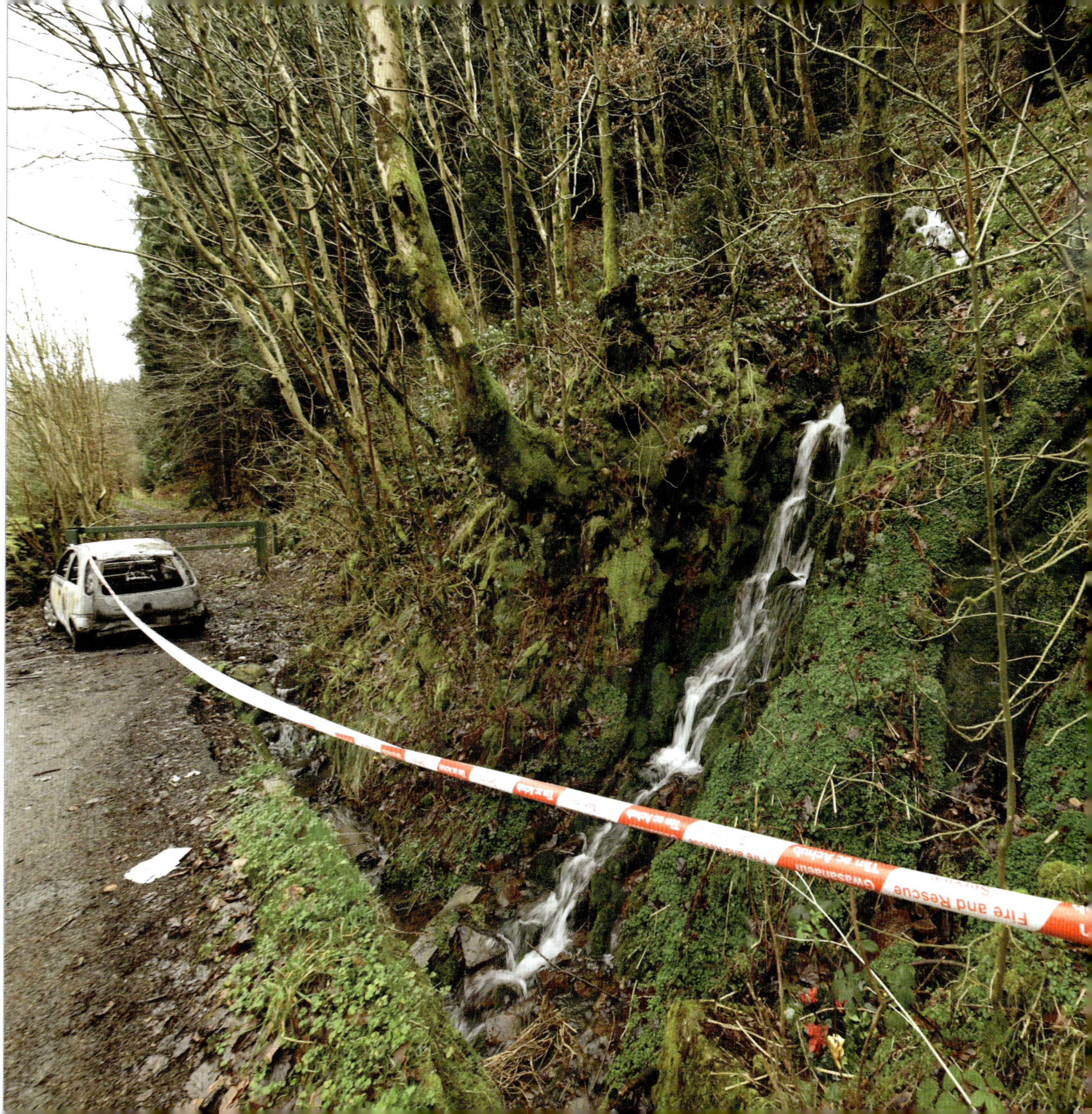

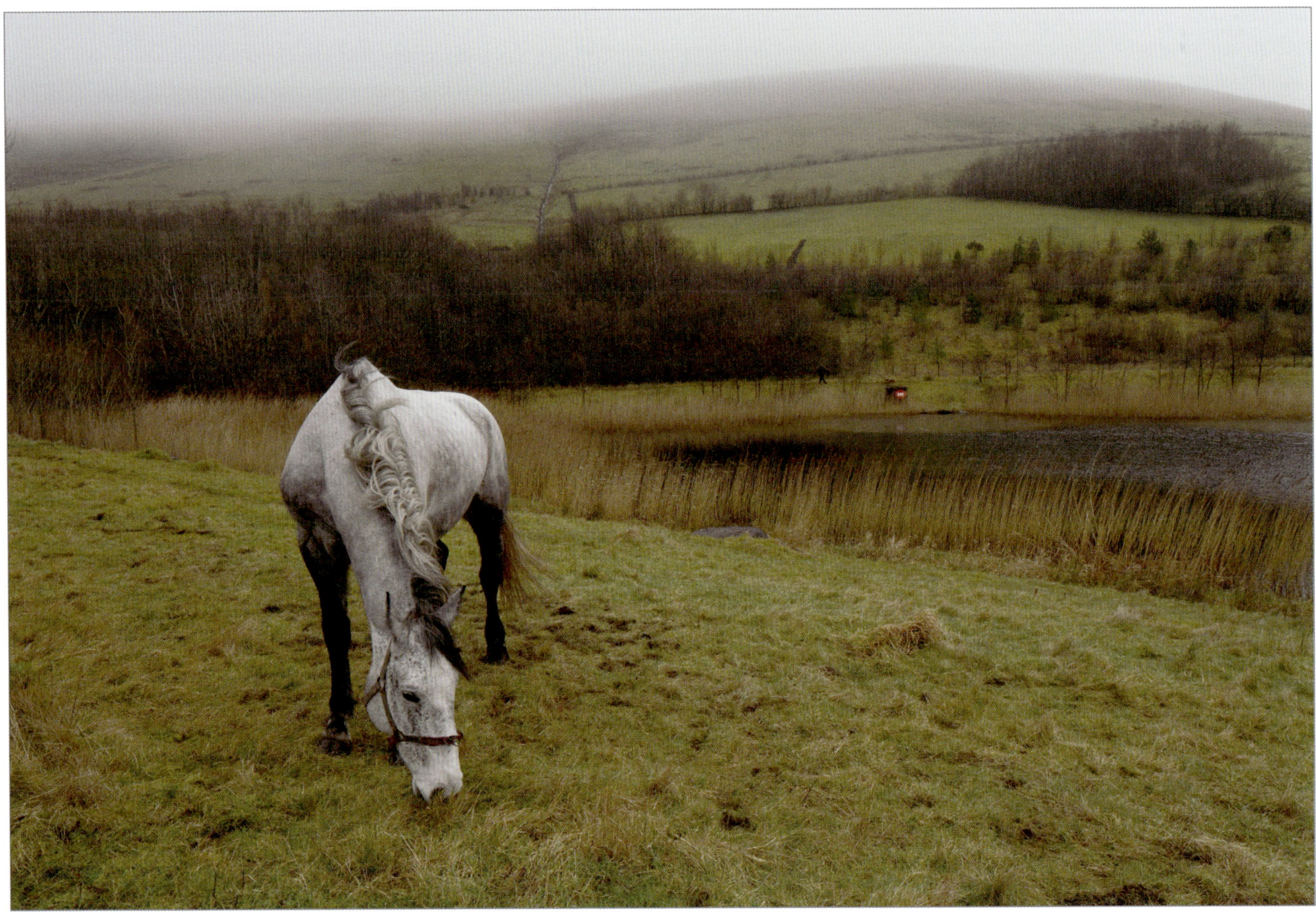

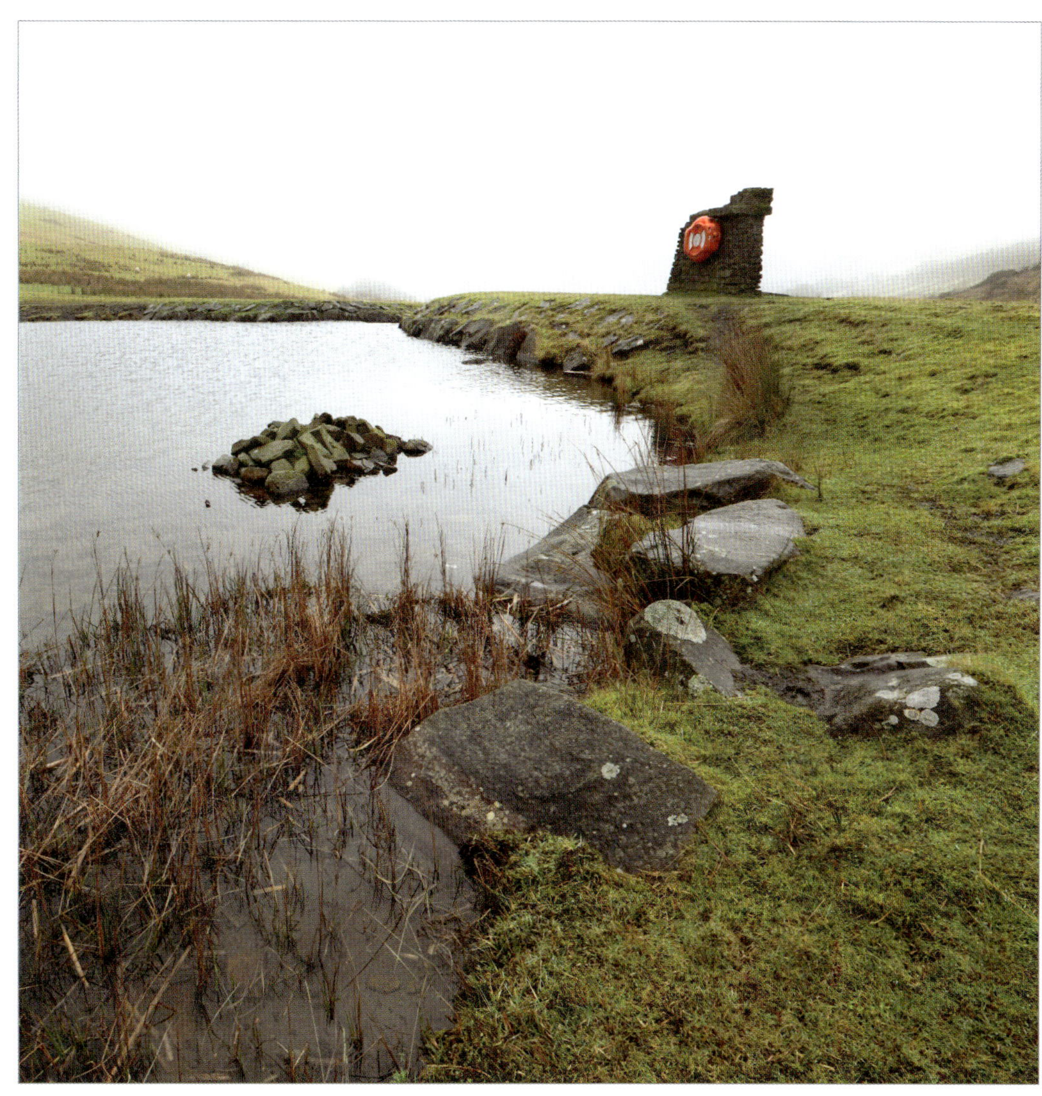

the two upper lakes at Nant Hir, Blaengarw, constructed during the Valley's reclamation scheme, on the site of the Ocean / Garw Colliery

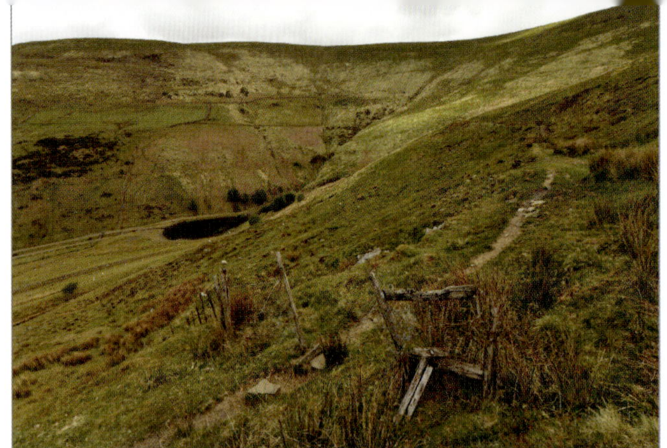

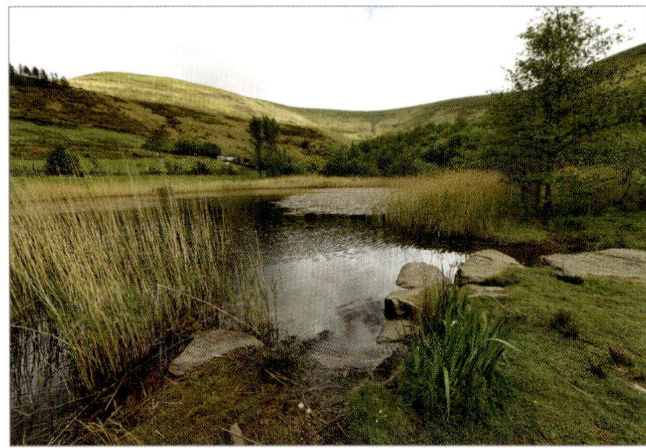

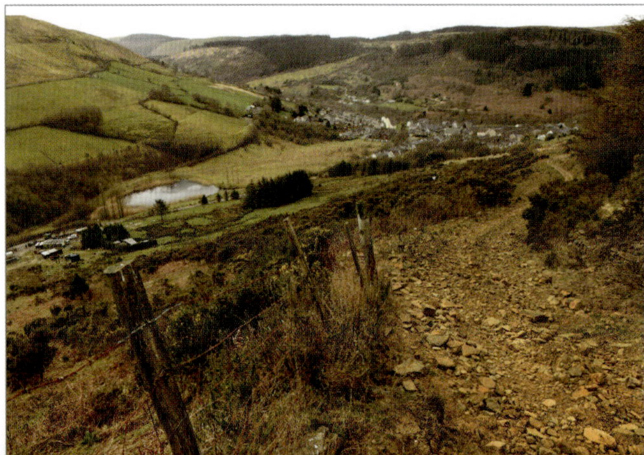

the upper
lakes,
Nant Hir,
Blaengarw

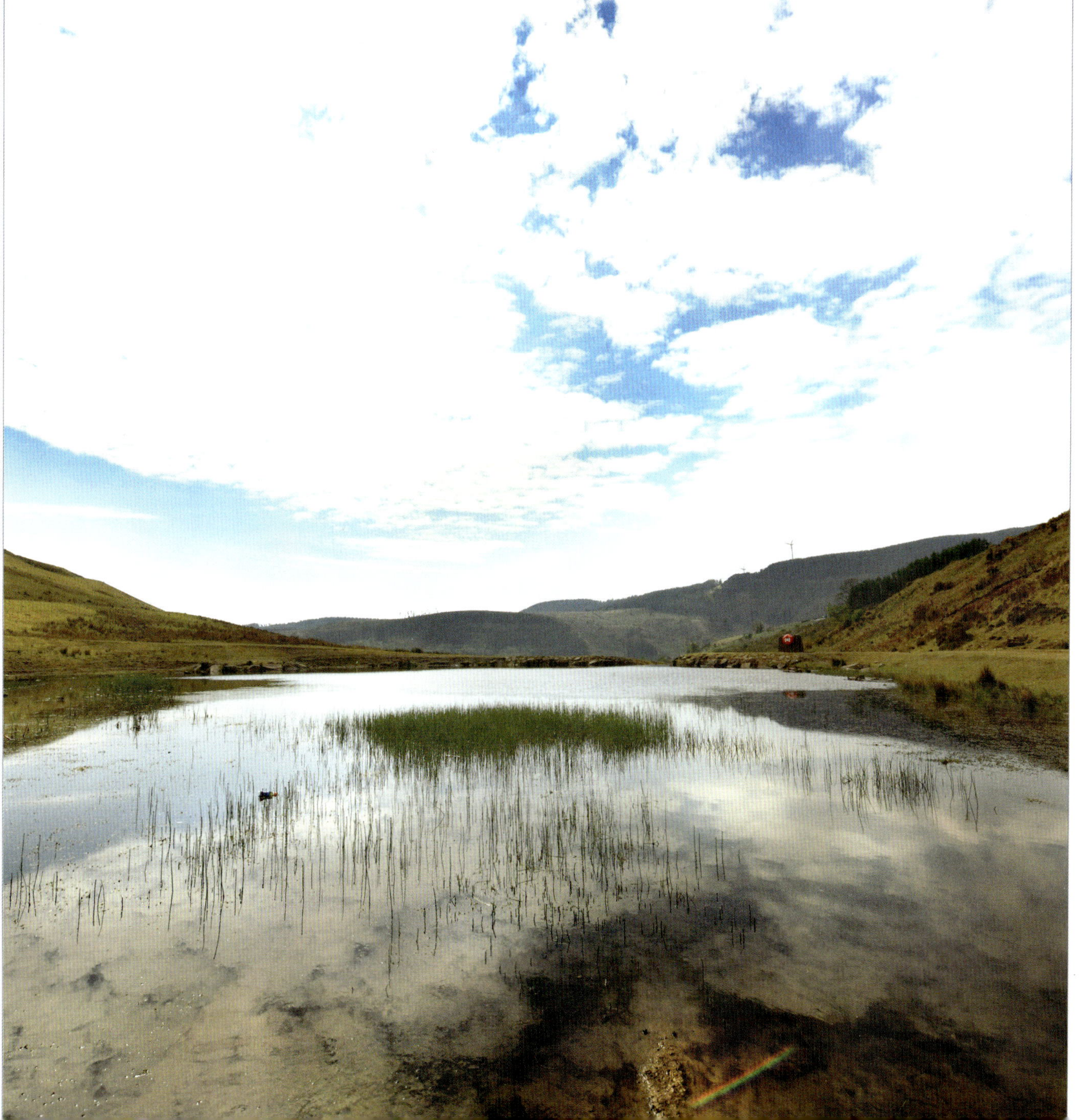

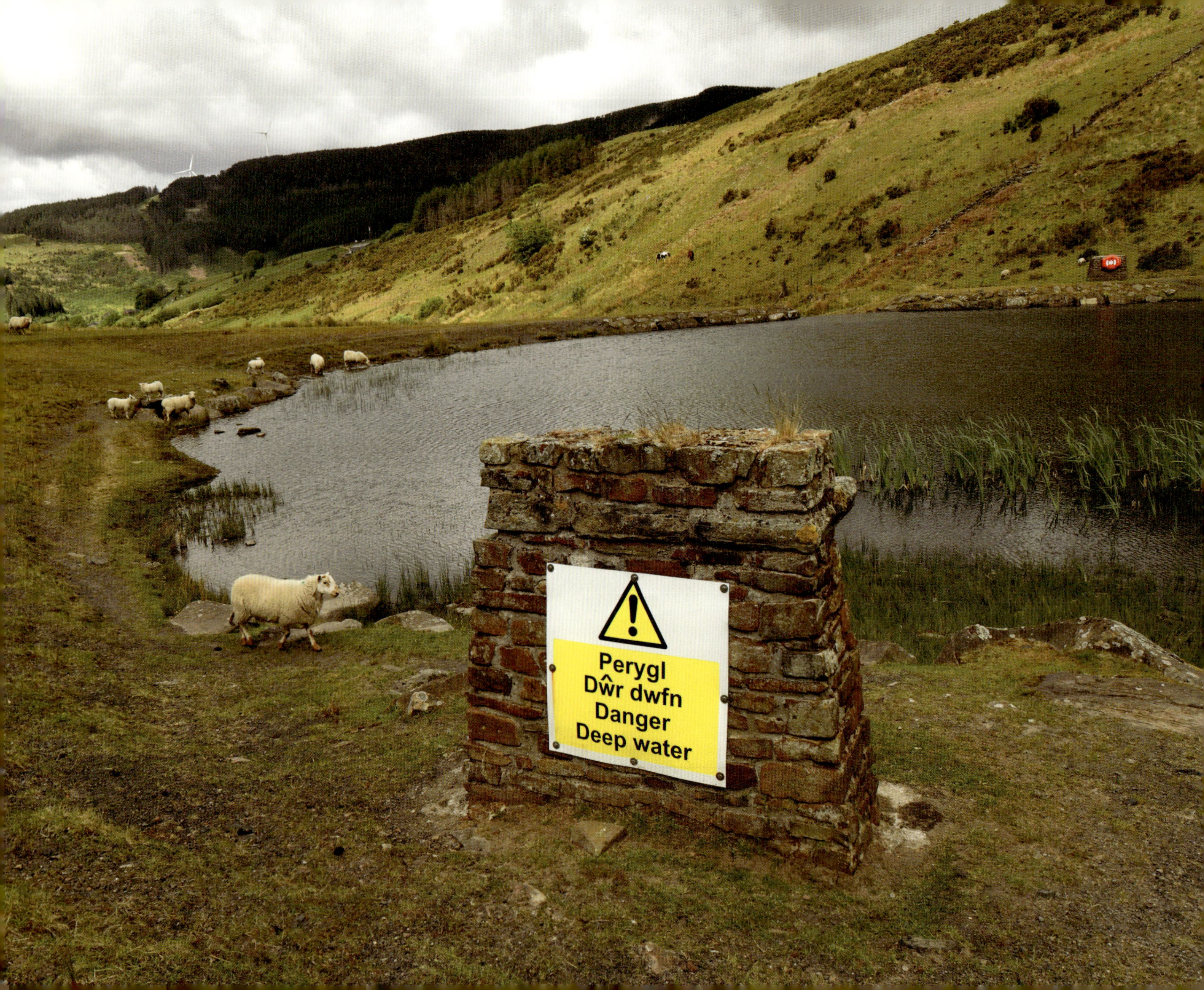
Perygl
Dŵr dwfn
Danger
Deep water

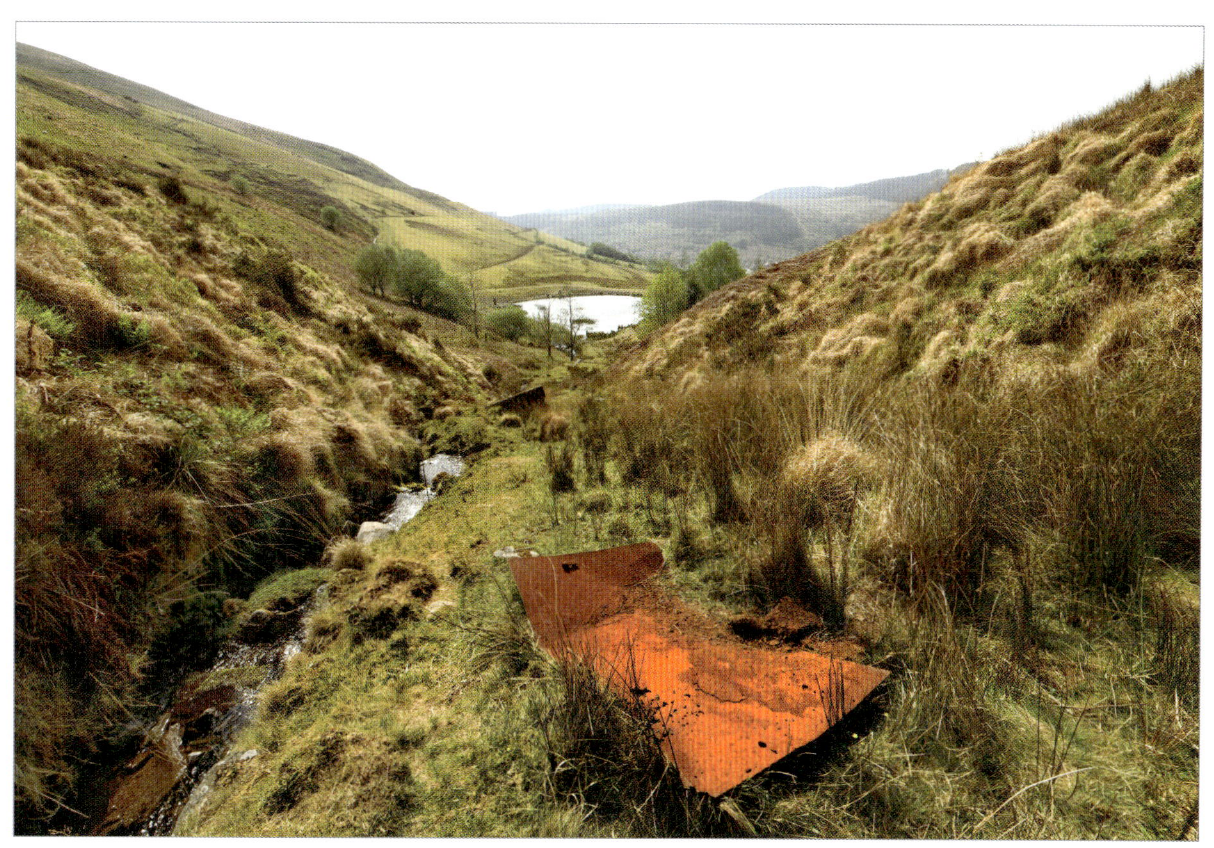

the upper lakes

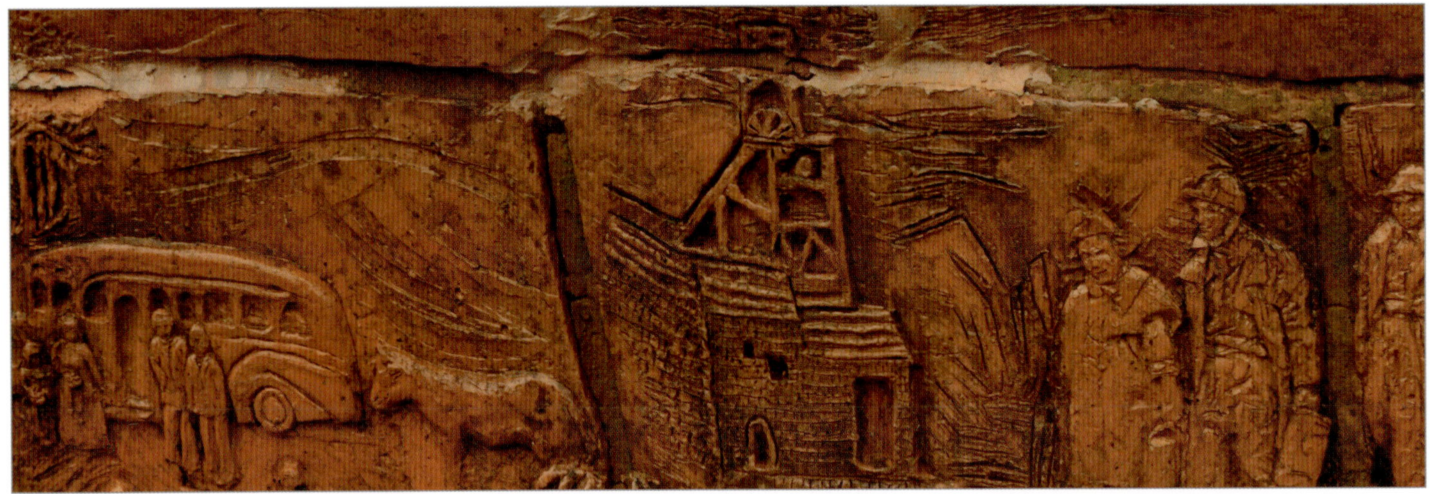

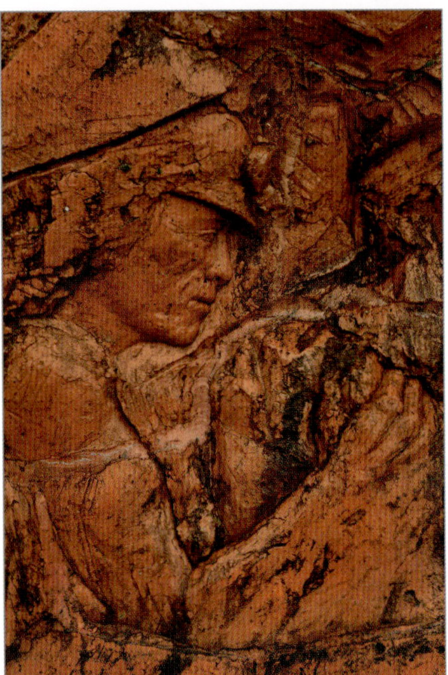

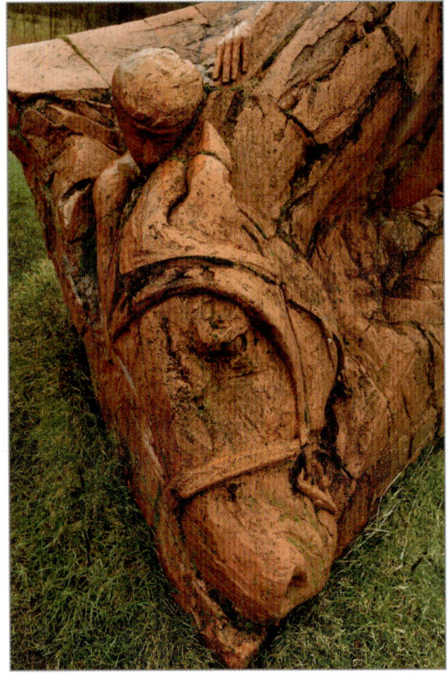

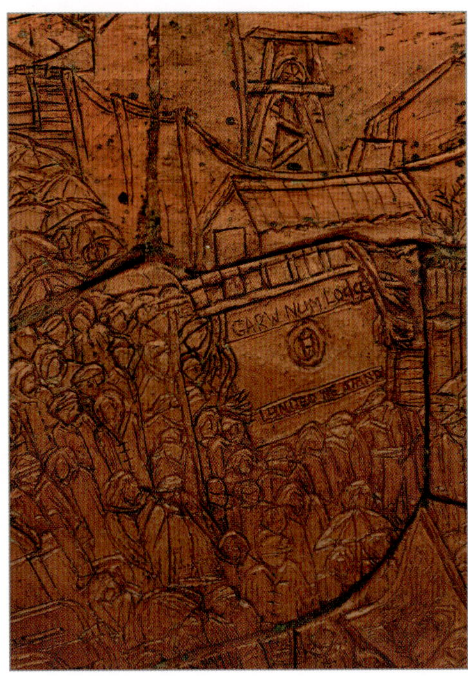
GARW NUM LODGE

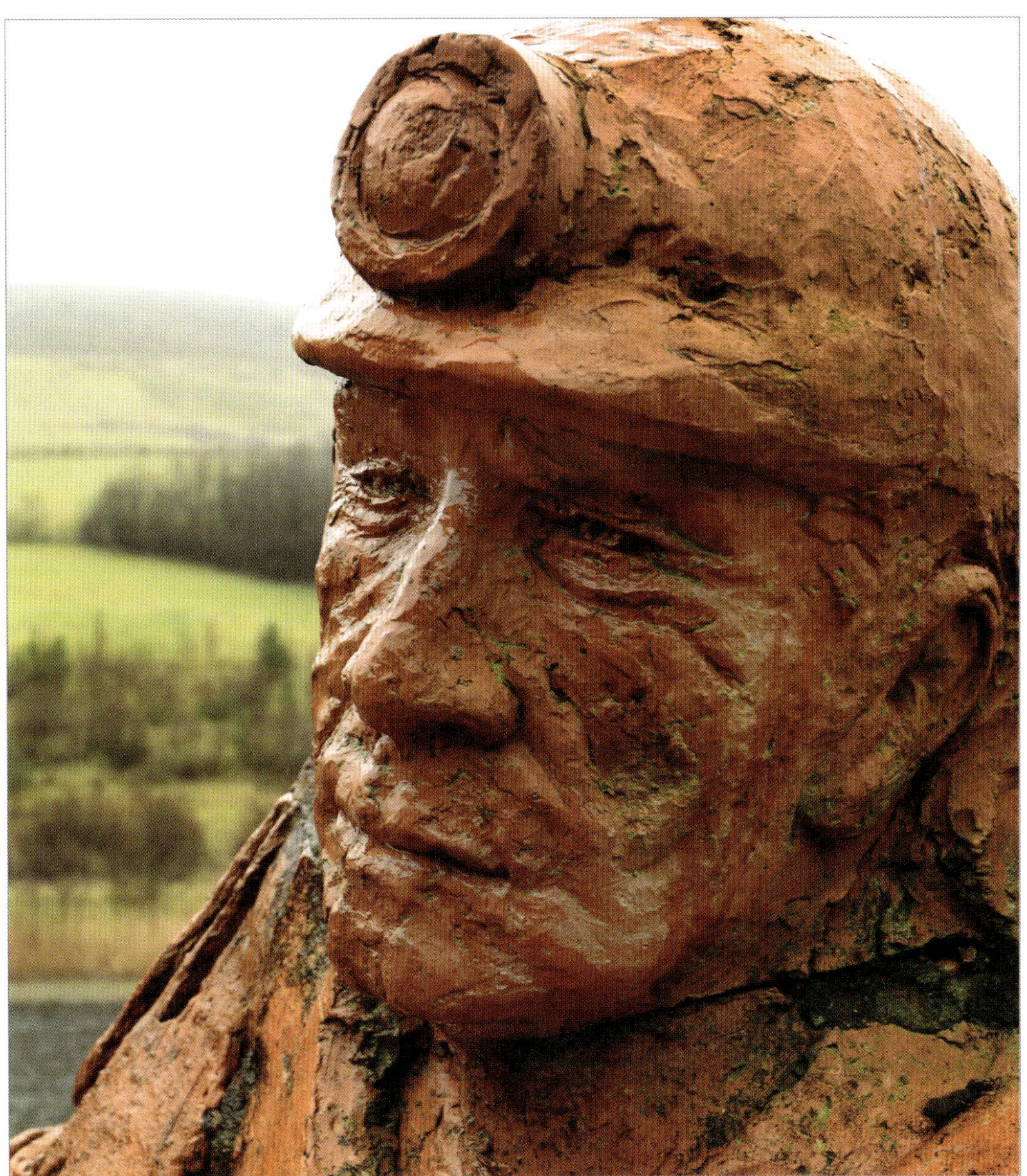

details from the
Ocean Colliery
Pit Marker
ceramic sculpture
of miners trying
to free a pit pony
trapped
underground,
Nant Hir,
Blaengarw
upper lakes

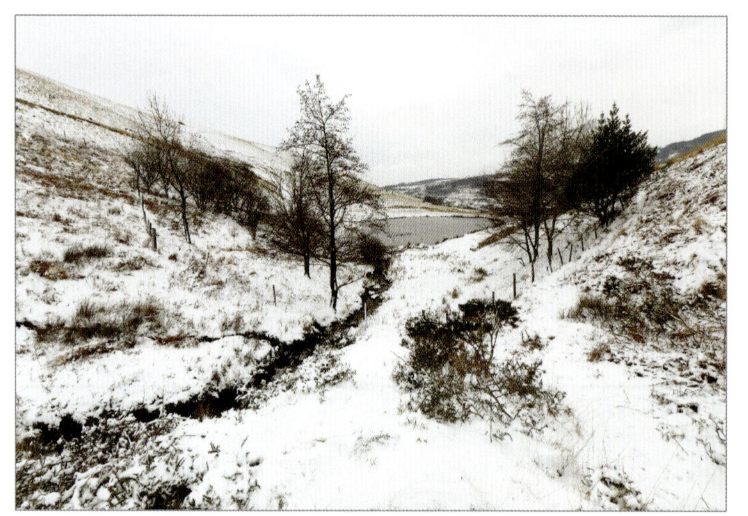

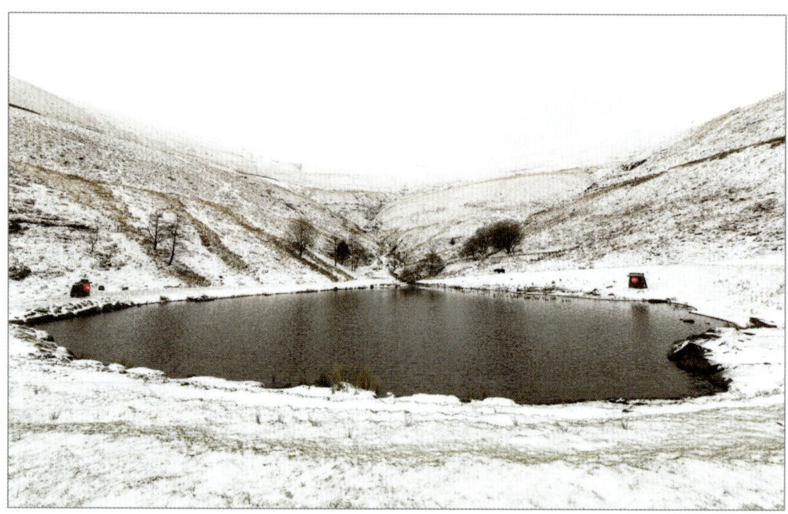

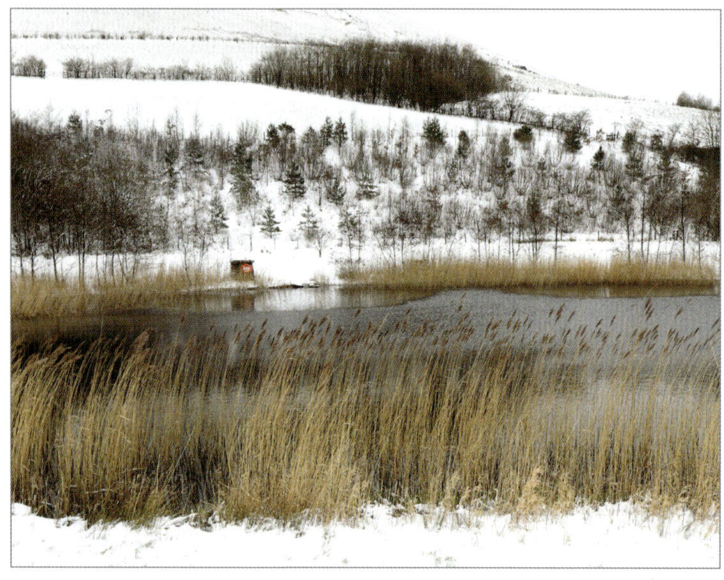

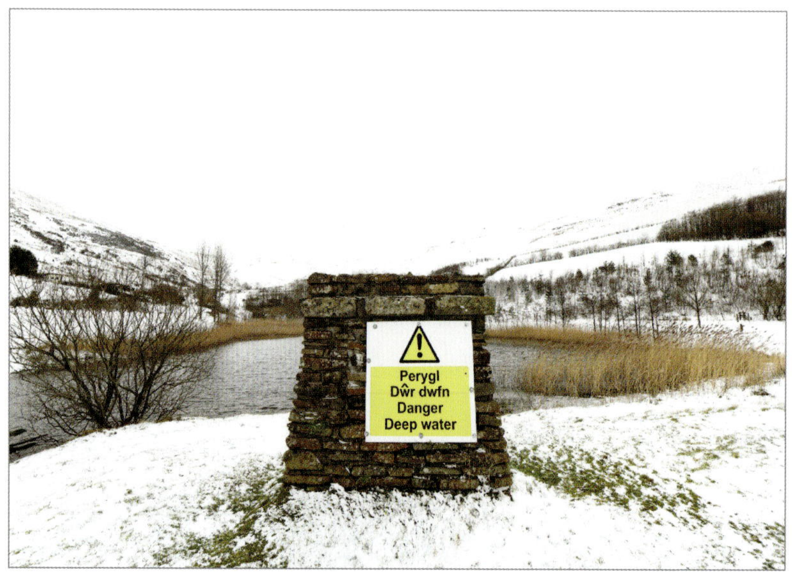
Perygl
Dŵr dwfn
Danger
Deep water

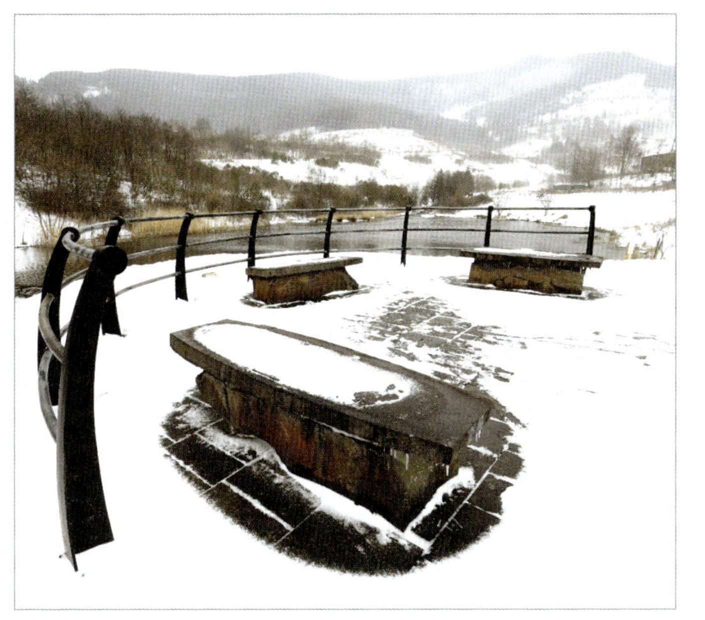

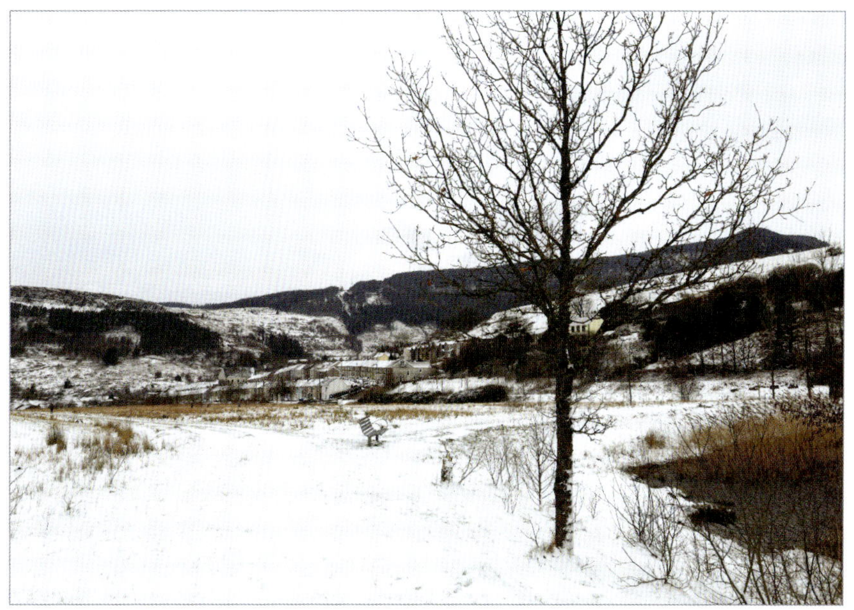

the upper and lower lakes, in snow,
Blaengarw

Driving north from the confluence of the Garw and the Ogmore rivers at Brynmenyn, your first impression always was and still is of a landscape of trees and fields, of isolated houses and farms. But, then, you reach the outskirts of the coalfield, and a new and confusing post-industrial, rural-urban world presents itself … a pastoral landscape masquerading as a town or, alternatively, a town with fading memories of when it used to be the countryside.

Following the closure of the Valley's *raison d'etre*, its inhabitants were largely abandoned with no alternative employment opportunities on anything near the scale that the pits and their support industries had offered … and with nature seemingly defeated, too. This had been a time of war against the land, with people as the collateral damage … or, to mix metaphors, a marriage to coal which was always an abusive relationship, the rock always unfaithful, terminating our brief affair when it had taken what it, or perhaps its pimps, had come for. Thousands were attracted to the Garw for bread, but were given a black stone, baked in time's deep earthen ovens, within a land where everything since the ages of ice and water had been worn down and away.

Well before the last pit had closed, there had been serious discussions on whether there was any future for our Valleys, even whether they should be abandoned in a process of 'deliberate depopulation'. Some, however, argued for a revitalisation, the modernising of existing communities to provide the infrastructure to attract new industry. While this has been successful to a degree in some other much larger valley towns, the Garw's lack of substantial level sites and its dead-end geography means that those bigger and better-connected places were always going to win in this kind of bidding war. (And, perhaps, we should have learnt our lesson, anyway, of the false promises of coal's overnight introduction and almost just as swift disappearance, and of industries arriving and leaving when it suited them, best illustrated locally by the heavily-subsidised Ford factory upping sticks from Bridgend in September 2020, with the loss of more than 1,000 jobs.)

Today, there are limited opportunities for employment within the Garw Valley itself. There's a handful of shops, a (once) family-run garage and petrol station, and a few small businesses in the Ffaldau and the Old Co-op Yard industrial estates; and there's the parachute manufacturer, IrvinGQ (with its 200 people, currently the largest employer in the Valley), and Corilla Plastics providing jobs for 25.

Current thinking concentrates upon the heads and the mouths of the South Wales Valleys where road and rail communication and land availability are more favourable. In the Garw, we have no 'head of the valley', just a towering mountain at the dead-end of the road, so no direct links with this northern promise. The river Garw only flows south and the road beside it rolls downhill to the industrial estates of Bridgend which have provided the mainstay of employment since well before the last pit closed. (Bridgend Local Development Plan for 2006-2021 proposed a 'Valleys Gateway Area' around Bridgend to function as 'a services hub' for the Ogmore and Garw Valleys.) In addition, some people make longer commutes to work in Swansea, Port Talbot, Cardiff and beyond, leaving the Garw mostly empty by day, a dormitory settlement serving the growth areas of the coastal belt, and often resulting in the permanent relocation of the most-employable away from the Valley.

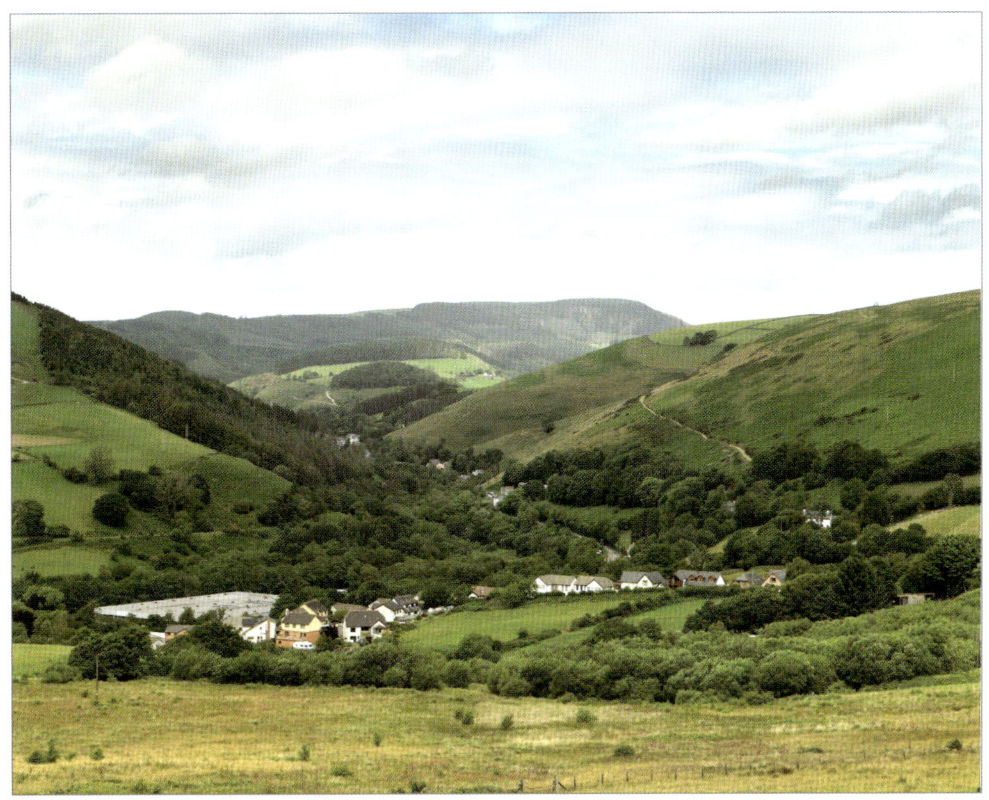

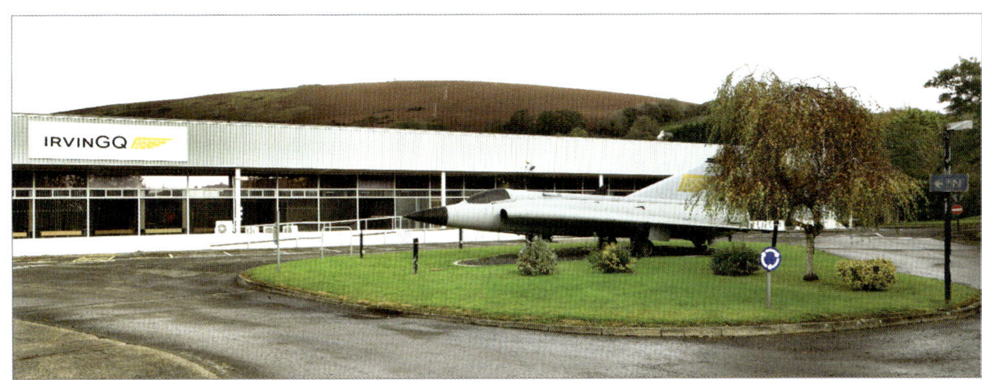

IrvinGQ, Llangeinor, parachute manufacturer, currently the Valley's biggest employer

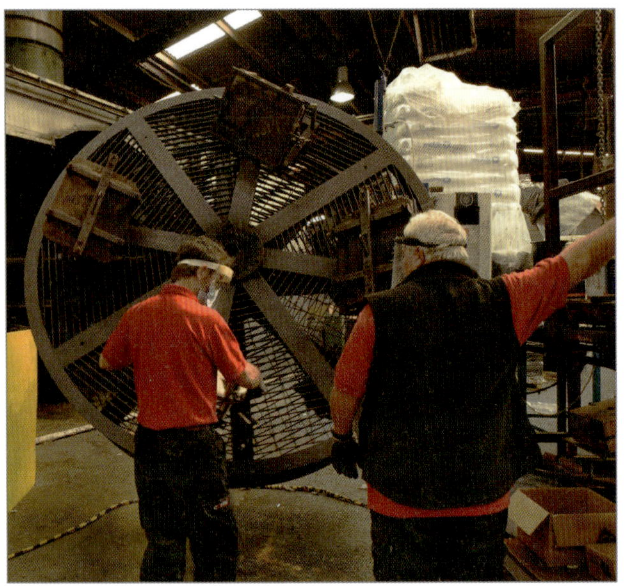 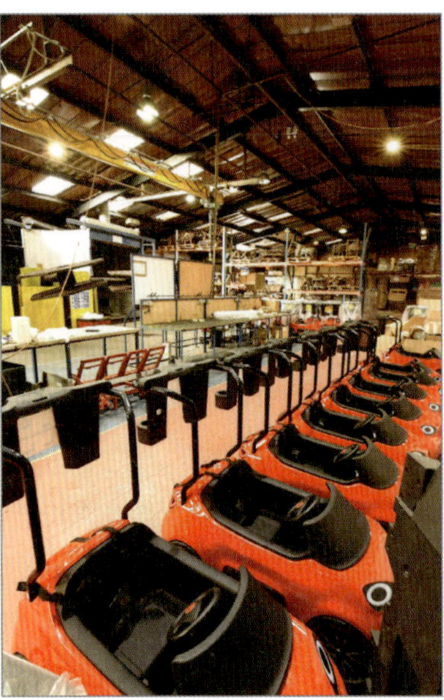 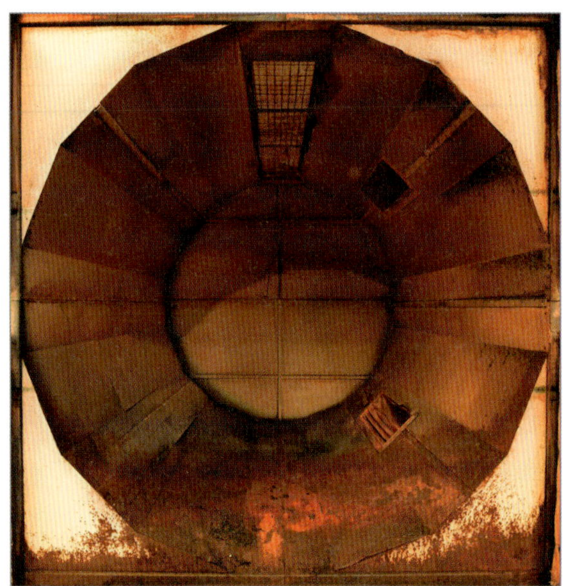

Corilla Plastics in Pontycymer is a UK-based rotational moulding company.
It makes playground equipment, marine navigation buoys, storage boxes,
disability aids, fuel tanks and car parts.

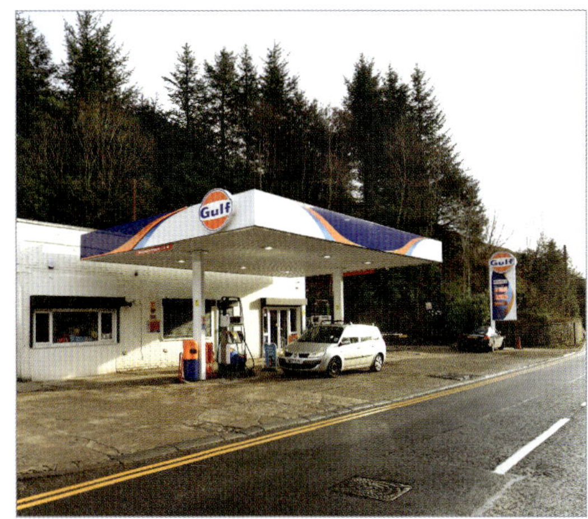

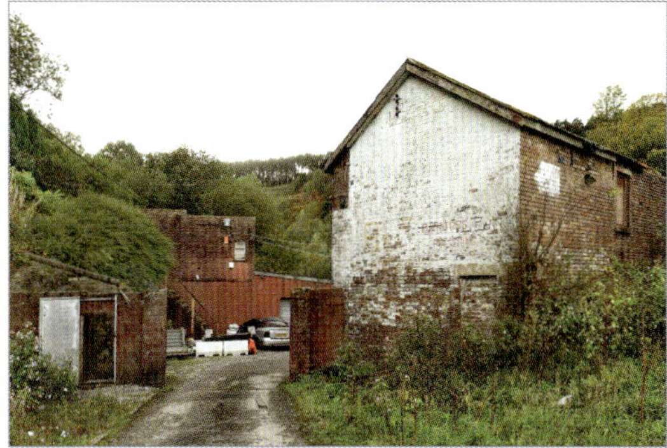

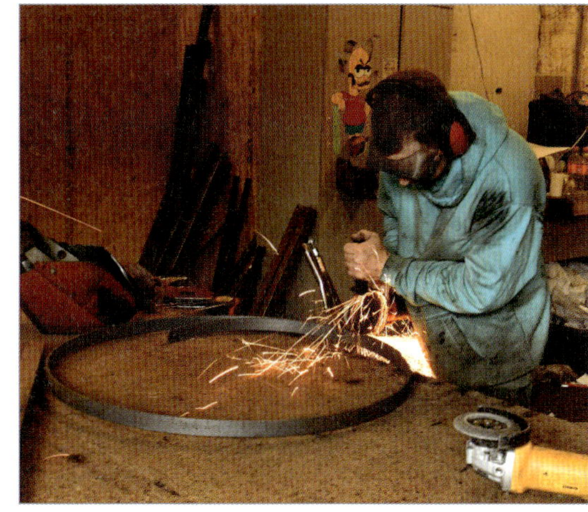

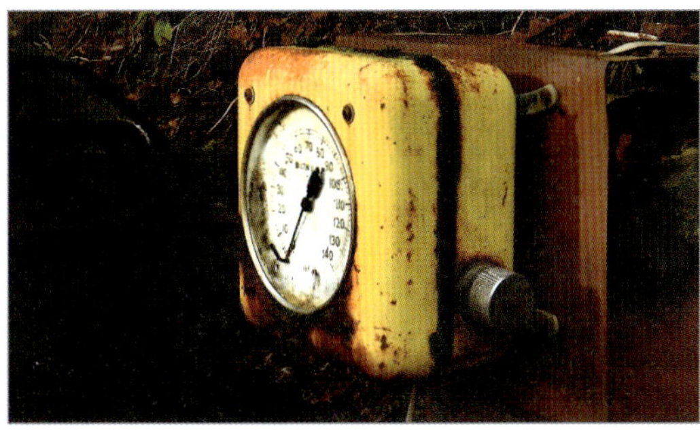

clockwise,
from top left:

Family-run for more than seventy years, Braund's Garage in Lluest has recently been sold to Gulf / Spar; the entrance to the Old Co-op Yard, Pontycymer; Croyden Griffiths, CAG Ironwork, the last business occupant at the Old Co-op Yard; the Old Co-op Yard; Kev's Autos at Ffaldau Industrial Estate; an old tyre pump, Braund's Garage

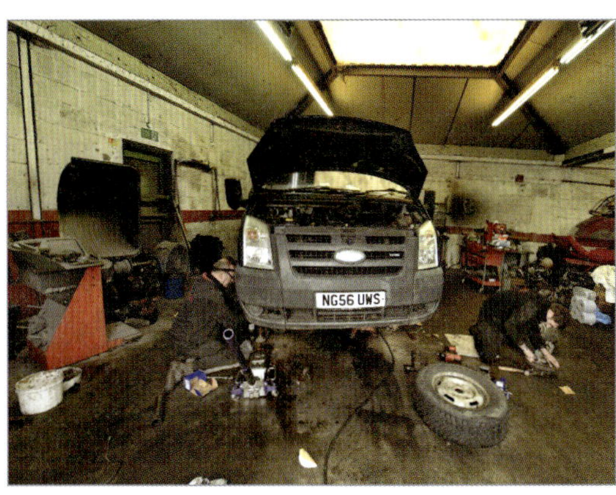

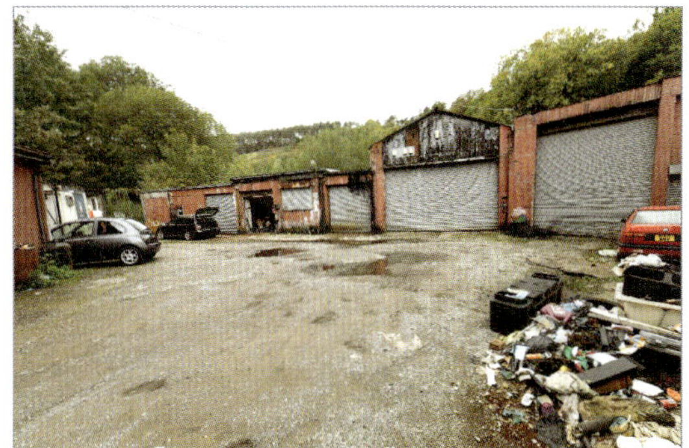

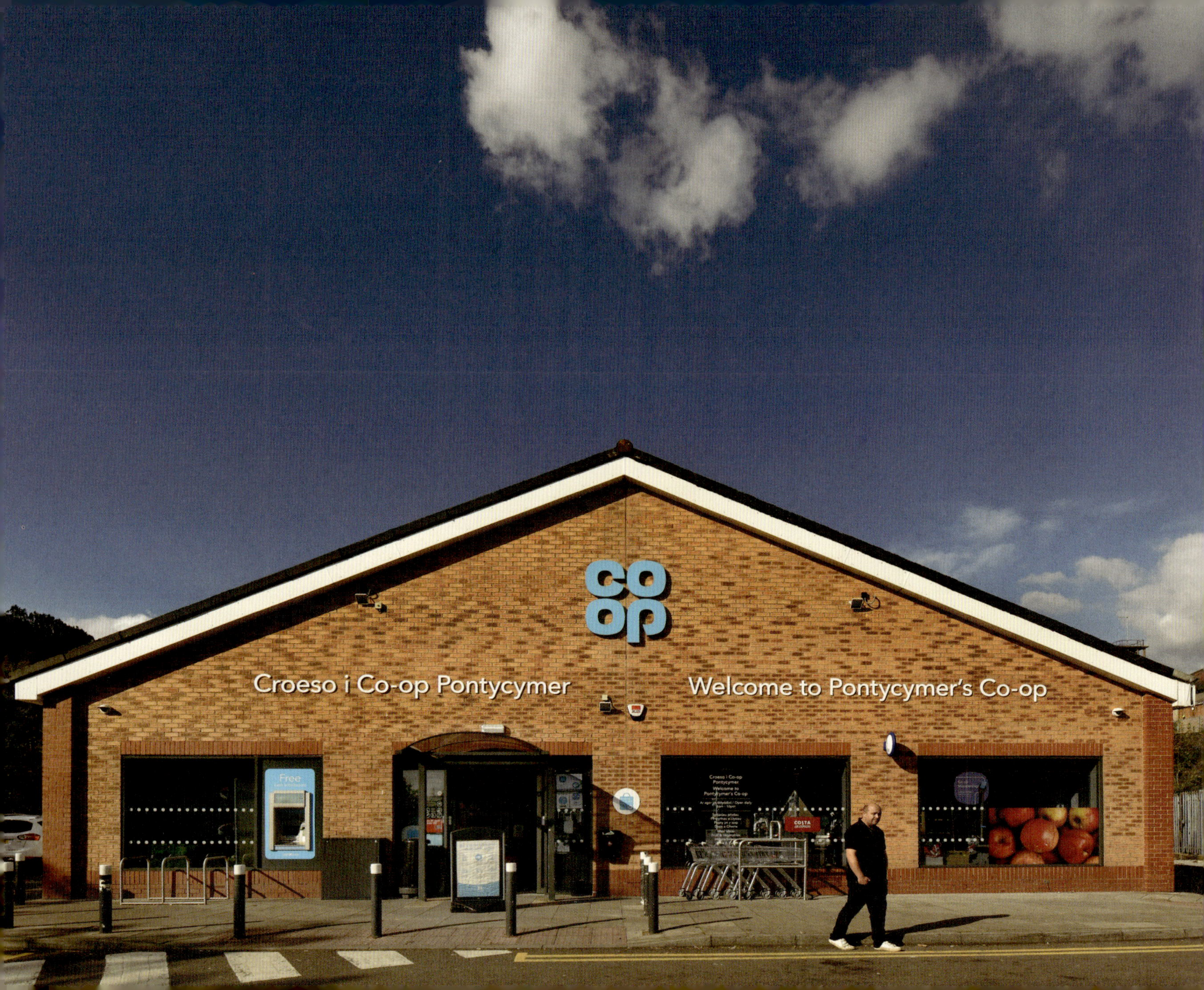

CO-OP
Croeso i Co-op Pontycymer
Welcome to Pontycymer's Co-op
Free

a few more
Pontycymer
and Blaengarw
shop fronts

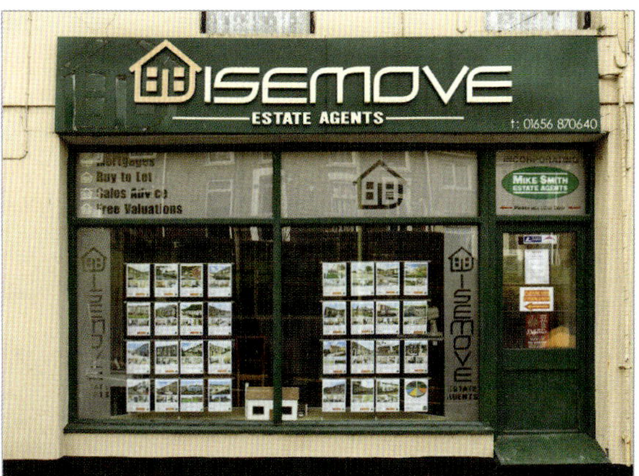

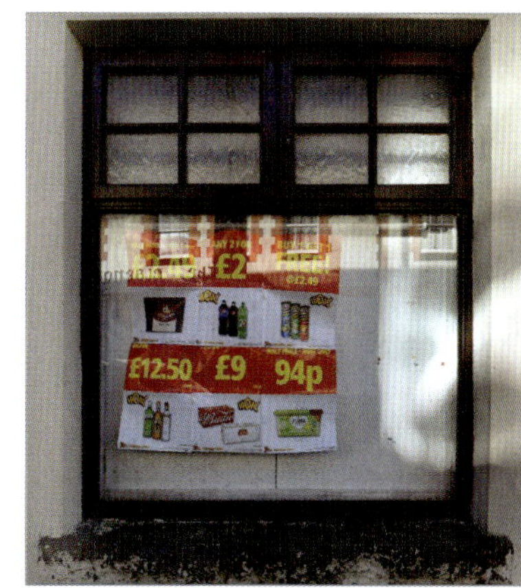

opposite:

The new Co-op store,
Pontycymer,
built on the Ffaldau
Colliery site:

The idea of an enterprise
owned by its workers
and customers was first
developed in Wales by
Robert Owen of Newtown.

Working people often
established their own
shops, in opposition to
those run by the coal
owners who sometimes
paid part of their wages
in tokens only re-
deemable in their own
establishments where
they were able to
dictate the prices.

The 'divi' or dividend, paid
out when the Co-op was
in surplus, was an early
form of savings for
working people.

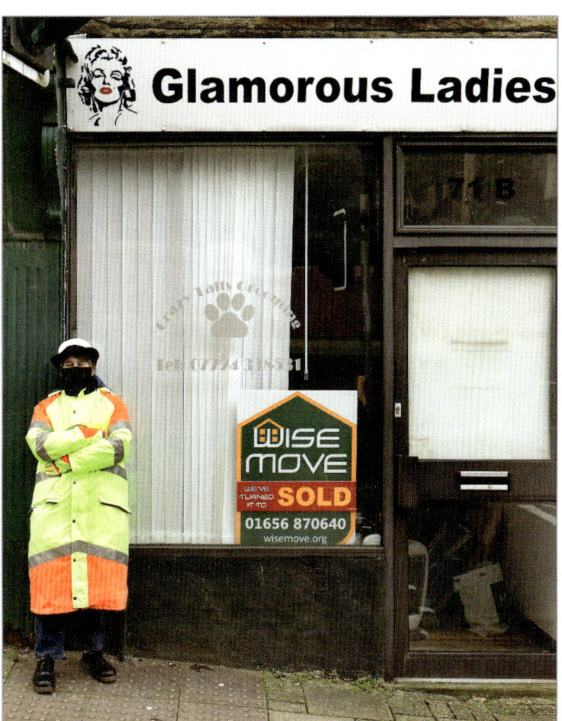

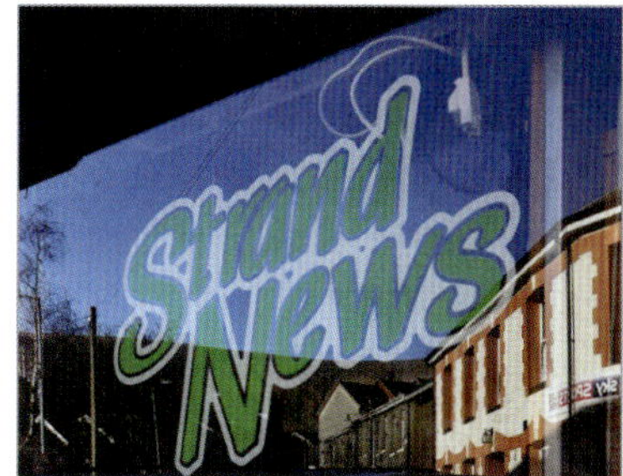

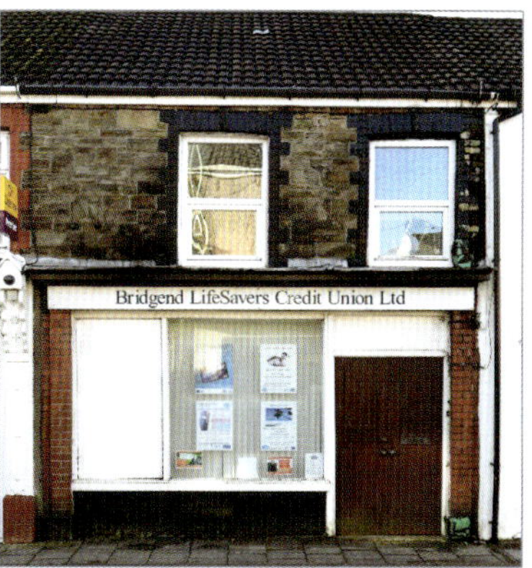

While the Garw's proximity to Bridgend, the M4 motorway and thus the rest of South Wales and the world has always provided an escape route for some, it also offers an easy connection in the opposite direction, for visitors to come and explore what the Valley has to offer, potentially providing new ways for the Garw to prosper. And there are many good reasons to visit.

The Bridgend Local Development Plan for 2006-2021 reported what we all already knew, that, despite our "exceptional scenery, fascinating history, and various activities the areas have to offer", few visitors stayed for more than a single day, arguing for the "capitalising on its rural surroundings and high quality environment to grow the tourism industry".

Nature, of course, offers the greatest promise of all. Much of the old agrarian Garw remains: stoutly-built walls running from river to mountain tops, field systems, waterfalls and silent valleys. Where there were once mineshafts there are now lakes … and the railway lines that carried people in and coal out are now walking and cycling paths.

Richard Price from the
Blaengarw Workmen's Hall mural

And another potential attraction of the Garw is its (largely-neglected) place in history … beyond coal. The Valley's ancient cairns are largely unknown and unexplored, rewarding the climb up to them with their connections to our earliest ancestors as well as superb views, on a good day as far as the Vale and across the Channel to Somerset.

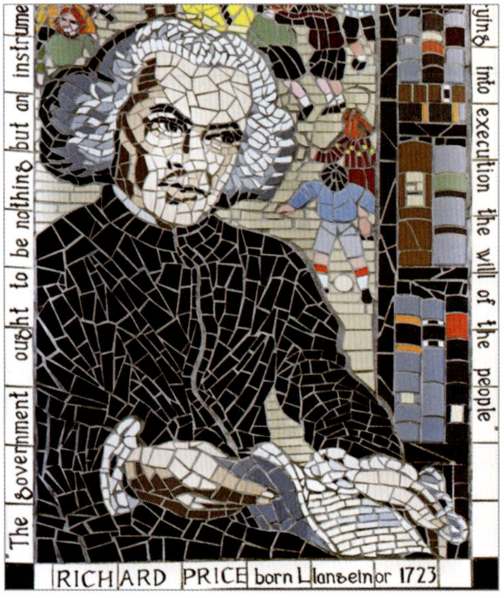

There's also, of course, our *"apostle of liberty"*. I wrote a report while running Valley & Vale suggesting that the late seventeenth-century Tynton Farm above Llangeinor – Richard Price's birthplace and childhood home – be bought by the Council and turned into a visitor centre for the study of Price's life and ideas. Though little known in Wales, there is huge interest in his life and work abroad, and particularly in the USA and France. He inspired the American Declaration of Independence, and was a catalyst for French revolutionaries. I argued that, as well as offering something else to make the Garw proud, the opportunities this purchase could provide for high-end tourism were significant.

Much later, in 2015, when the farm was put on the market, a petition was submitted by Martyn Hooper MBE, the chairperson of the Richard Price Society, calling on the Welsh government to *"acknowledge the important contribution of Dr Richard Price …. and develop his birthplace and childhood home into a visitor information centre where people of all nationalities and ages can discover how his significant contributions to theology, mathematics and philosophy have shaped the modern world."*

In an action that could never be described as 'enlightened', Tynton Farm was sold to a private buyer in August 2018, the Garw and Wales missing a huge trick here to rechristen our Valley as the home of Dr Price and the birthplace of democracy.

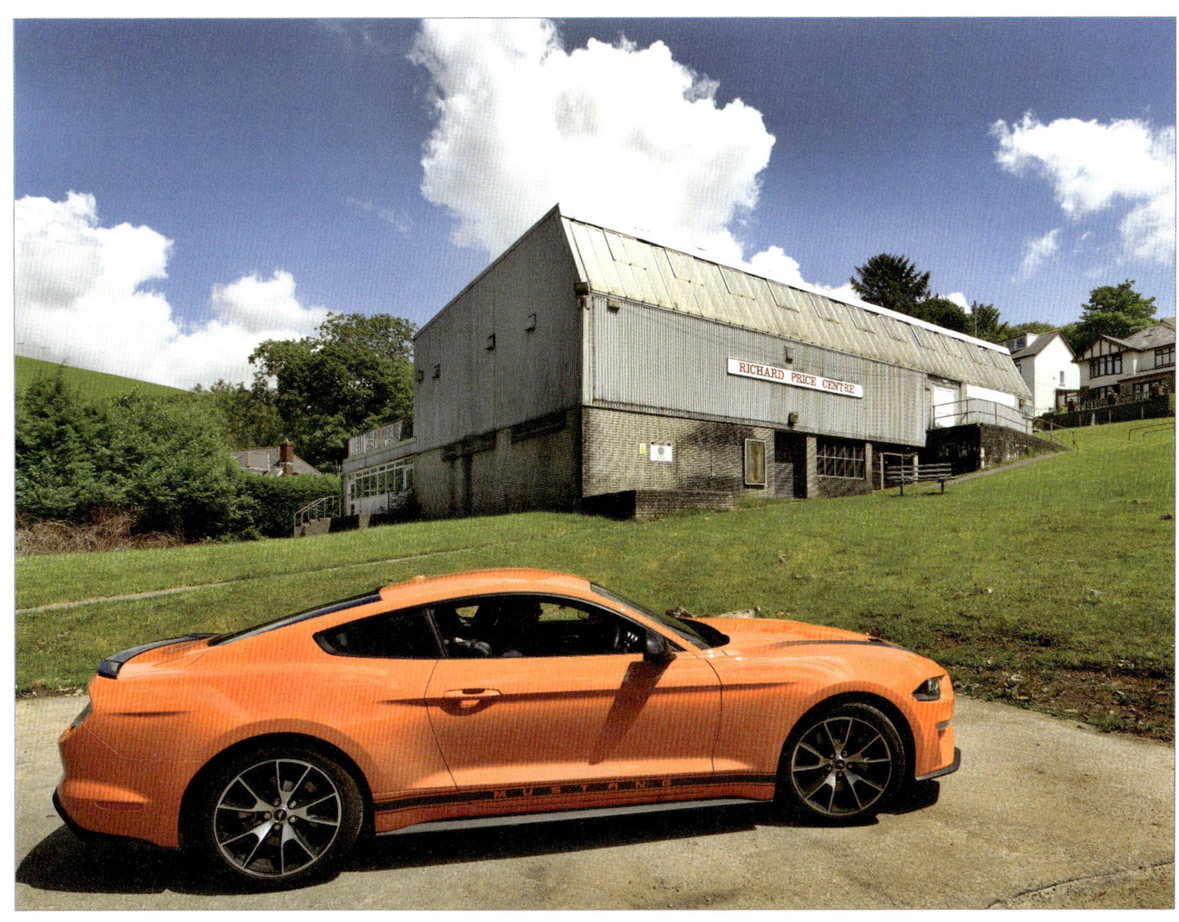

the Richard Price Centre ...
and a Ford Mustang,
Llangeinor

The Valley no longer has the unity it once had as a consequence of the removal of a shared workplace and shared way of life.

We've seen snapshots of this re-emerging during Covid but it's all been more ephemeral than permanent. The days of clapping the NHS, street quizzes, bingo and karaoke have all faded away.

People always say they are proud to come from the Garw, but I'm no longer sure they know what they are proud of. I think much of that pride comes from what the Valley was ... rather than what it is.

We wanted to cling onto the past instead of embracing the future.

Dr Wyn Price

Throughout the Garw Valley, new uses are being found for many old and historic buildings: chapels and workmen's institutes are being turned into homes, workshops and warehouses, and one into a gymnasium.

And there's also the more anarchic – and probably quasi-legal – re-possessing of bits of the Valley's skin to extend homes and gardens and create smallholdings, making confident new demotic claims for local people and their animals in a kind of bold reclamation of what was never ever ours.

top to bottom:
Ffaldau Workmen's Institute;
and Sardis Chapel, Bettws,
renovated as one of
the bases of Valley & Vale
(now Tanio);

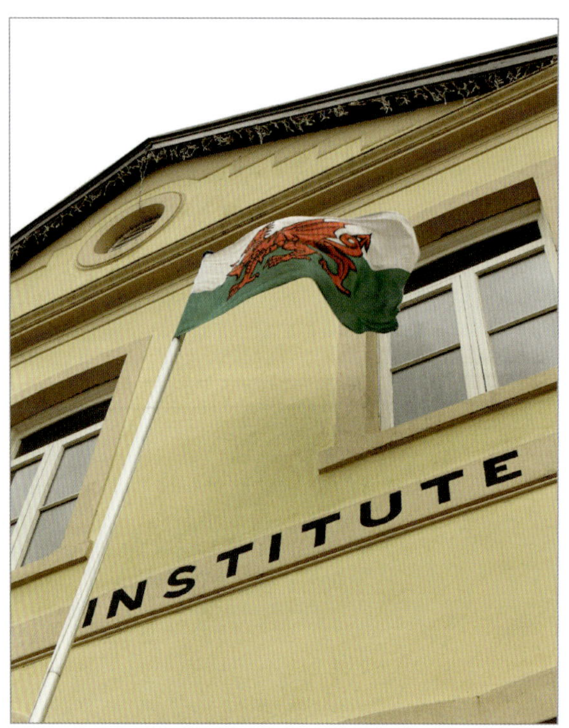

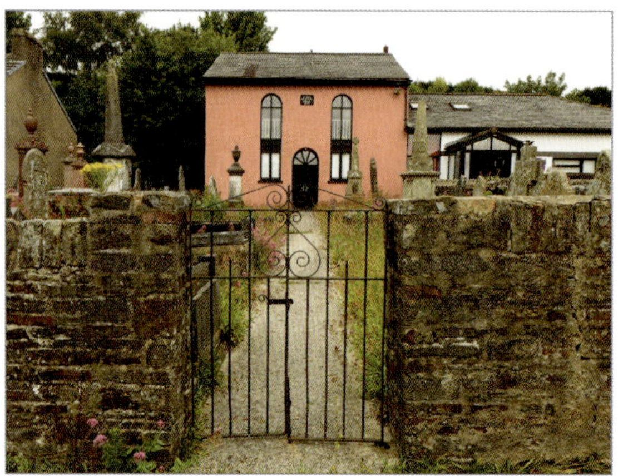

opposite:

the sensitive
renovation of
Ffaladau Institute,
in progress

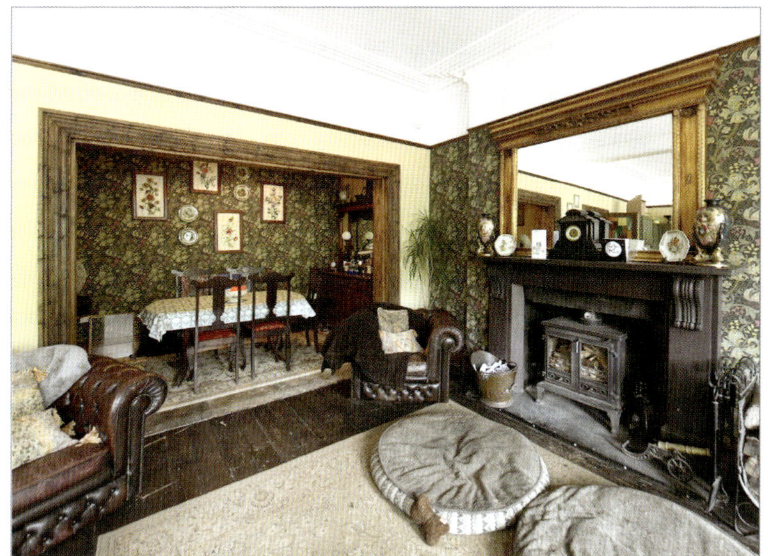

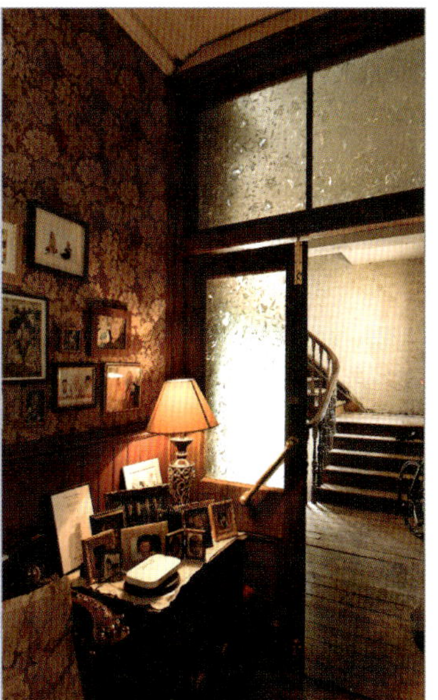

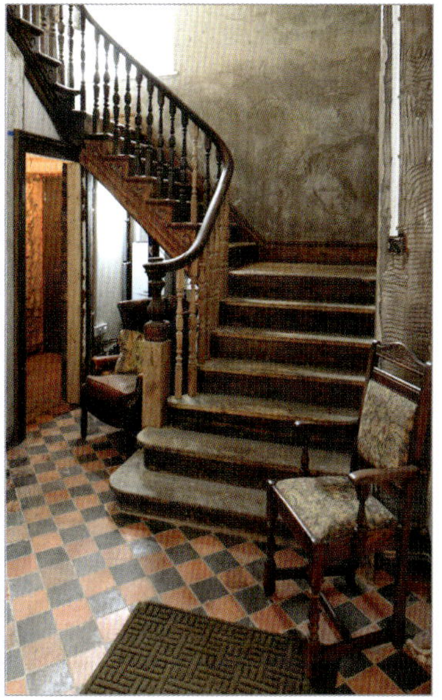

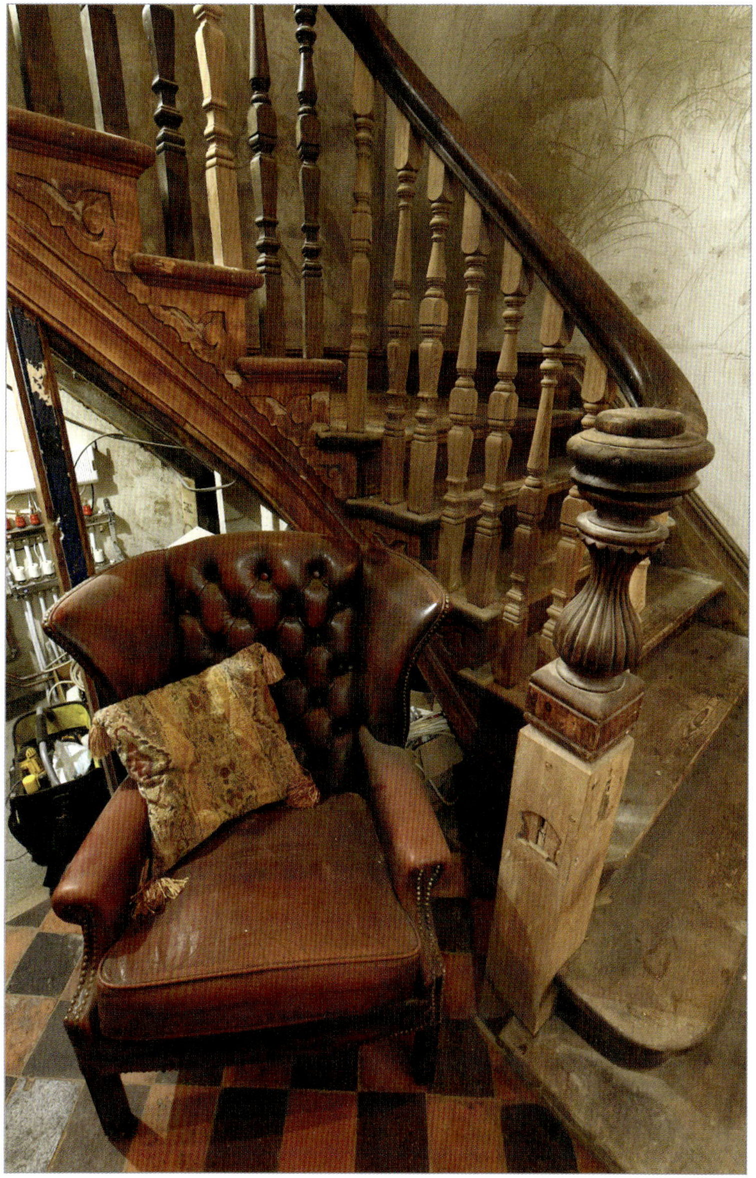

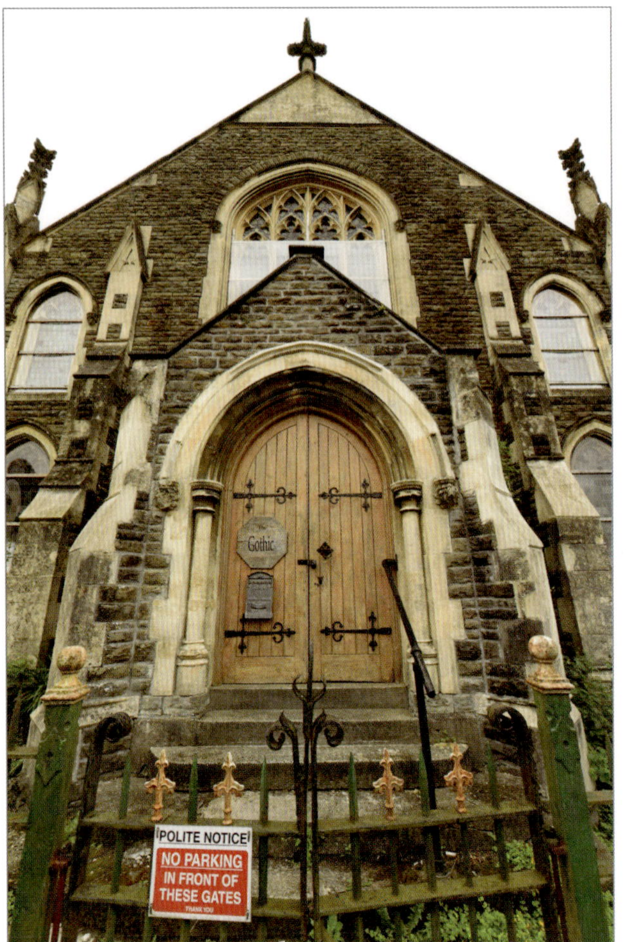

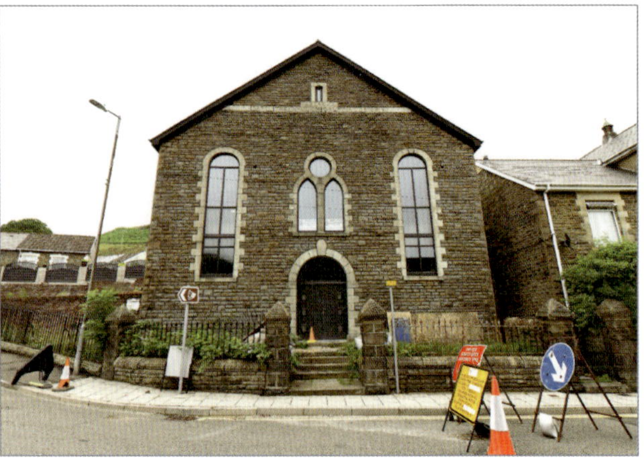

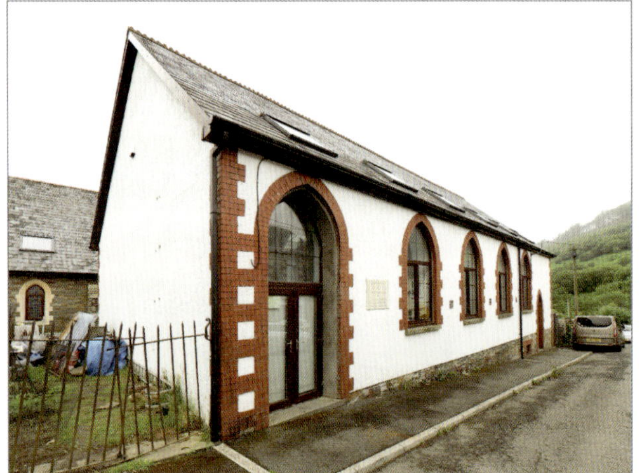

clockwise, from left:

English Congregational Church, 1893, (now known as 'The Gothic'), Alexandra Road;
Capel Trefnyddion Calfinaidd, 1881, Katie Street, Blaengarw (currently being renovated);
Fudgey's Health & Fitness Club, which was once St John's Church (in Wales), Blaengarw

opposite, clockwise from top left:

void where Mount Zion English Baptist Chapel once stood, King Edward Street, Blaengarw; Bethel Baptist Chapel, Oxford Street, renovated; site of Tabernacle Baptist Church, Katie Street, Blaengarw; flats (centre) built upon the site of Trinity English Baptist Chapel

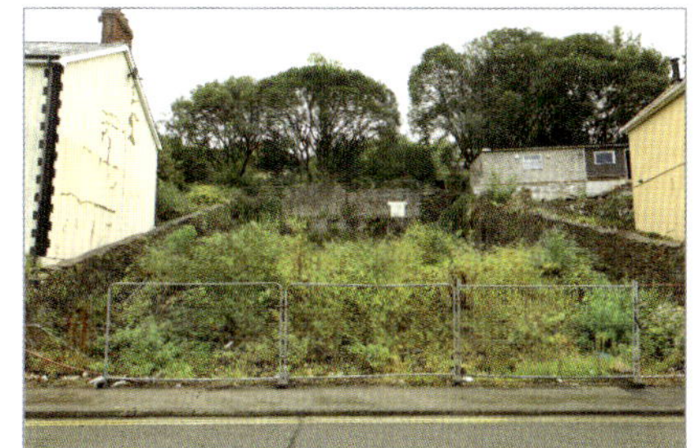

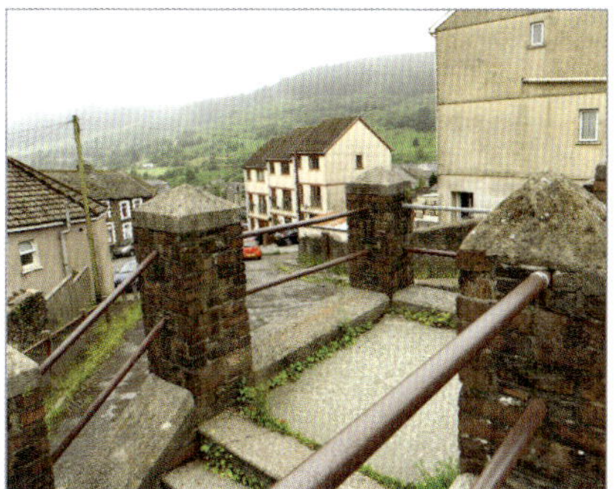

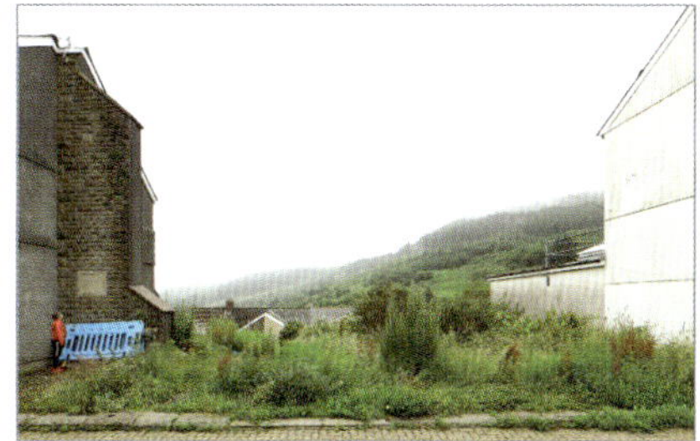

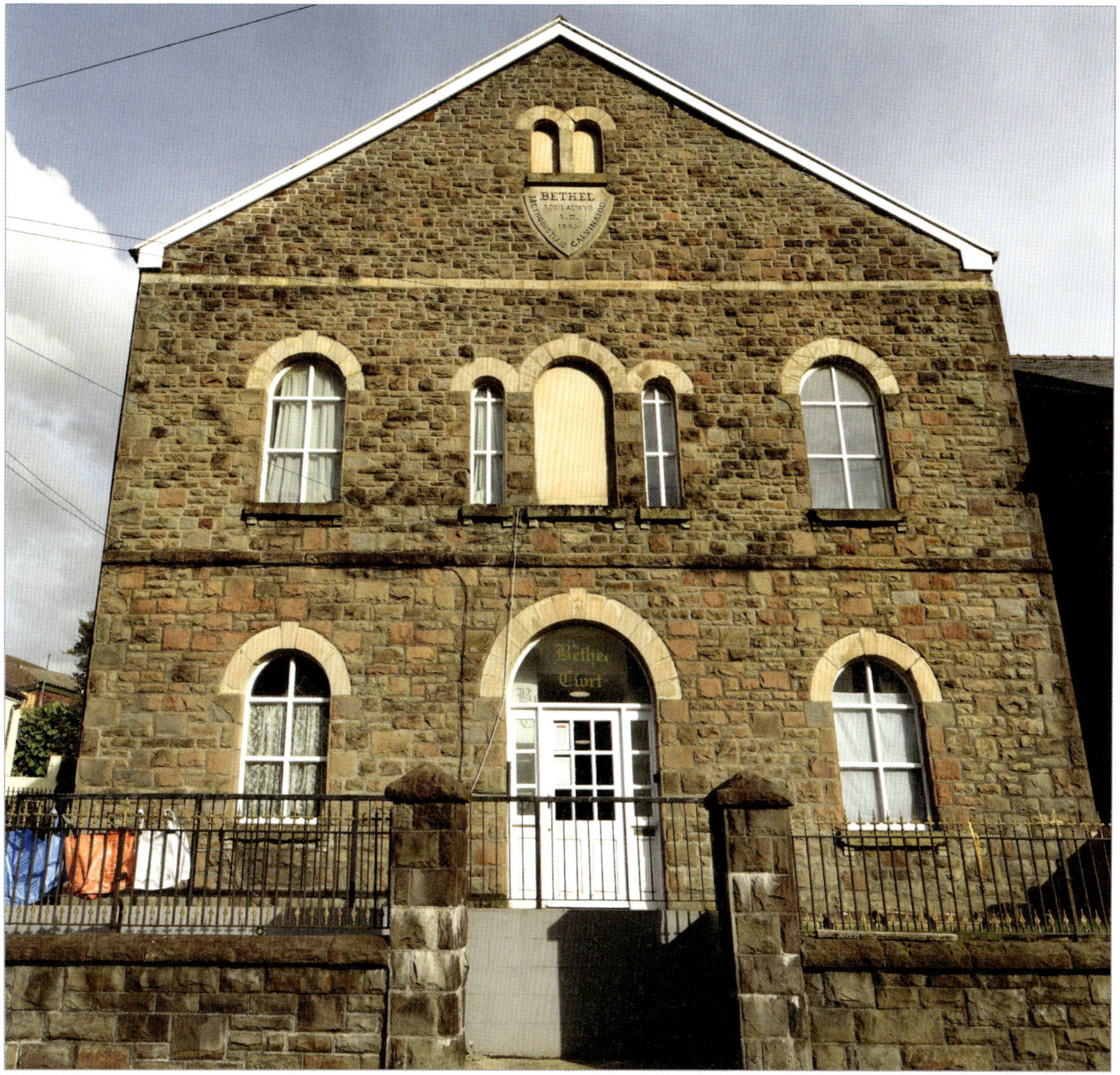

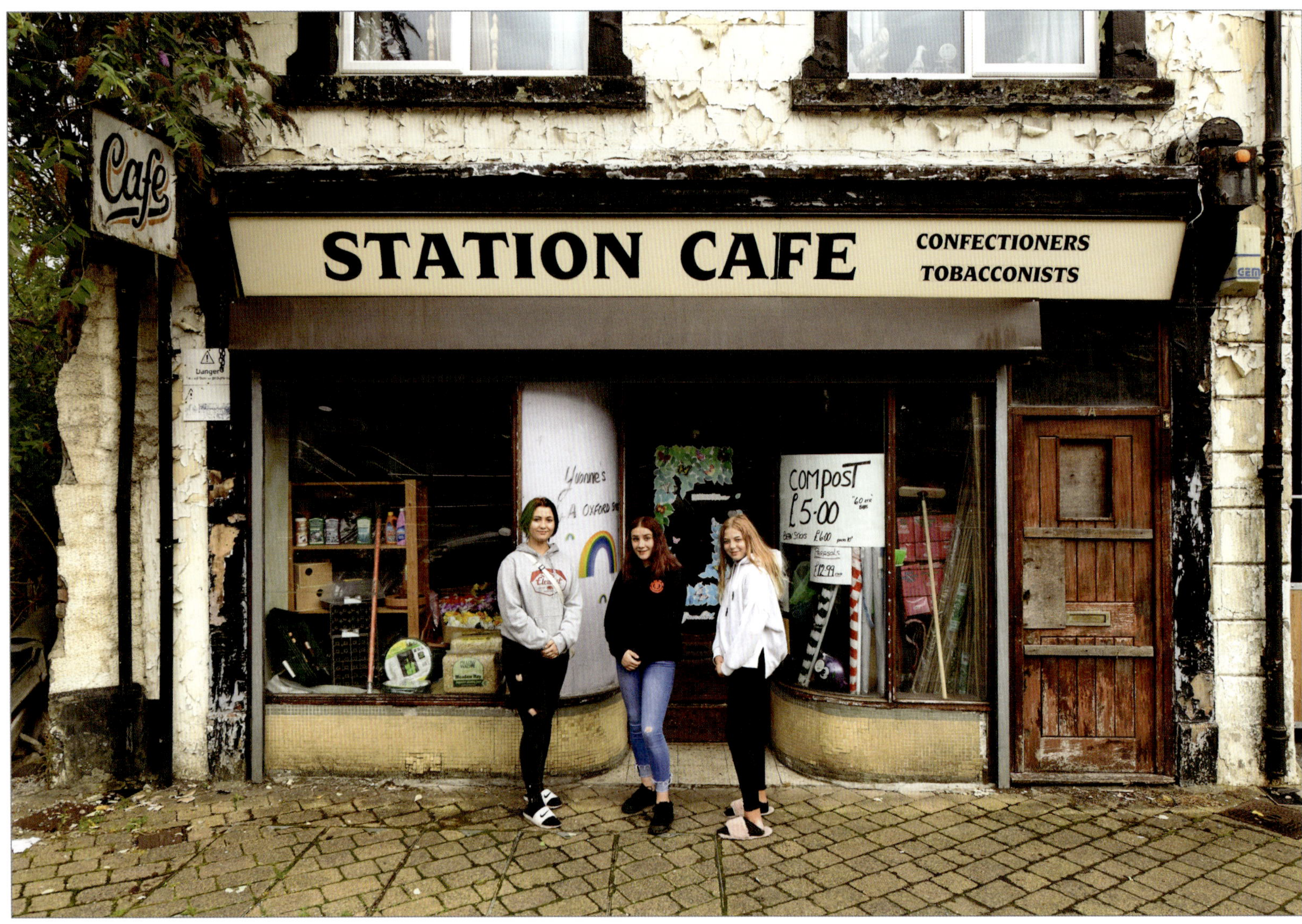

Station Cafe,
Ffaldau Square,
Pontycymer

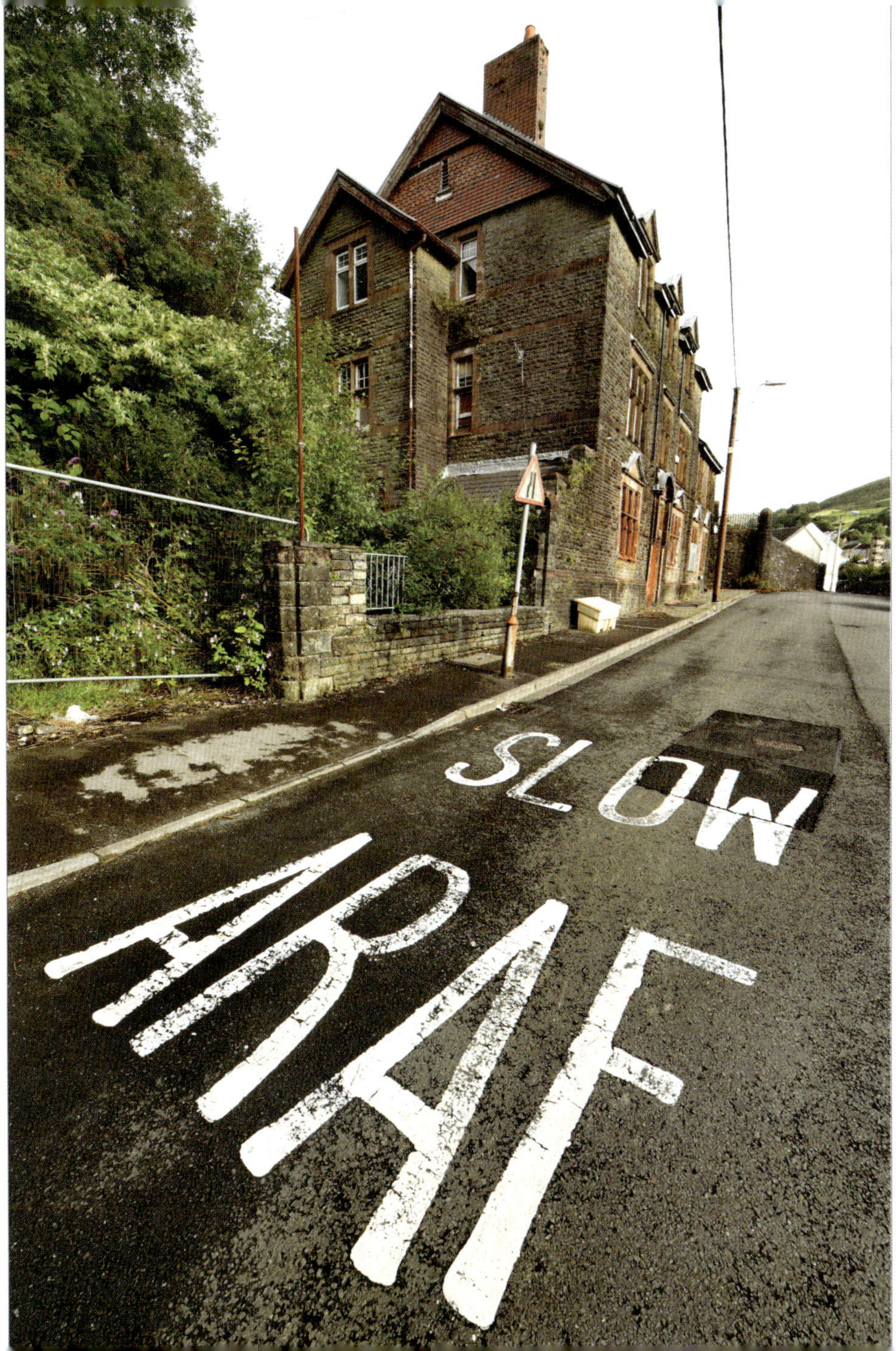

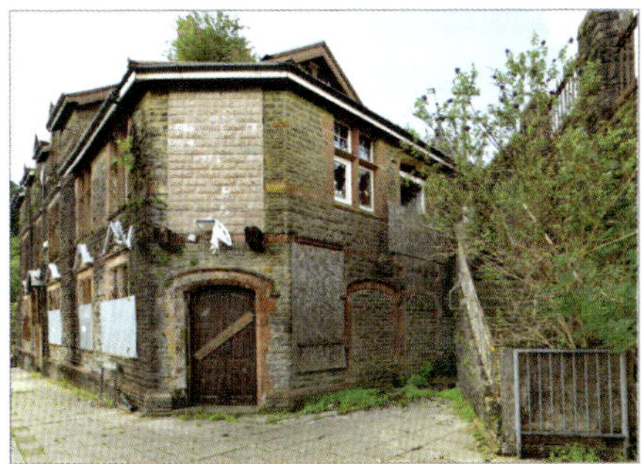

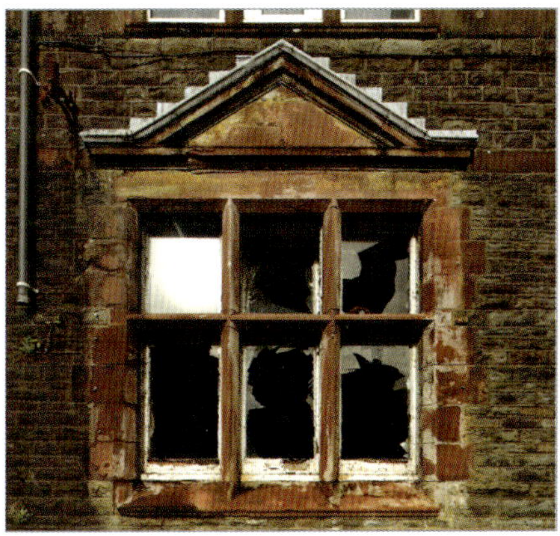

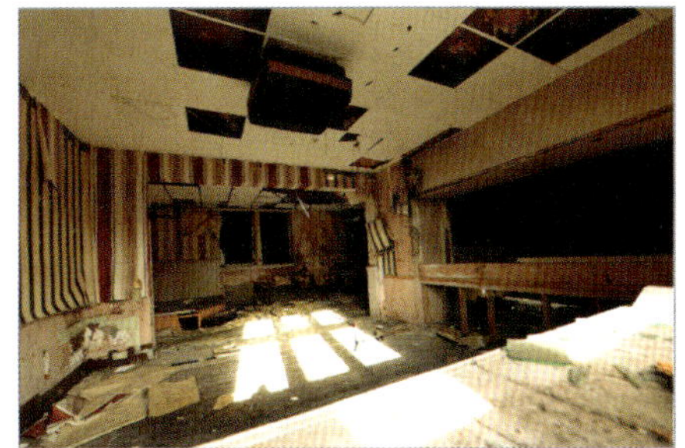

Not all of the historic buildings in the Garw have survived, however. These are the sad remains of the once-fashionable Royal Hotel in Pontycymer.

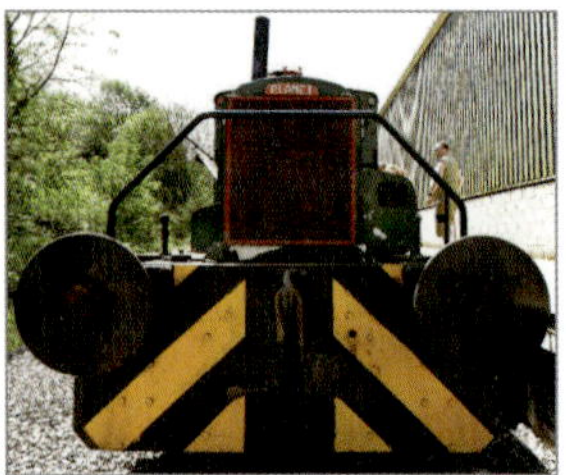

The community route for walkers and cyclists (National Cycle Route 884) runs in parallel with the old railway line that opened in 1872.

Ending its services for passengers in 1953, its final coal train trip was in 1986 (though it re-opened in 1995 to support the land reclamation scheme, before its final outing on 7 April 1997).

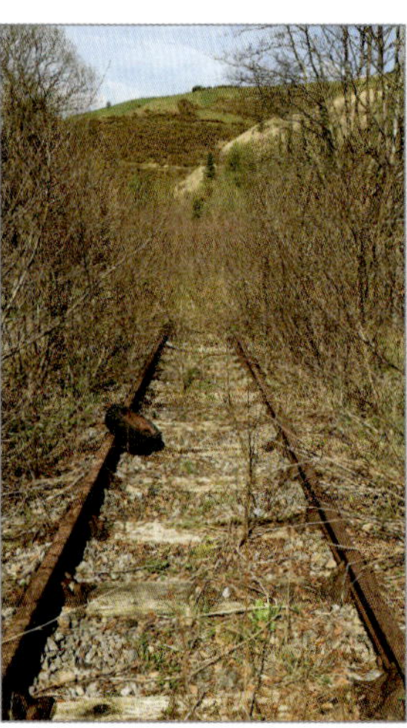

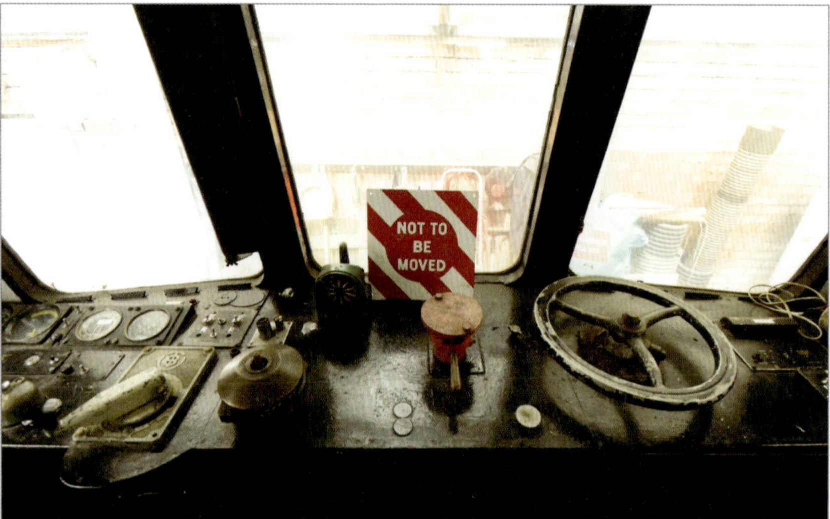

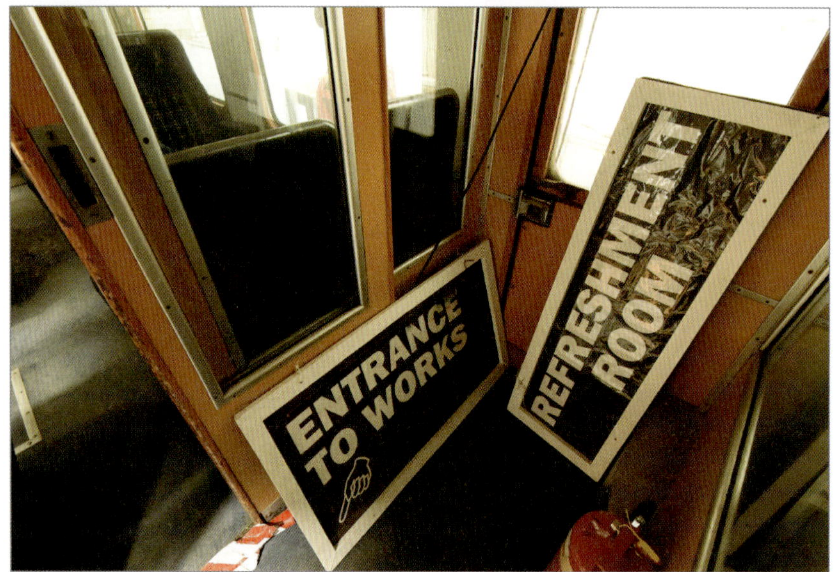

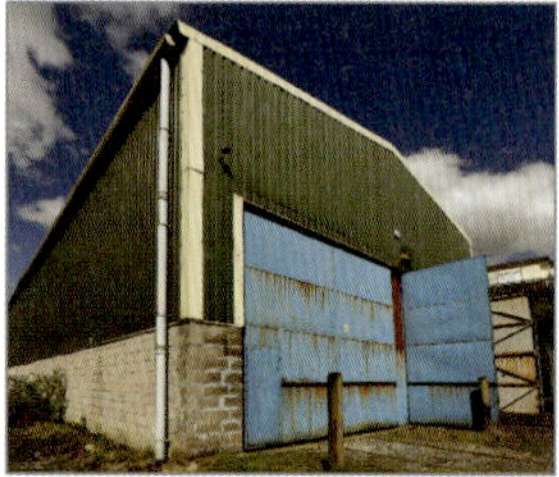

Over the next decade, the Bridgend Valleys Railway Company plans to run trains once again between Bryngarw Country Park and Pontycymer, with special tourist steam days on the weekends.

In addition, a museum and archive of local industrial railways is being developed at Pontycymer Station with the long-term objective of extending the line as far south as Tondu, to link up with the national rail network between Bridgend and Maesteg.

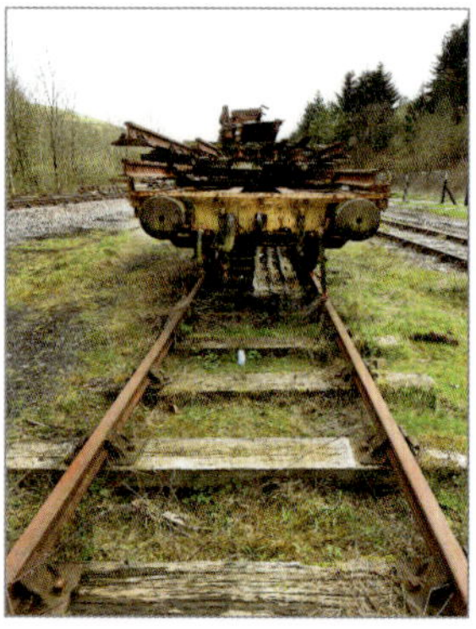

above and opposite: Garw Valley Railway shed and yard, Pontycymer Station

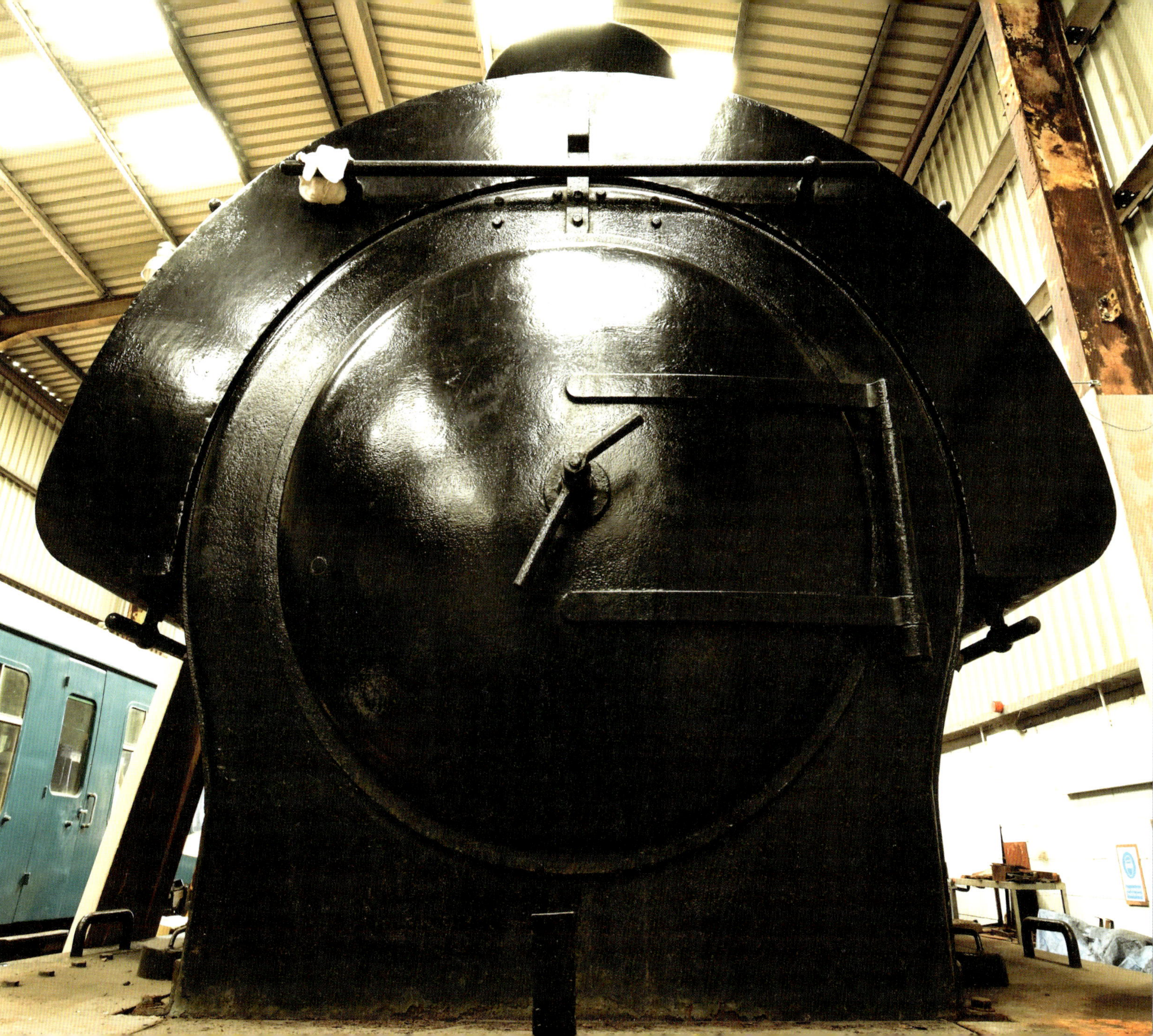

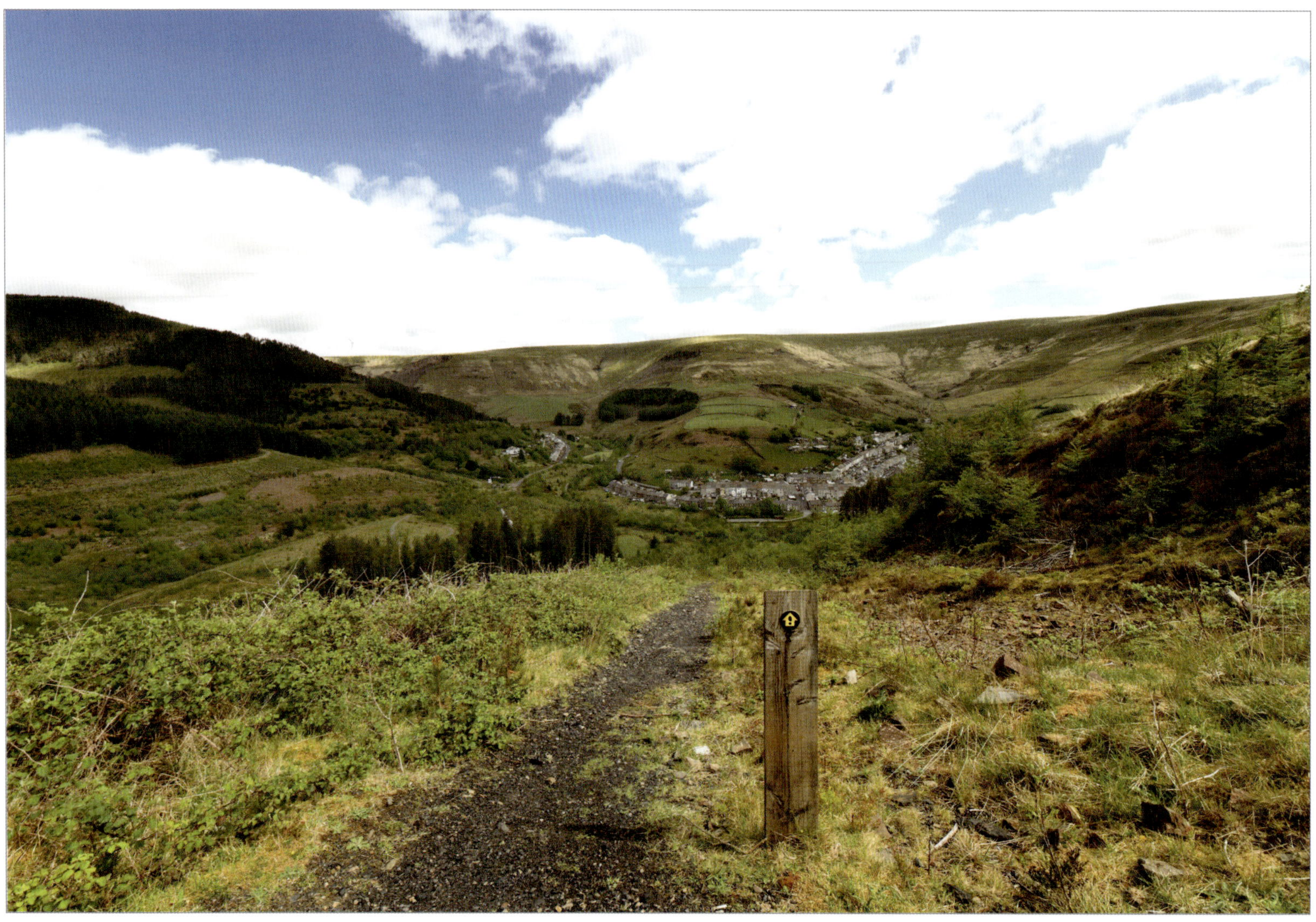

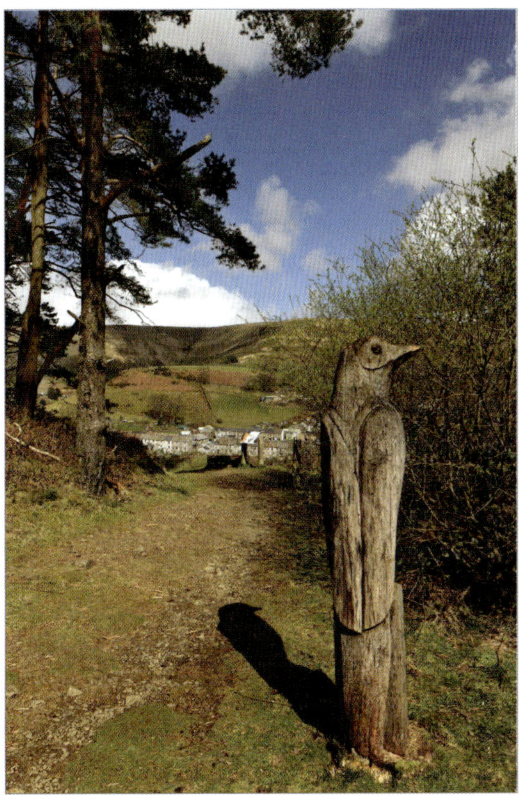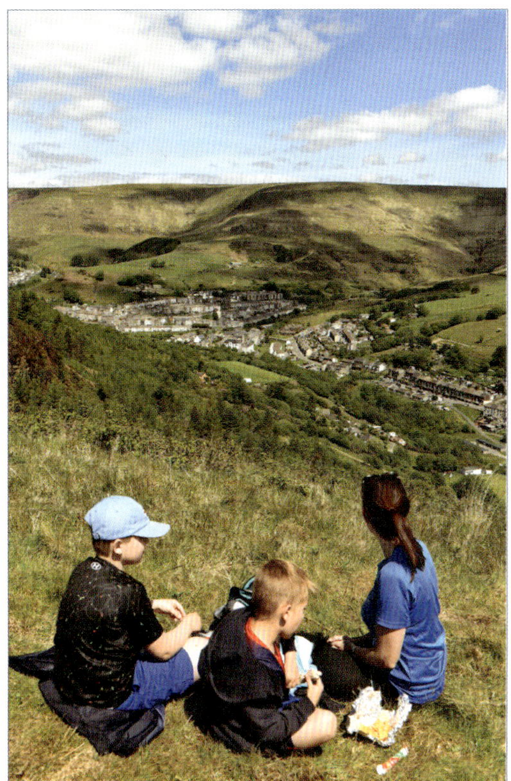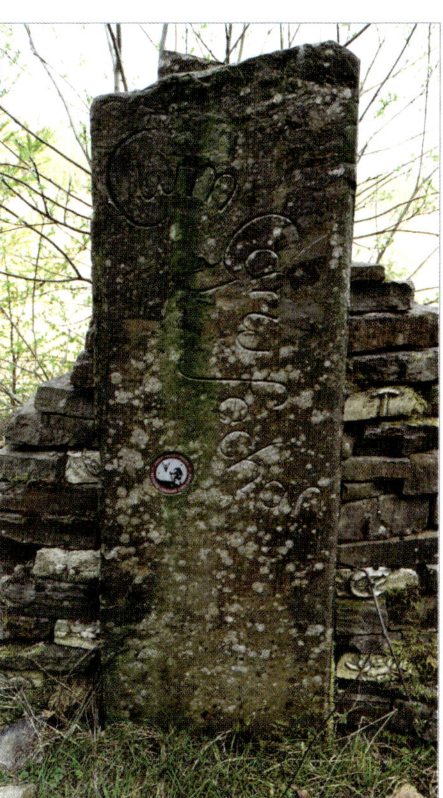

cycle and walking trails, above Blaengarw, Pontycymer and Braich-y-Cymer

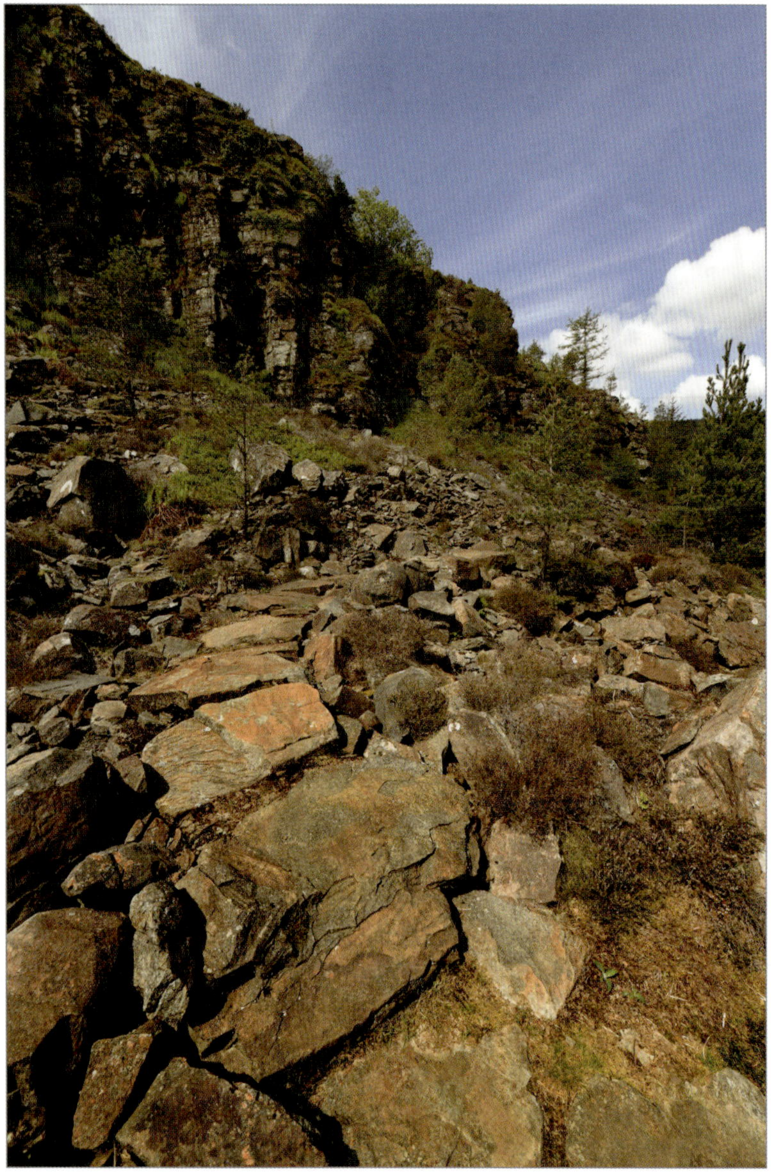

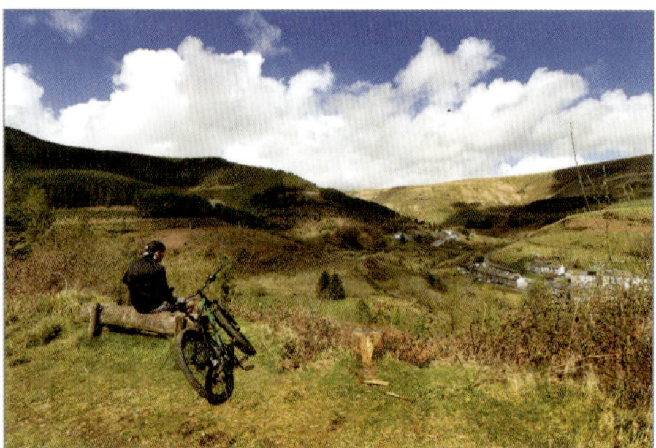

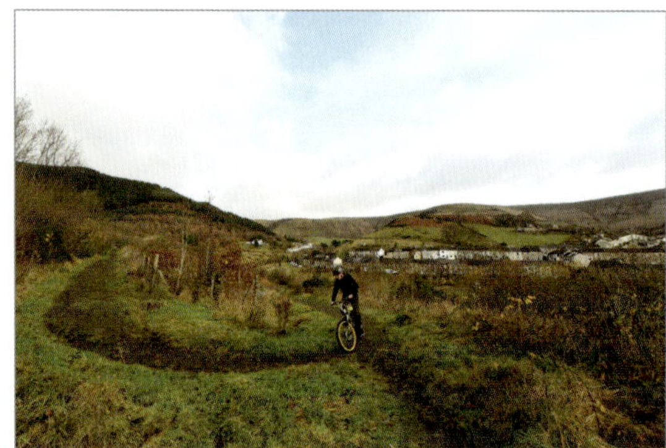

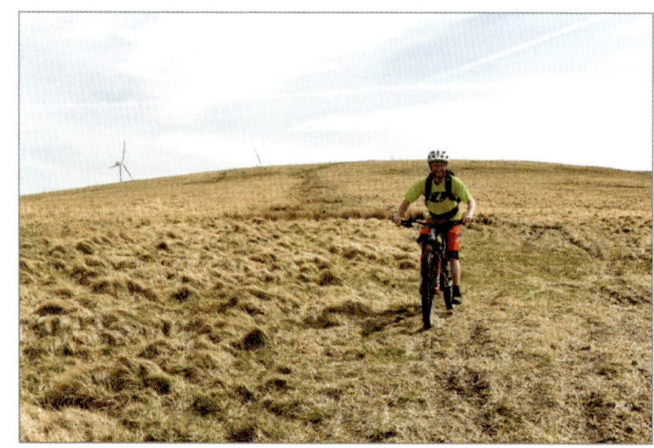

cycle and
mountain
bike trails

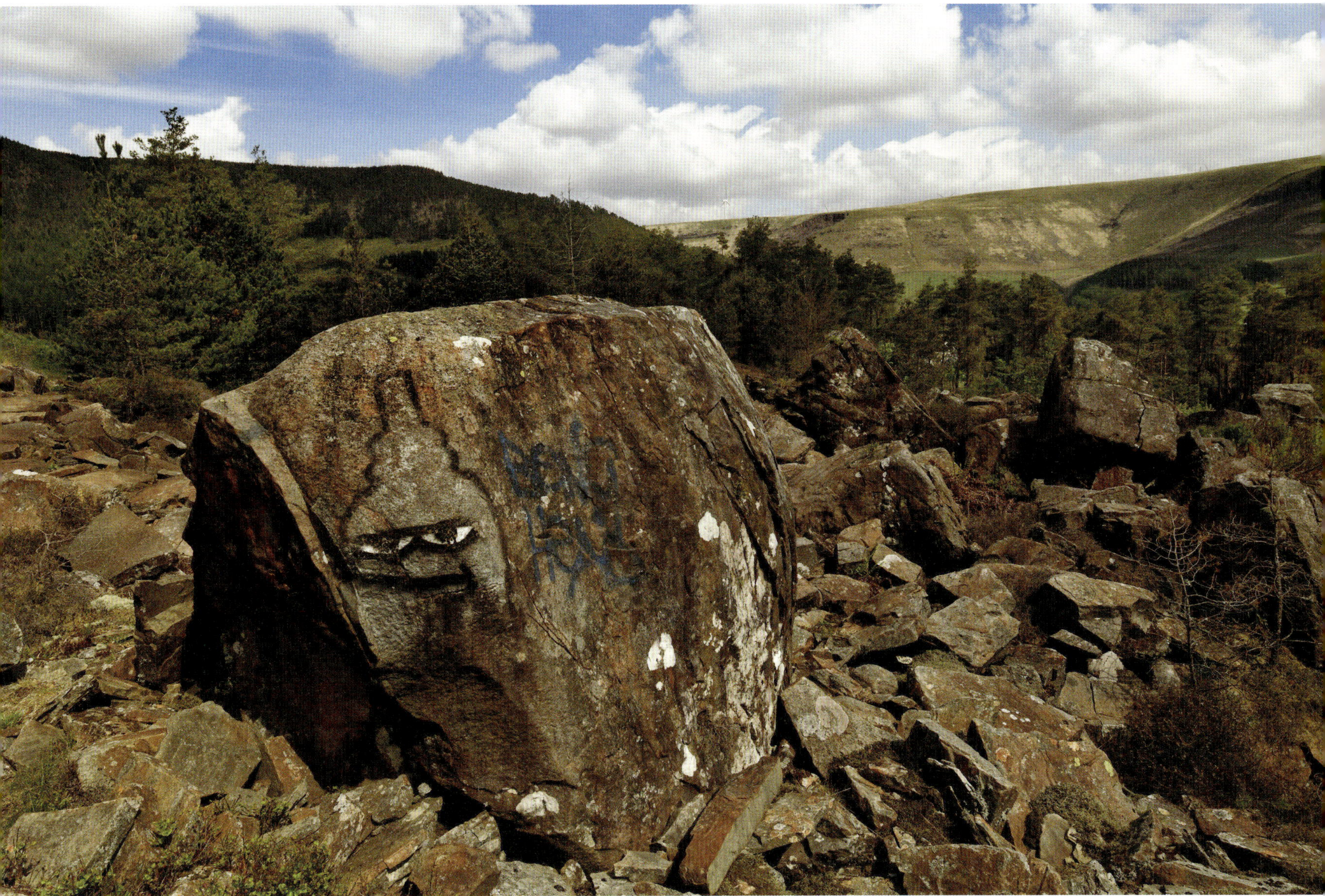

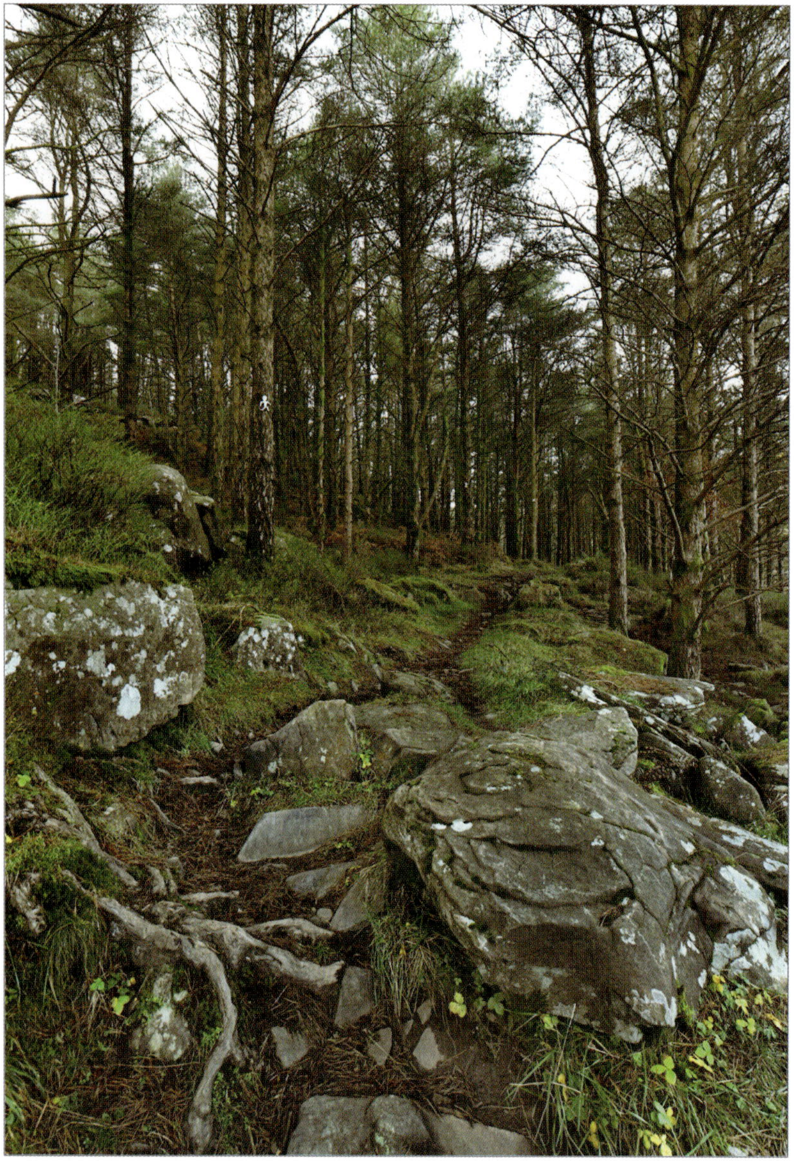

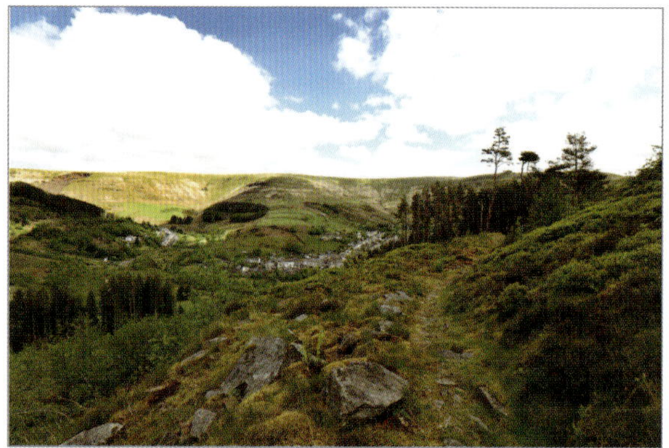

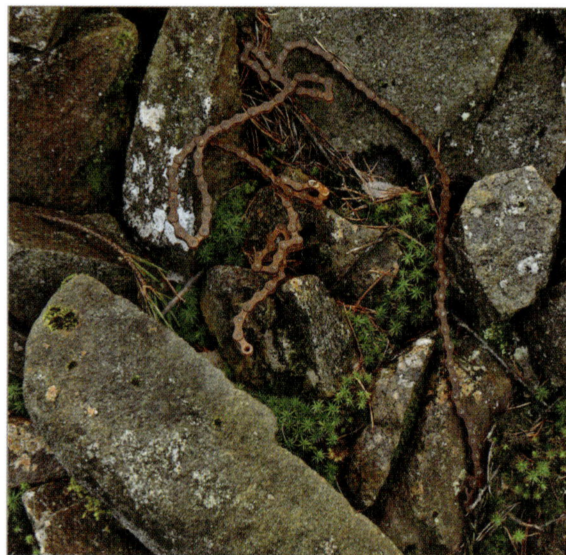

challenging
mountain bike
trails

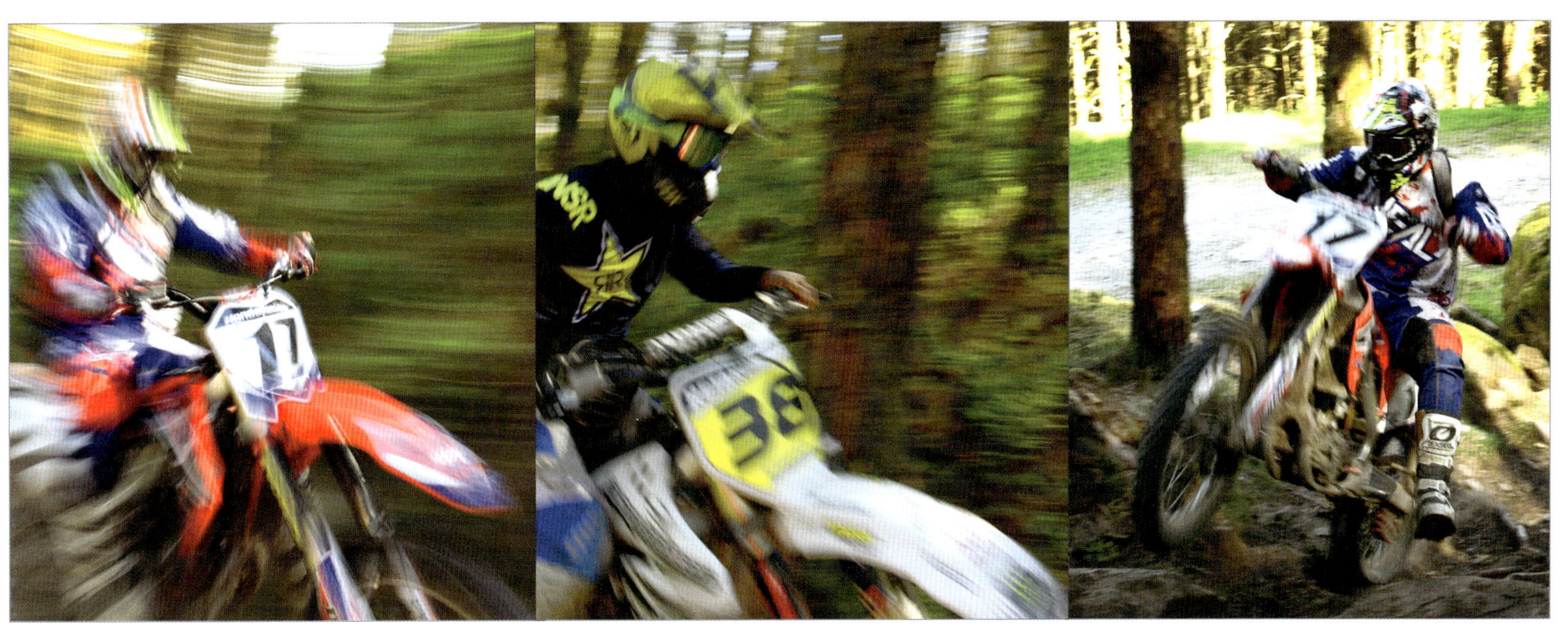

motor bikes also make use of
the Valley's forestry trails

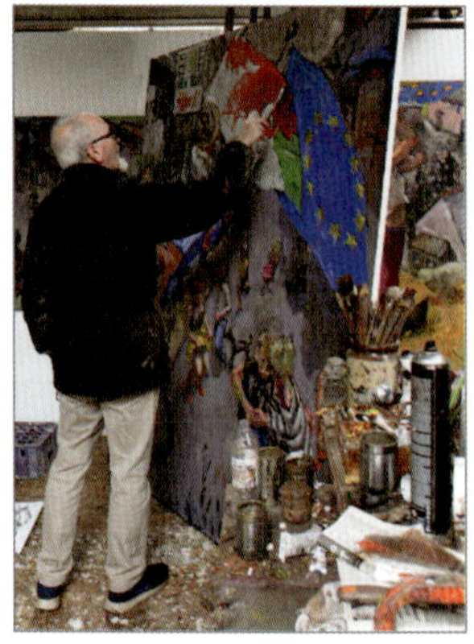

Kevin Sinnott returned to the area of his birth in 1993. Today, his studio is raised up on the Valley's west side, in the large roof space of his converted church home, and his new gallery, *Studio 18* sits proud on the Garw's main street.

Sinnott's work has explored the main chapters in the history of the Valley as well as the lives of its residents (including in a time of Corona and Brexit), but always with the landscape as the principal character.

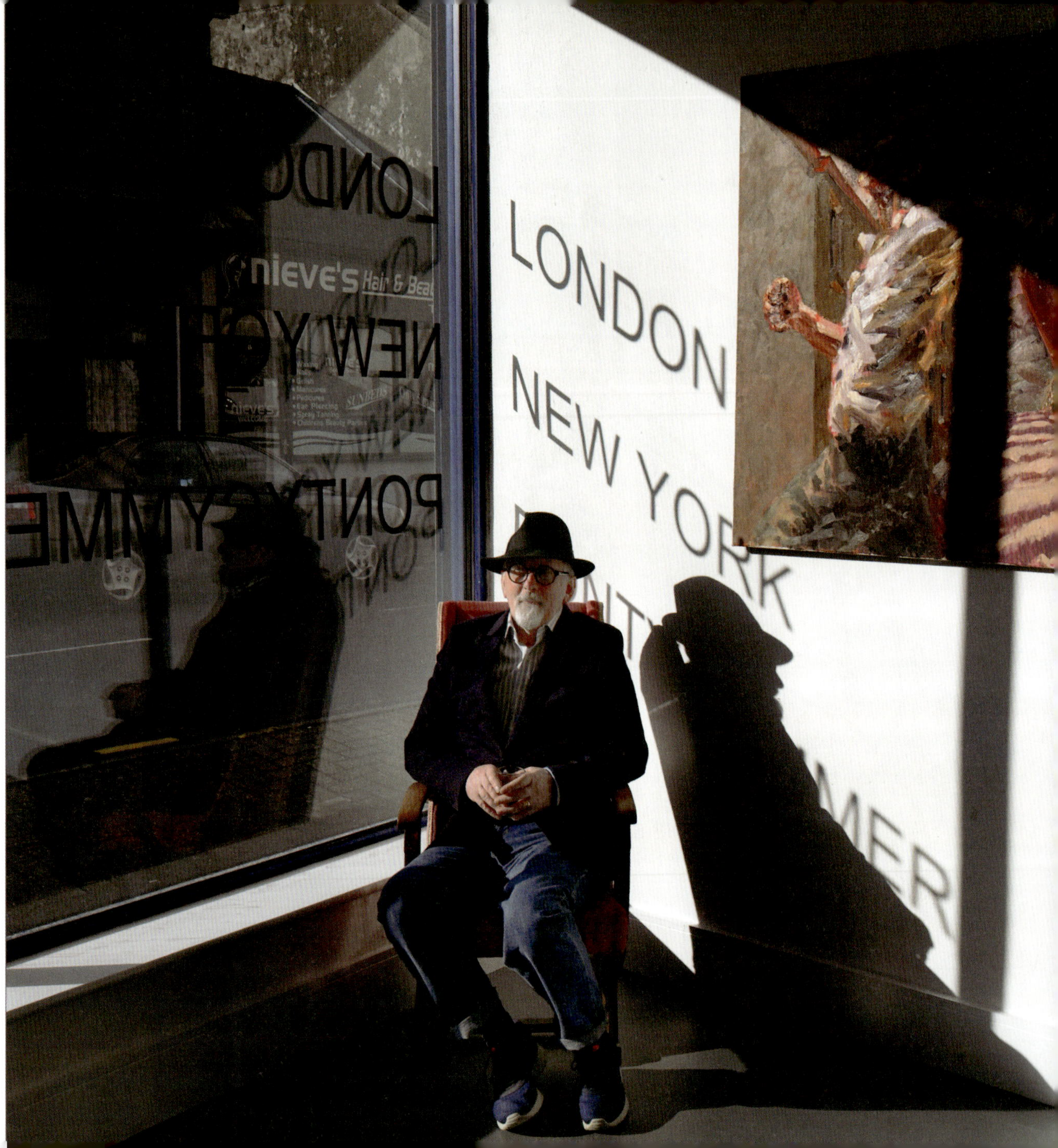

BINGO IN THE TIME OF CORONA

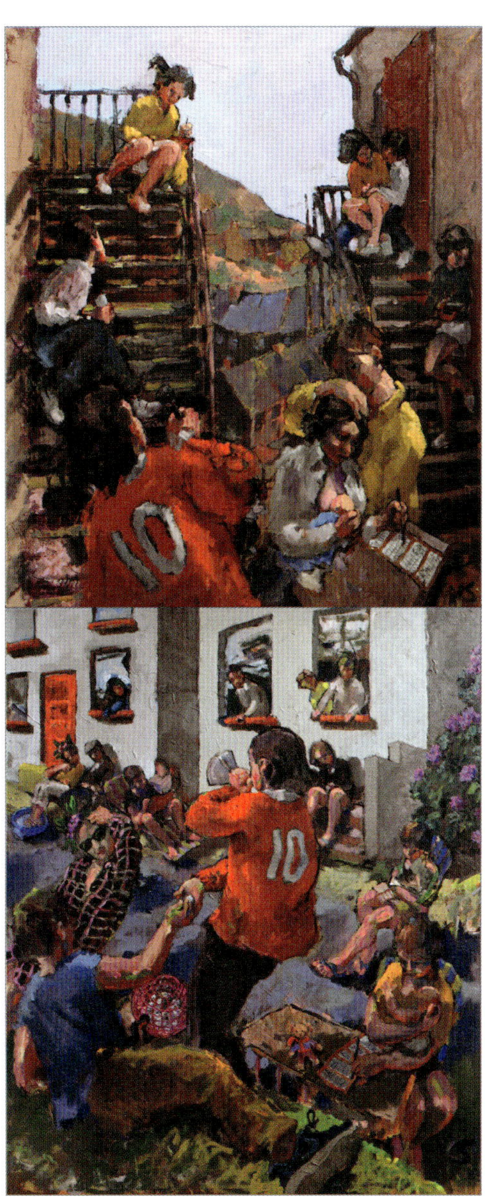

Coming down from the hills,
strange sounds,
Legs 11 in lockdown,
booming from house speakers in

our rediscovered maths
of contact and community,
our new fragile algebras of faith.

In a time of bad numbers –
those infected, lack of PPE
and ventilators,
the newly-unemployed,
businesses going to the wall,

no toilet rolls, and death –
we're playing (distanced) bingo in
the streets
– Staying Alive, 85 –
for charity … and hope.

On the lower lake,
Two Little Ducks (22),
and Mary behind her Garden Gate,
locked-down safe at Number 8.

In our full houses,
we're keeping our distance –
Number 2, Me And You,
In A State, 28 –

in danger of not knowing
where we're going,
forgetting where we've been,
trapped inside the geometry of
Covid-19,

beating the pandemic
with our caring beating hearts and
rediscovering we're much much
more than
the sum of all our parts.

Under Doctor's Orders, Number 9,
Red Raw, 64,
Duck and Dive, 25,
Down On Your Knees, 43.

Hitting The Floor at 74.
67 … Stairway To Heaven.

opposite:

Kevin Sinnott in his 'London /
New York / Pontycymmer'
Studio 18;
and painting in his
workshop home

top to bottom:

Kevin Sinnott's
Lockdown Bingo
and *Lockdown Bingo II*,
both painted
in 2020

Kevin Sinnott
outside his Studio 18,
Oxford Street, Pontycymer

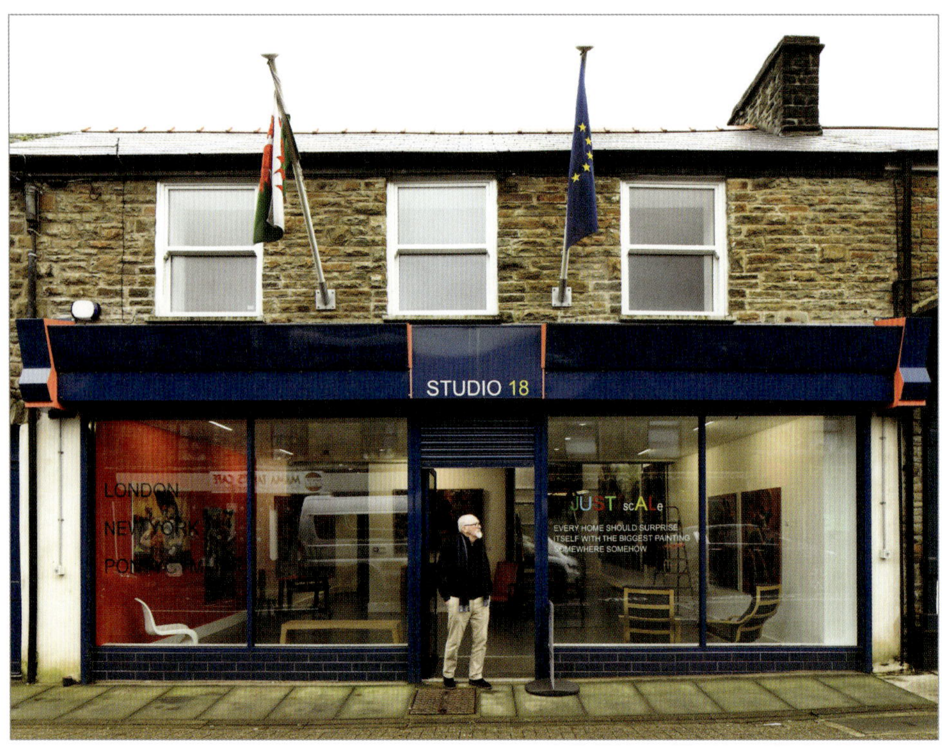

*The Relieving of New Town,
Pontycymer* by Kevin Sinnott,
painted in 2020, featuring
Welsh and EU flags flying
above his studio

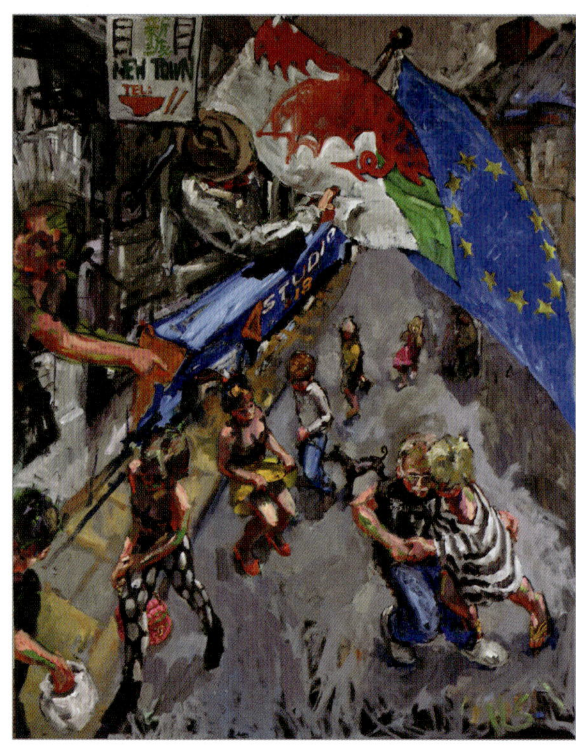

opposite:

Kevin Sinnott's
Pegging Out (2020)

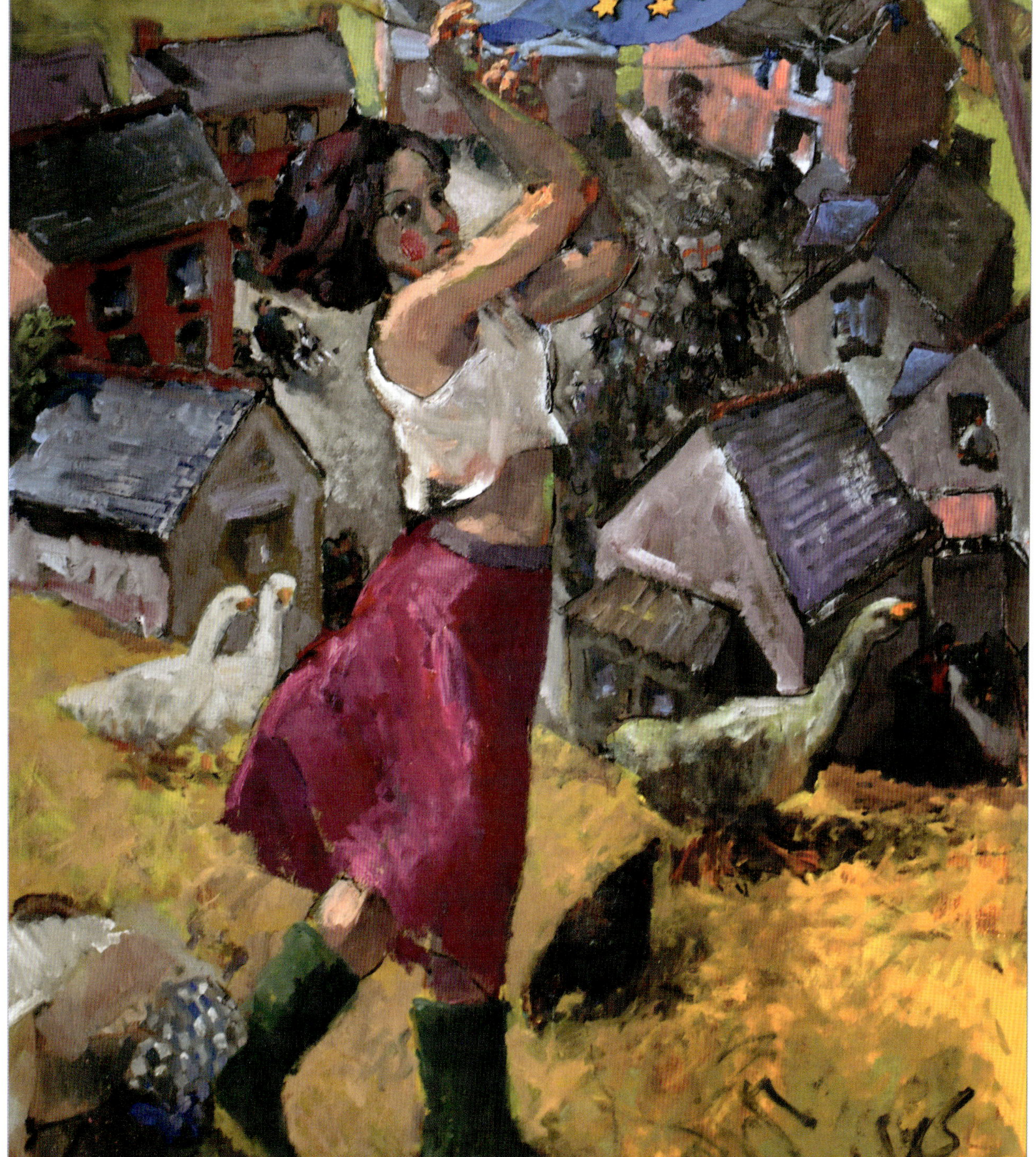

Self-taught artists are not uncommon within the South Wales Valleys, where auto-didacticism has always been the principal cultural direction. Bred from within the stones of Workmen's Halls and Institutes, theirs was (had to be) a philosophy of self-help and mutual aid. And this culture, creative and oppositional, is clearly reflected in the work of three of the Valley's most interesting artists:

Merlin Madog MBE [1935-2015] was one of the Garw's great characters, a harp-maker and a wizard of invention, regularly seen travelling up and down the Valley on his (self-made) penny-farthing or in his wind-up clockwork car. Merlin's great uncle, Captain Hopkin Thomas Madog was the first Welsh rugby international from the Garw Valley.

Lovespoon-maker Siôn Llewellyn became Merlin's apprentice in 1976, and after his death took over his workshop in Meadow Street, Ponty-cymer. Each of award-winning Siôn's lovespoons are individually hand-crafted from home-grown hardwoods … with pride and passion .

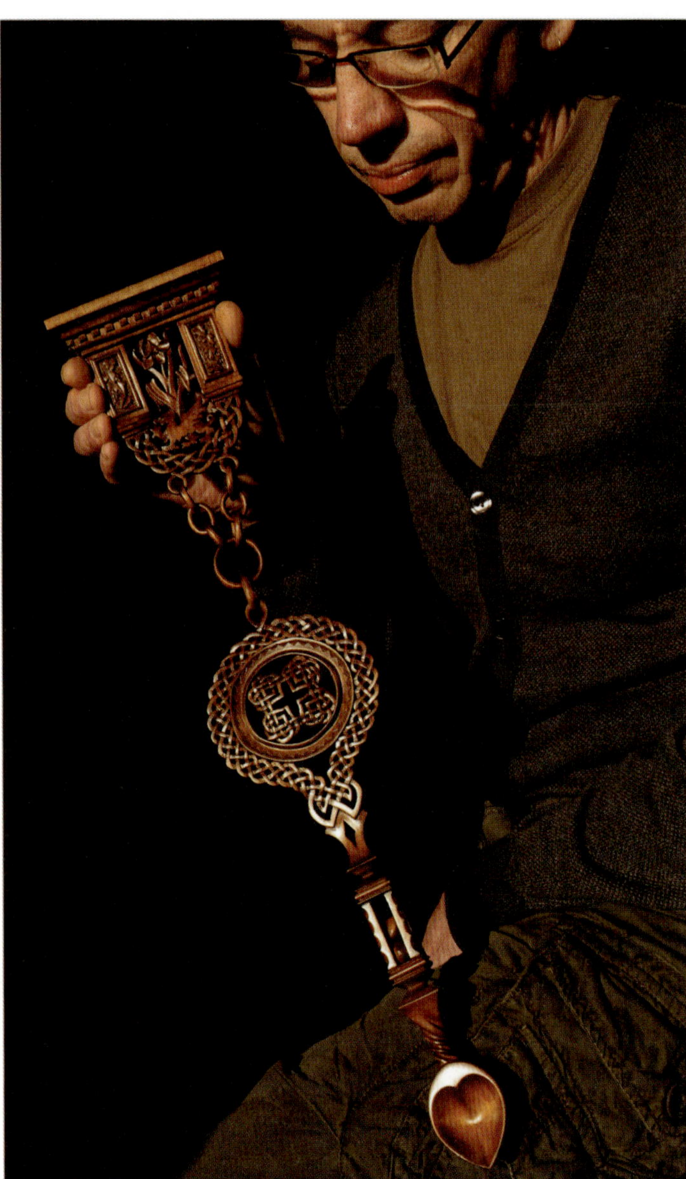

Siôn Llewellyn and the lovespoon he donated to the Museum of Welsh Life, St Fagans:

The cornice at the top, like those found on Welsh dressers, was included to show Siôn's cabinet making background. (image by Sean © Wales News Service)

Merlin Madog's old harp studio
in Meadow Street, Pontycymer;
and its new occupant,
lovespoon-maker, Siôn Llewellyn

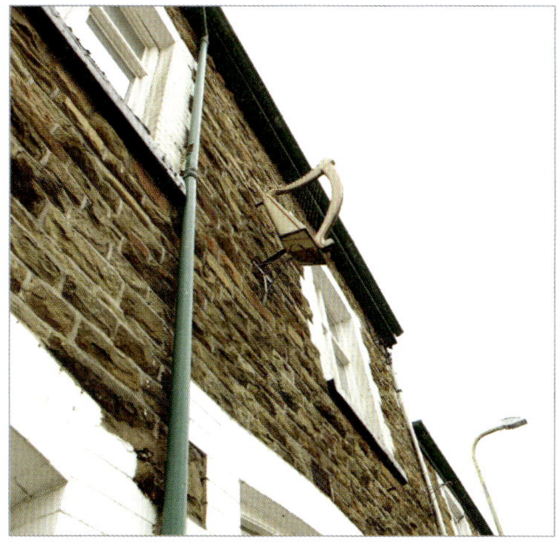

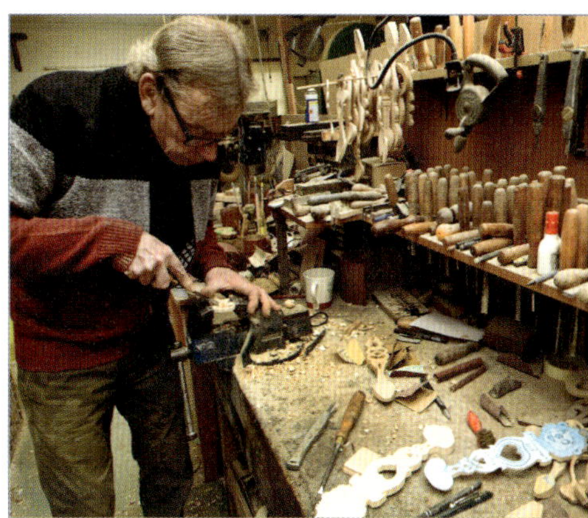

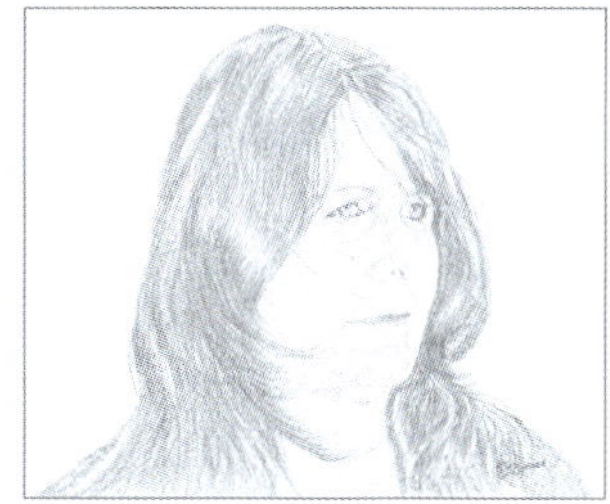

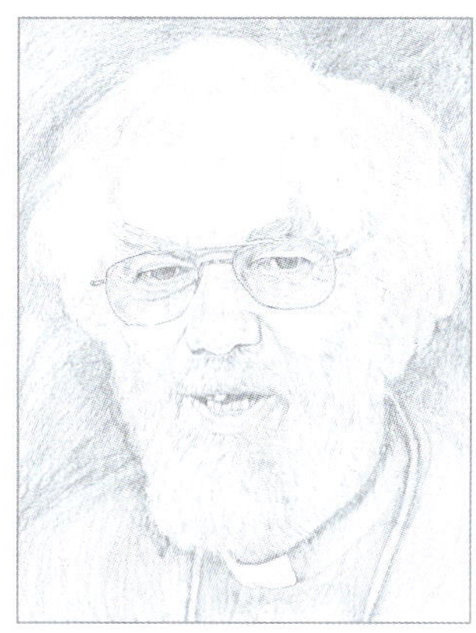

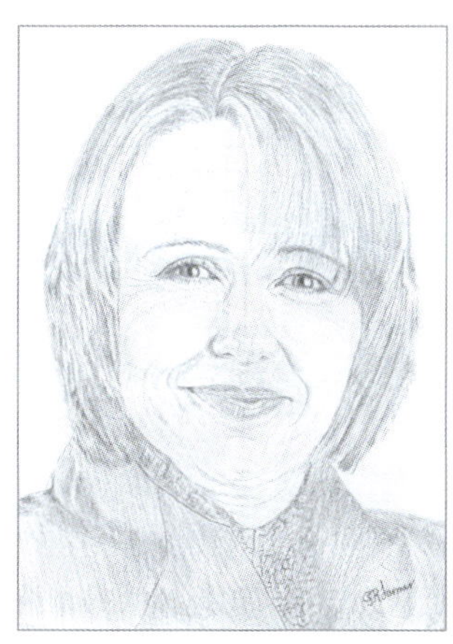

Disabled, ex-miner Gordon Farmer took up drawing after an accident ended his working career. His graphite pencil portraits celebrate – alongside the great and the good, the famous and the infamous – the lives and the faces of ordinary Valleys folk.

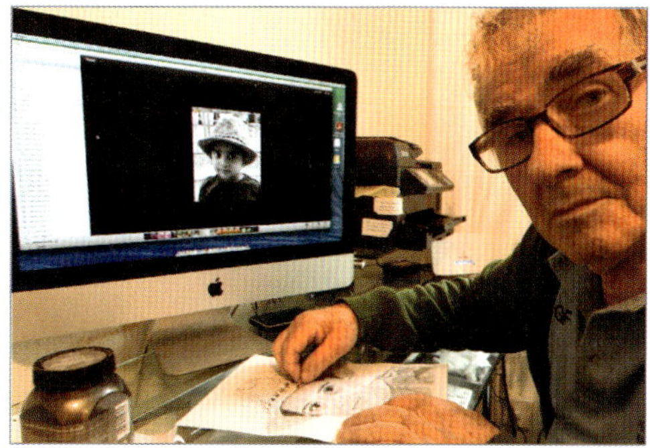

Graphite is another form of carbon like the coal which defined so many of our Valleys' stories, created through millions of years of the compression of animal skeletons and plants. When subjected to high temperatures and pressures graphite can convert into diamonds, and today, George's new armchair excavations are revealing the abiding riches of Valley peoples' identities through the infinity of reflections and shades from black to white ... the miner's palette.

Gordon Farmer in his home in Pontyrhyl,
and his portraits of Ali Carter, Rowan Williams
and Dame Tanni Grey Thompson

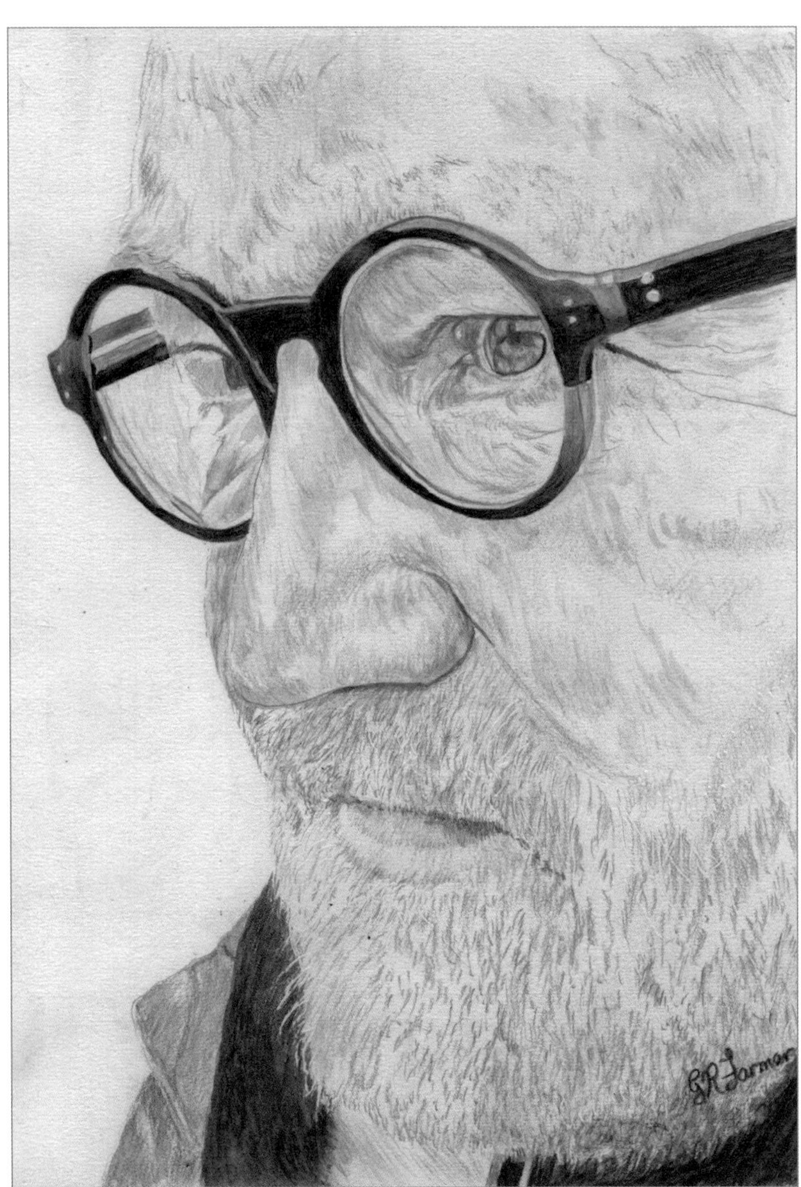

Gordon Farmer's
portrait of
The Golden Valley
author

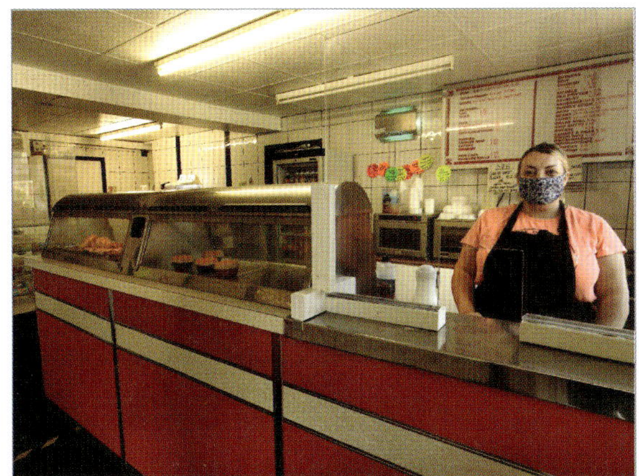

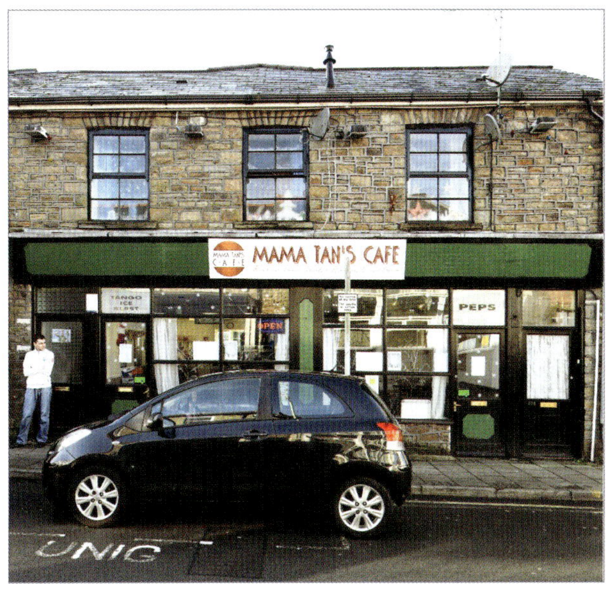

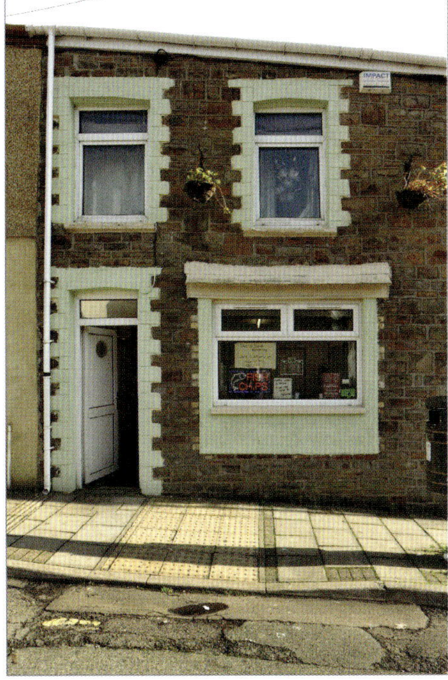

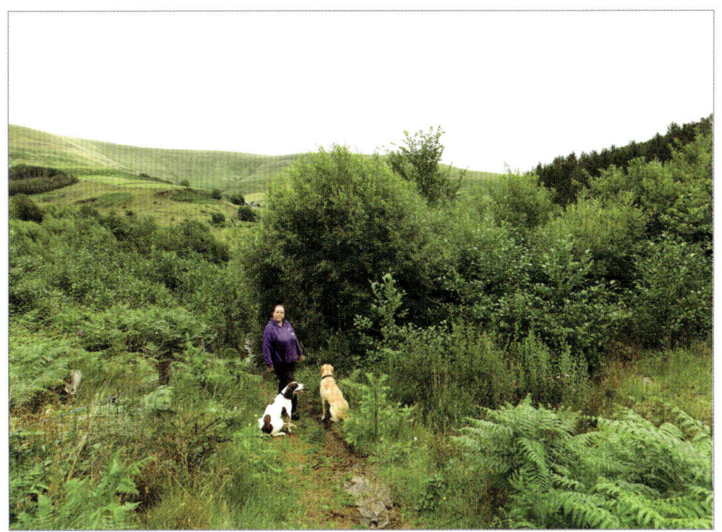

clockwise from bottom left:

Waun Bant Fish Bar, Ffaldau Square, Pontycymer; Tracey Edwards serving; Mama Tan's Cafe, Oxford Street, Pontycymer; Kirsty Williams of Kirsty's K9 Cwtches (a dog walking and sitting service), with Thor and Charlie

While we are certainly losing people from the Valley, others are arriving (I was one of them, 36 years ago). With the trend in business away from large-scale industrial, often dirty and dangerous monoliths towards more localised, targeted units of production, connected digitally with the rest of the world, the geography of the South Wales Valleys – even those few dead-ended ones like the Garw – offers an attractive location for this alternative approach.

In 2000, Rob Cowell bought the historic Fforchwen Farm (the subject of the BBC Wales documentary). Today, Rob is employed as a software builder by a multi-national company, his main work – undertaken from one of the best views in the Garw / Wales – being in South Africa.

The most recent of the Covid pandemics has taught many of us that we can work without 'going to work'. I've certainly learnt a great deal about the possibilities of delivering online events for people in the USA, Ireland, England and throughout Wales, and the ability to create and design books, like this one, without leaving my home.

What this Valley offers is a working environment second to none, at least for those who can work digitally and/or make a living from the land.

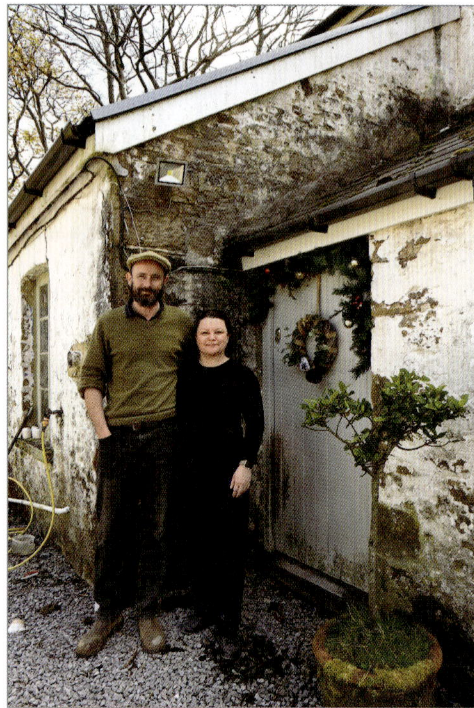

With the Garw's environment of mountains, trees and lakes, fresh air and very little crime, and the avoidance of the daily commute's traffic jams, rush hours and pollution, why wouldn't anyone want to make their homes and their workplaces here?

Rob and Karen Cowell at their Fforchwen farmhouse:

Karen is a graphic designer, potter and candle-maker who is currently building a workshop at the farm which she hopes will one day employ local people to help with her creations.

opposite:

one of Karen and Rob's workplace views!

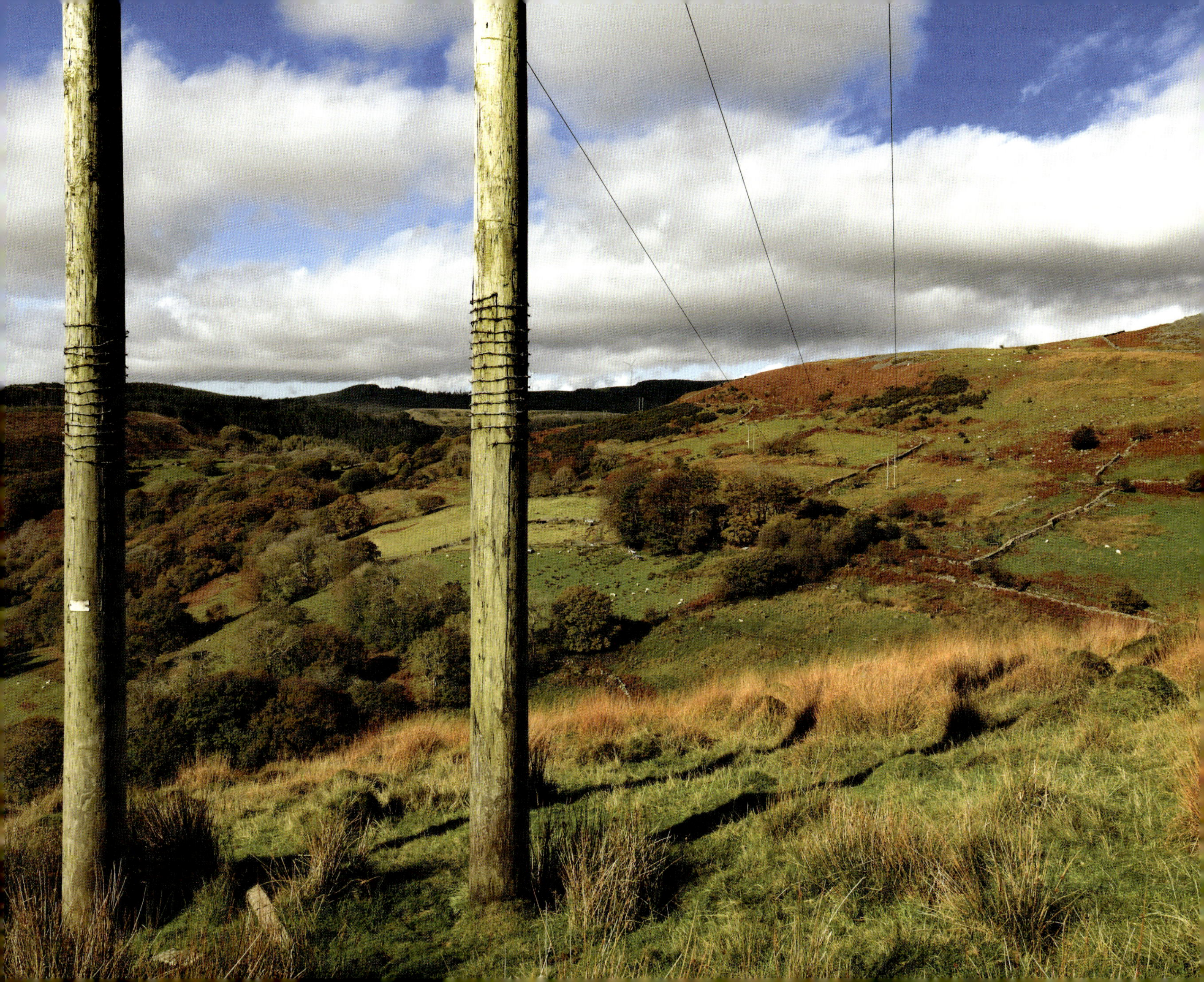

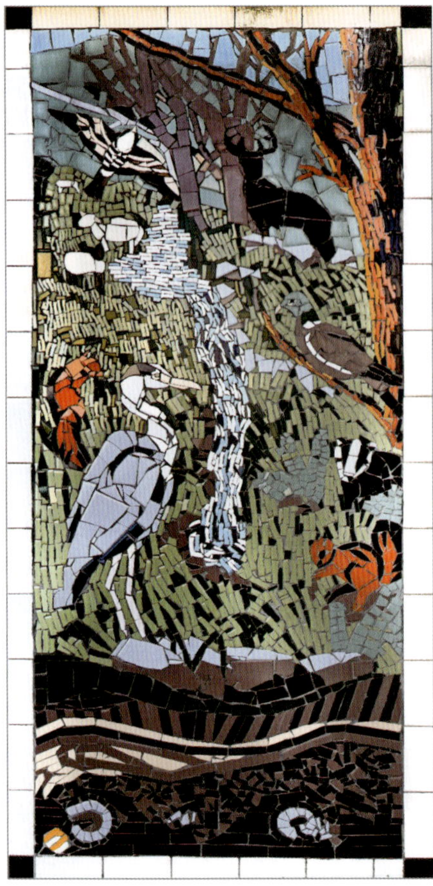

above and far right:

the 'imagined future' images
by young people from the Garw,
Blaengarw Workmen's Hall mural

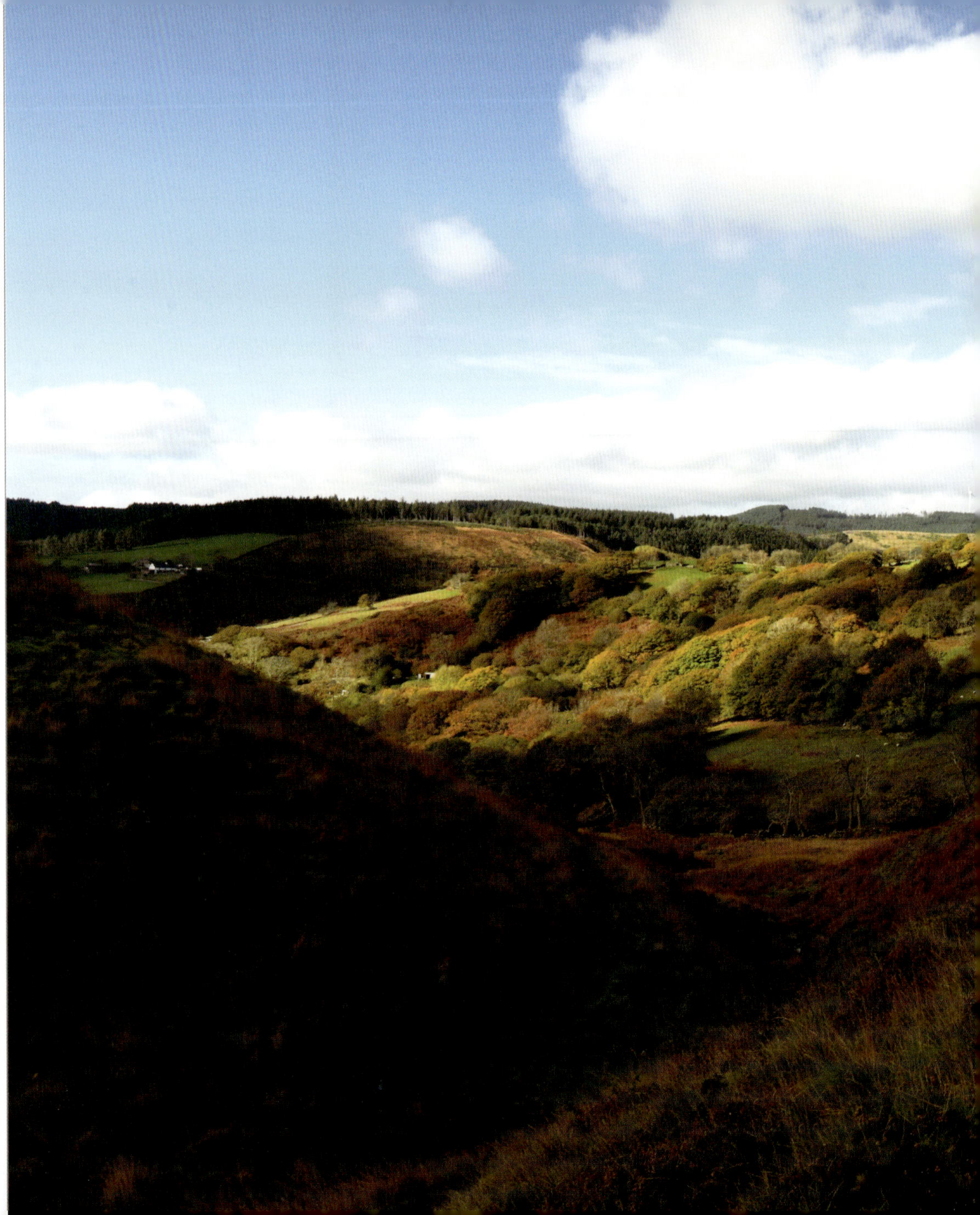

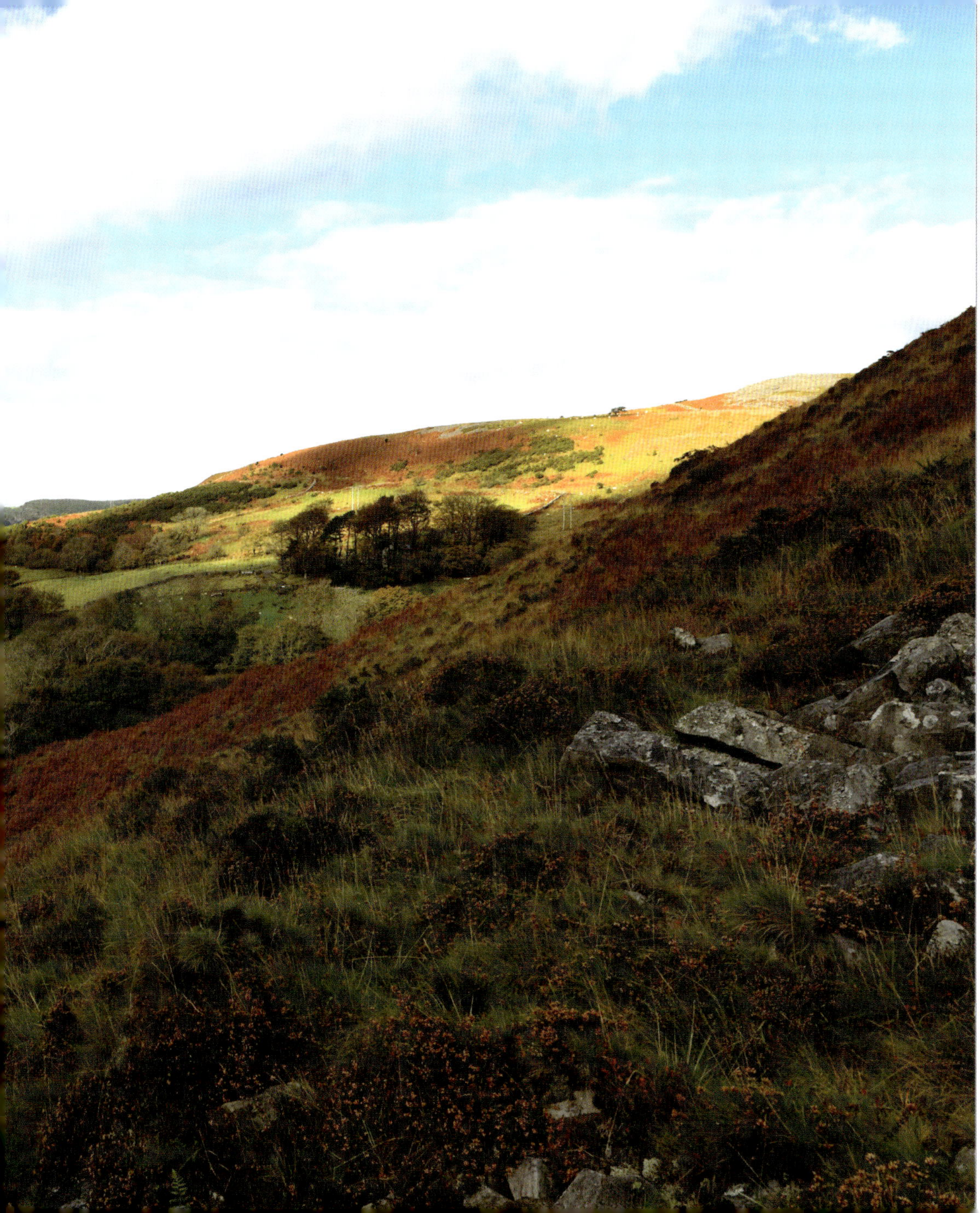

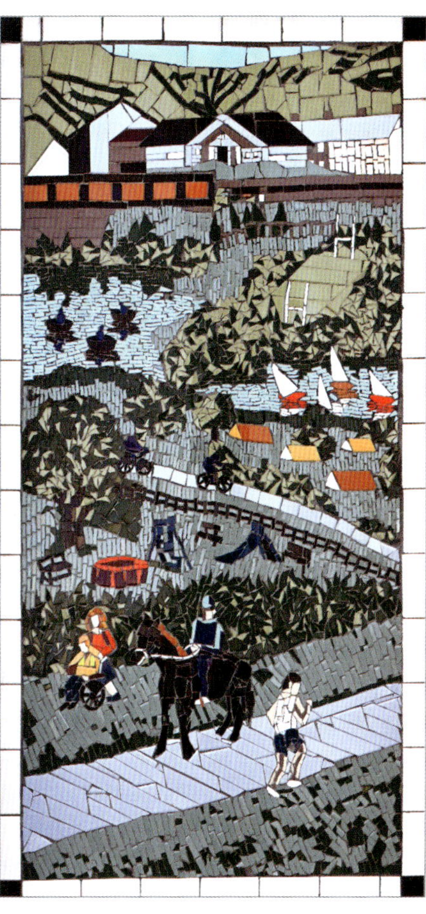

left:

Nant Fforchwen

Today, the only things which stand higher than the elevating piles of stones where our ancestors lived and were buried are the new turbines turned by the same winds which brush over the long history of these hills, breathing new life where life began.

Wind farms are a major part of the strategy to reduce our reliance upon fossil fuels as they convert the wind's kinetic into electrical energy, making a significant contribution towards our renewable energy targets.

We have plenty of wind in the upper Garw, though unlike coal, it is a freely-available resource, with the new wind-mills emitting no greenhouse gases, producing few waste products, and costing a fraction of the former's heavy toll in lives and the despoliation of the land ... and, even more impor-tantly, in the existential danger to our increasingly-fragile planet.

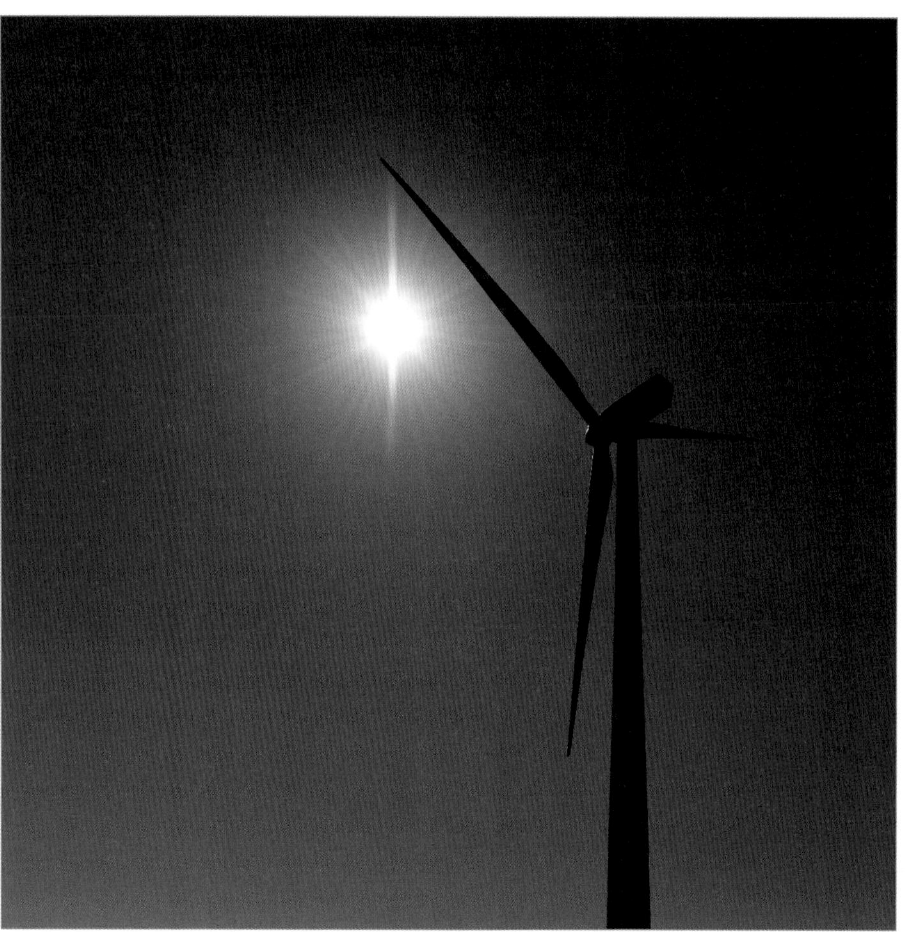

I recognise that some local people – while understanding the need for non-carbon-based, renewable sources of power – dislike what they see as the turbines' disfiguring of our mountain horizons. For me, however, they are often things of beauty which suggest the possibilities of a cleaner, more sustainable future

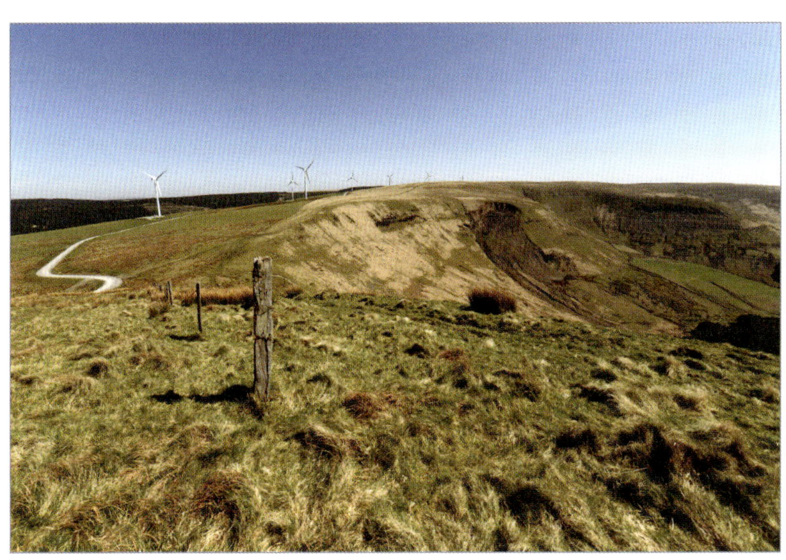

the summit of Bwlchgarw,
with a line of turbines
in the distance

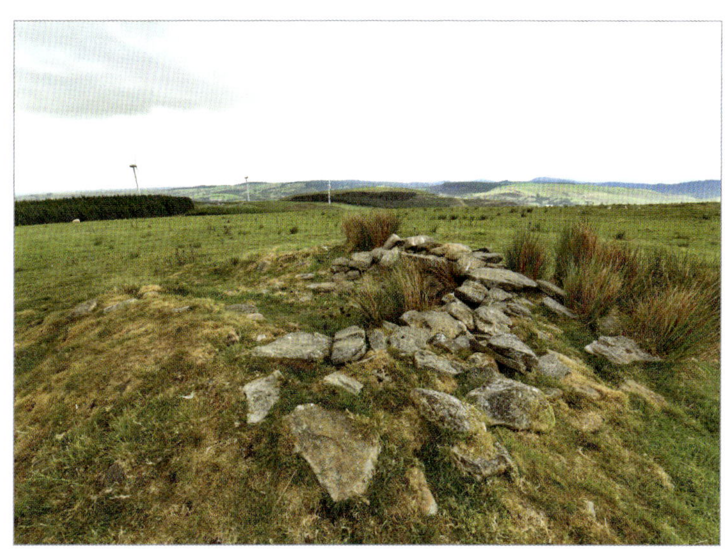

another round barrow,
one of ten on Llyndwr Fawr,
... and accompanying
turbines

The Garw Valley is certainly struggling today to recover something of its self from a century of abuse.

This was a place where the unspeakable happened, bit by bit, until it amounted to a great tragedy, a play in which few had written their own lines, swept along by an unseen director.

But today, a mixed cultural industries, new technology and tourism approach has the potential to offer valleys like the Garw a new reason to exist … and this time without the physical dangers of coalmining, offering a cleaner, more humane range of answers to the question of why we are still here, and how we can stay and even prosper.

What we can be sure of is that the solutions won't involve coal, not in its digging, or even in its historical examination in any significant sense: we have no major physical remains in the Garw to share like those at Big Pit in Blaenavon, Rhondda Heritage Park, or even our near-ish neighbour, the South Wales Mining Museum in Afan Forest Park, Neath Port Talbot.

It's time we all came up for air, anyway, removing the dominance of carbon from our story.

We need to replace the old single cash (for a few) crops of coal and of conifers with a new mixed economy that celebrates the magnificence of our landscapes, and the richnesses of our histories and cultures, turning in the process what were once seen as the Valley's disadvantages – its 'dead-end' nature, steep hills, small size, no through road, etc. – into the strongest of our merits.

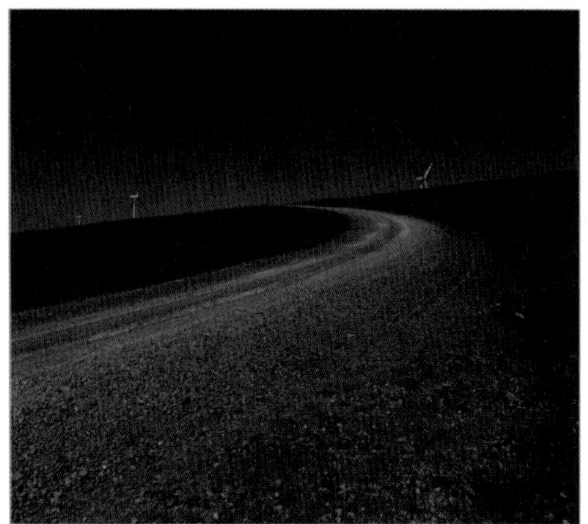

The excellently-named Plant Scheme ('plant' meaning 'child' in Welsh) is rooting a tree for every child born or adopted in Wales. Set up by the Welsh Government in 2008 and supported by Natural Resources Wales and The Woodland Trust, children have been encouraged to take part in the actual planting of a wide variety of tree species (including alder, white birch, hawthorn, hazel and ash) in four different sites in Carn, Blaengarw and Pontycymer, as well as learning about the critical importance of trees in absorbing man-made carbon dioxide emissions and helping to combat climate change.

The new ambitious triple blueprint of active tourism and the celebration of our history and our culture, alongside the harnessing of digital communication possibilities and the generation of clean energy will require a degree of vision and effort we don't usually see up here, at least not in the recent past since the shattering revolution that was coal.

But whether these dreams will ever be able to replace the levels of employment once provided by the mining industry; and whether these new uses of the land more akin to a partnership than an invasion could ever be enough to sustain the present population now that the pits have closed is the biggest question of them all … and one not just for the Garw but for all of our ex-coalmining valleys, and for Wales as a nation.

wind turbines,
Mynydd Caerau

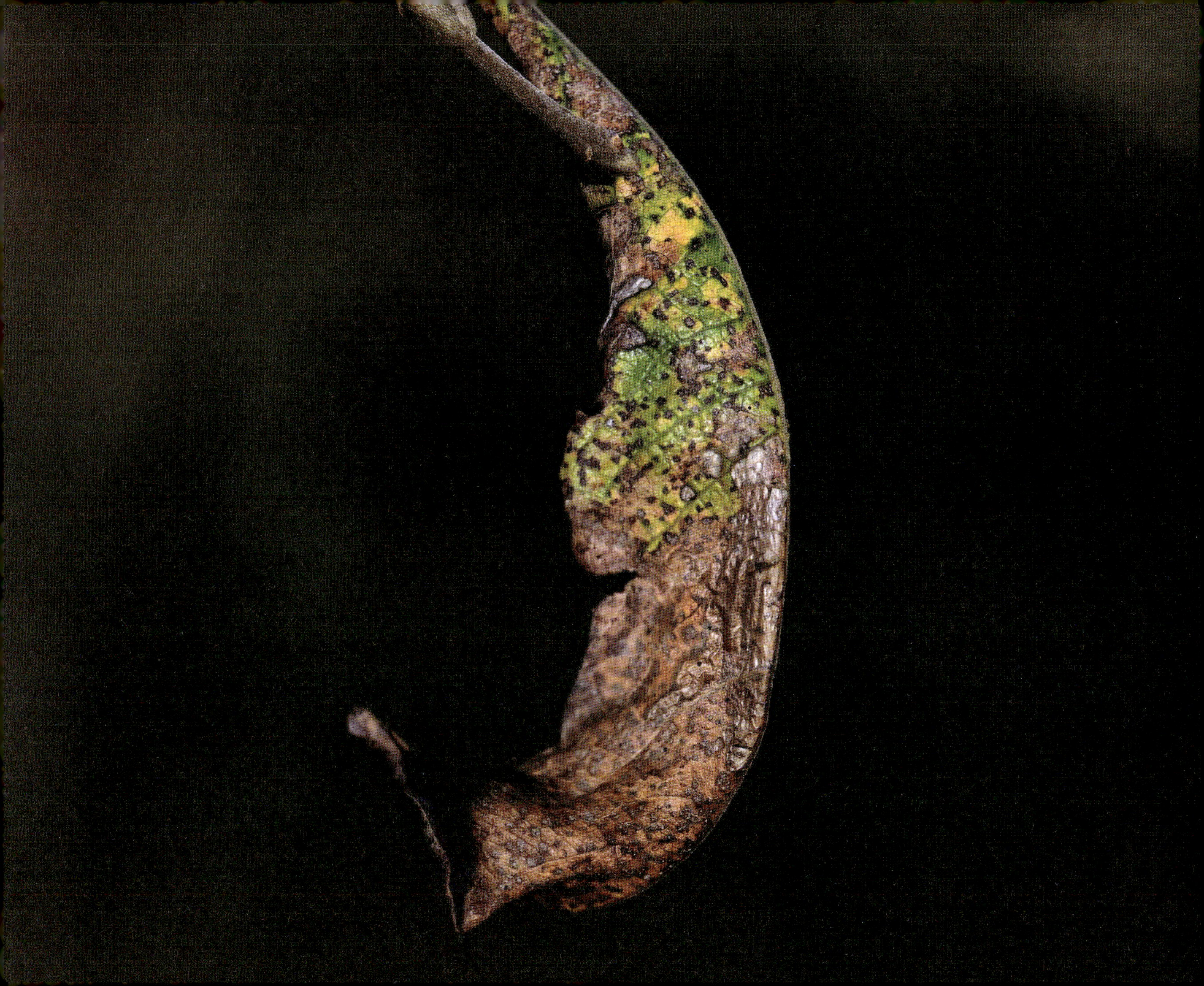

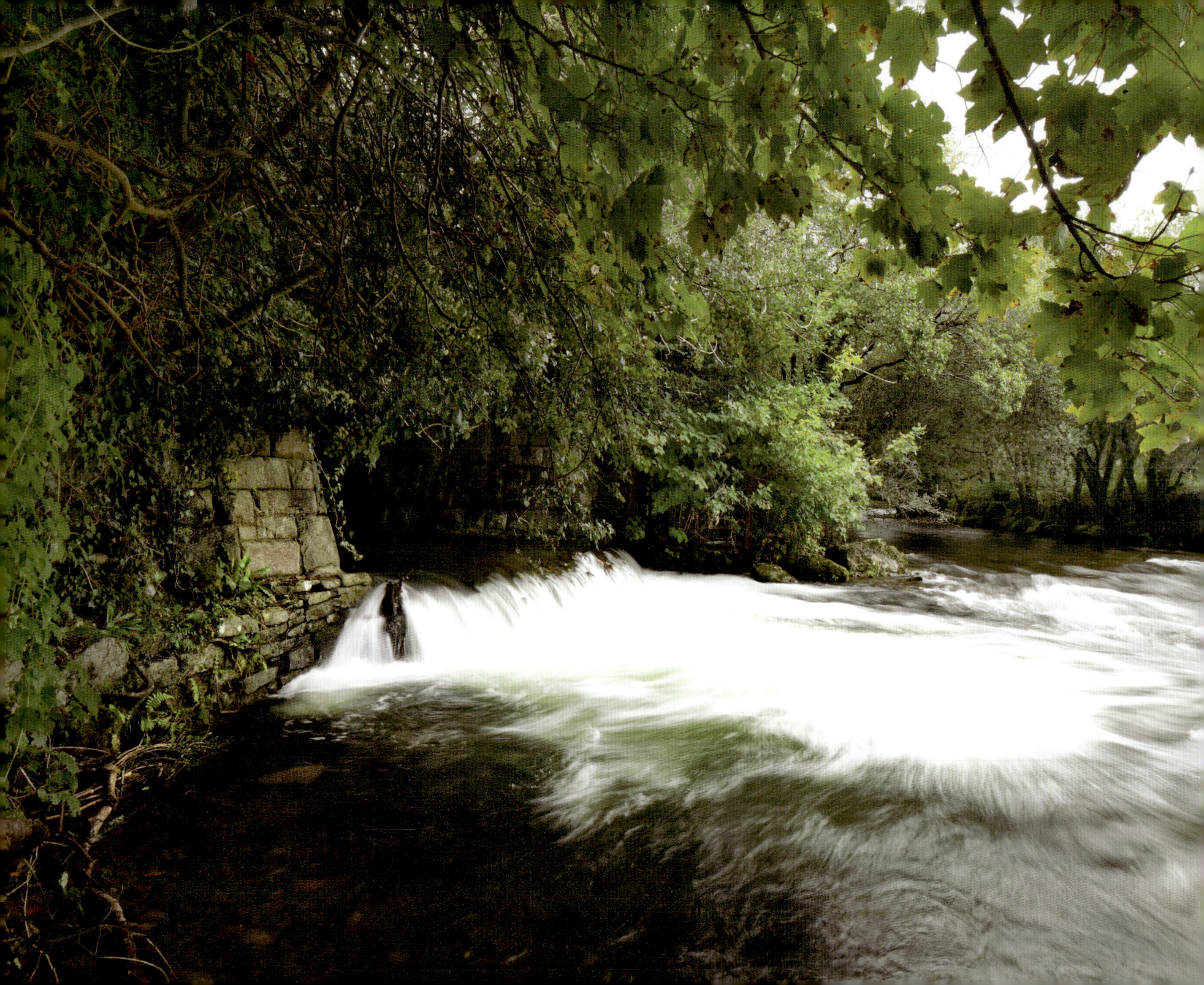

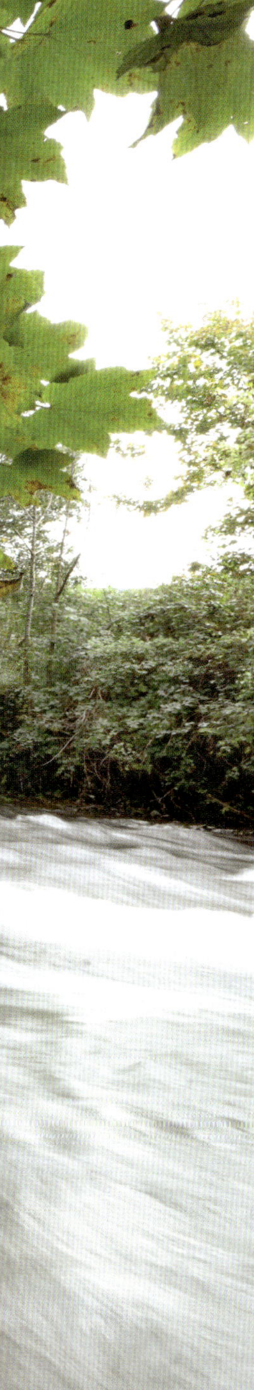

the confluence, where the Garw is swallowed within the river Ogmore's much deeper throat, on its way to the sea ...

* Dylan Thomas

EPILOGUE:
the force that through the green fuse drives the flower *

Richard Mabey, writing about his recollections of the Second World War in *The Unofficial Countryside* (1973), observed that *"The first summer after the blitz there were rosebays flowering all over three-quarters of the bombed sites in London, defiant sparks of life amongst the desolation"*.

He was able to see the beauty within the beast.

Perhaps these are the Garw's post-blitz days, after our own war with nature and ourselves, made more resonant today as we try to survive yet another man-made plague in Covid-19.

The Garw is undoubtedly **the** most beautiful of all of South Wales' ex-coalmining valleys ... but to visit you have to make a detour. It's not on the way to anywhere except itself (unless you're a bird or on a mountain or motocross bike and are making your way up and over to the Ogmore or Llynfi Valleys, or north to Blaengwynfi and beyond).

Any biography of the Garw must start, not with coalmining, but with these hills … as well as with water.

The land's best conjuring trick is the river, always emptying itself but always full, snaking from countless springs along the belly of the Valley, taking the steeply sloping land's easiest path, never uncertain in its simple objective, serpent-like in our once- and possibly-future Garden of Eden.

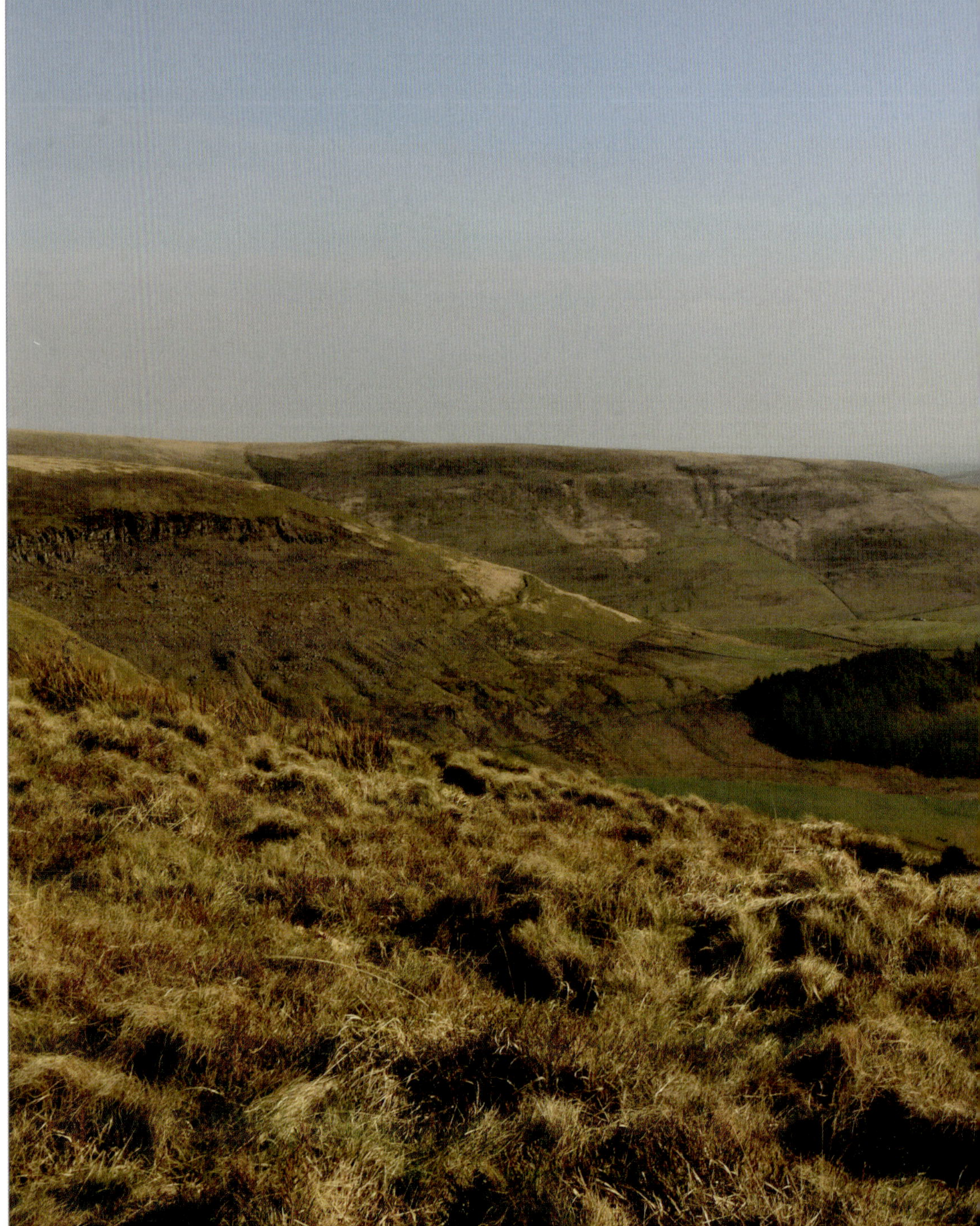

the view from Bwlchgarw, above Carn, down the whole of the Garw Valley, and – on a good day – to the Vale of Glamorgan, the Channel and across to Somerset

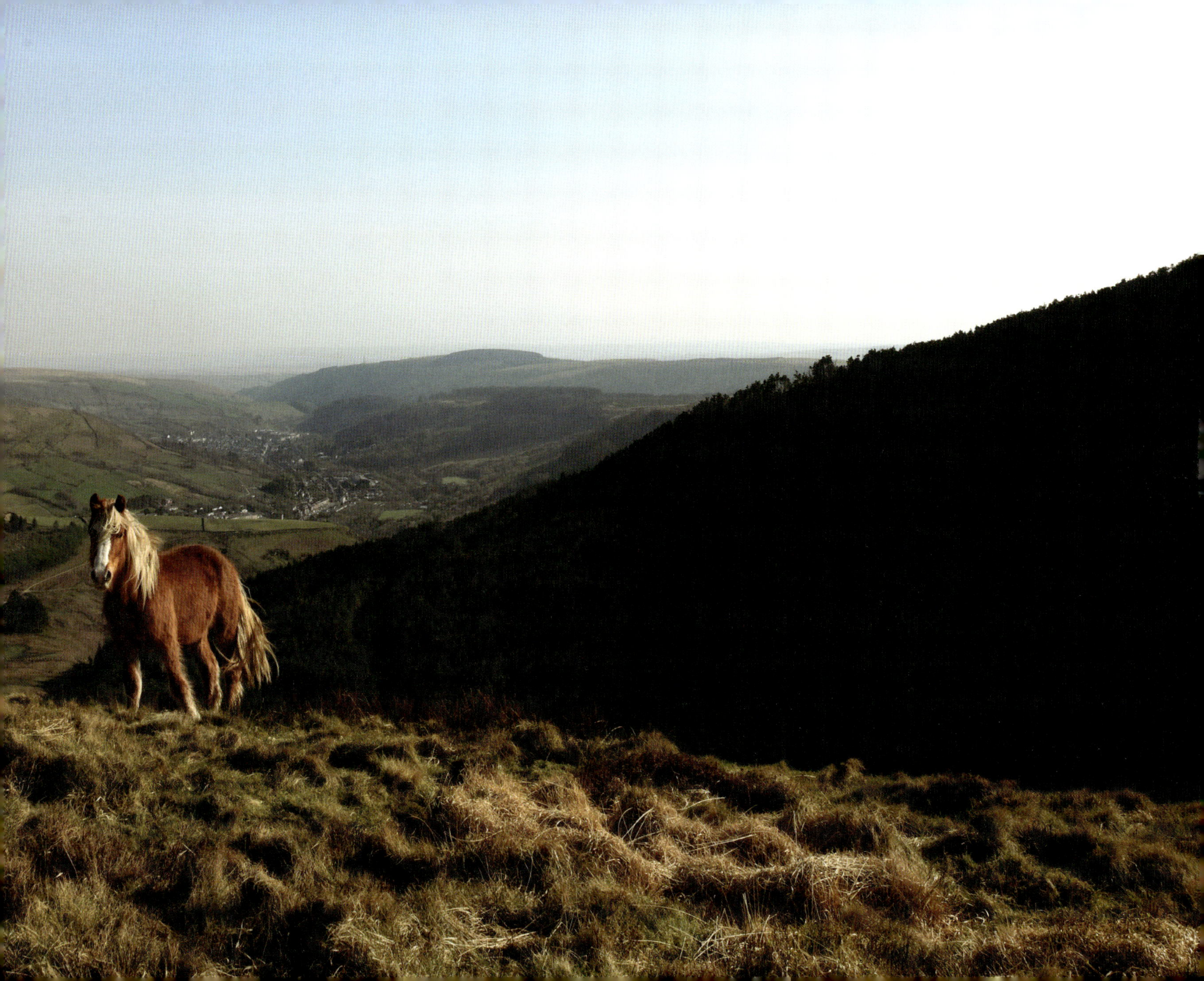

Our narrow Valleys separated by high passes, with poor transport networks (and, in the Garw's case, no through traffic), set alongside the lack of large areas of flat ground upon which to build has, post-coal, minimised the kinds of employment initiatives which see the footprints of factories as the only effective solutions. We need to be imagining a very different kind of future, laid out in human trails and bicycle tracks; in accommodation and decent places for visitors to eat and drink; in Sinnott's art and Workmen's Hall performances; and in the re-opening of the railway; with all of our energy supplied from mountain-top turbines by our nearly-always-available wind.

As history has made an about-turn in my *cul-de-sac* home, we're already returning to a more traditional relationship with the land. In a combination of humankind's efforts to say sorry and nature's own unstoppable reclamation scheme, greater celandine and common valerian, creeping buttercup and wood sorrel are flowering like parables through the cracks in Garw's ruins, suggesting something possible; and bramble, broom and gorse, feverfew and primrose are rising up in nature's quiet fight-back.

Our new lakes are alive again with brown trout and frogs, with dragonflies, ducks and dippers, coots and moorhens, and the always solitary and antisocial heron. A peregrine falcon couple make their annual visit, nesting confident in a wall of quarried cliffs where stone was once cut to build miners' houses, as our recently despoiled habitats are being recolonised, nature returning to its briefly-interrupted residences and reclaiming its goods.

And, according to local bird photographer and my sometimes walking companion Richard 'Cuffy' Evans, you can also now observe the red kite, buzzard, cuckoo, house martin and swift, jackdaw, rook and skylark; song thrush, starling, pied and grey wagtail, magpie, bullfinch, goldfinch, chaffinch and greenfinch; blue, great, coal and long-tailed tits, as well as the jay throughout the Garw. And, if you are lucky, you might even spot a kingfisher, kestrel, ring ouzel, tawny owl, lesser spotted and green woodpecker, goldcrest, nuthatch and stonechat, living here alongside foxes, squirrels, badgers, otters, mink, stoat, rabbit and hare.

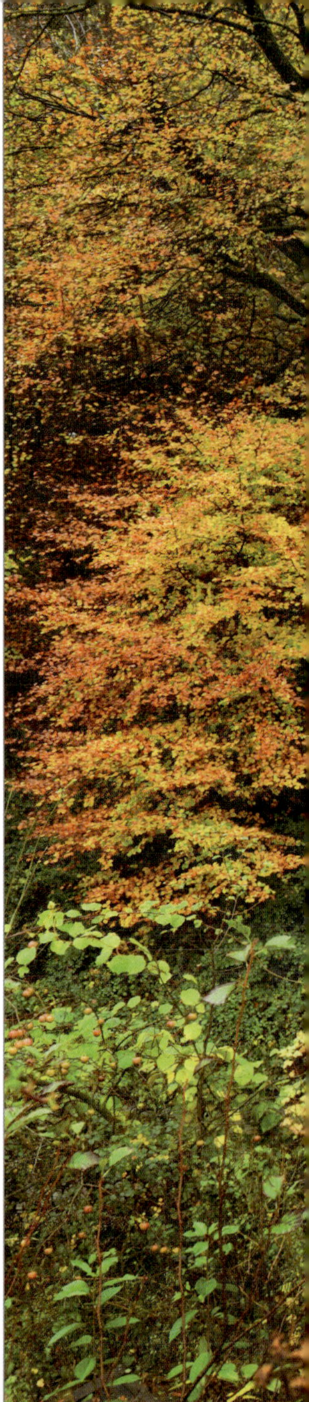

the river
Garw
in its autumn
colours

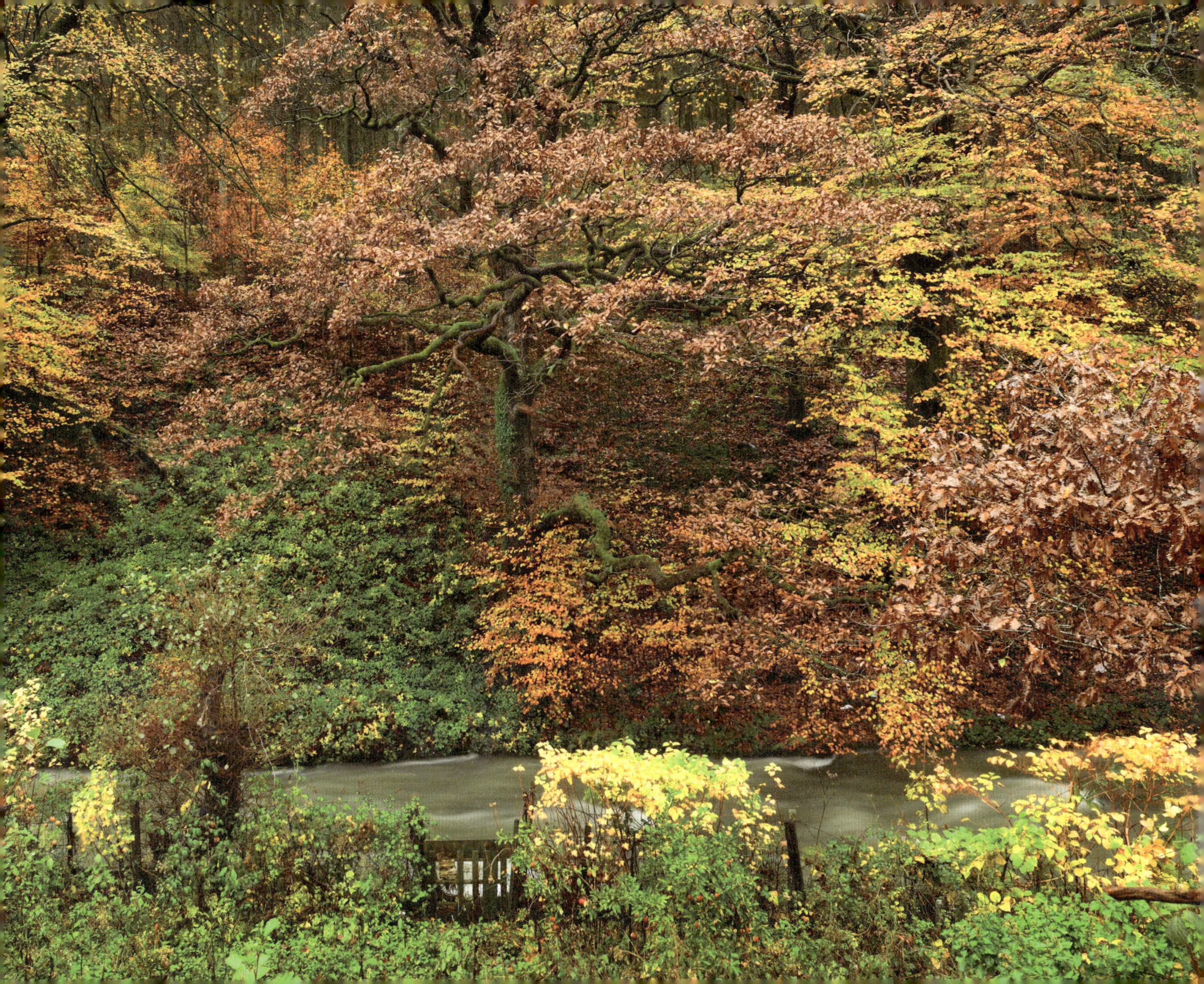

The land has remained – beaten up, of course, its flesh in places gored – but wounds heal, as the days of coal mining are now as unimaginable to most of us as the ages of ice, or those of the building of the ancient cairns to bury the dead, or even of Richard Price and 'Fanny Bloomers'.

And, even if none of our most recent schemes for survival work out for our complex and contradictory species … no matter. The grass, the trees, the bushes will soon grow high through the windows of our abandoned houses and shops, rising through the floorboards of our churches, schools, and workmen's halls and institutes, flourishing once again where they always used to flourish. The extremophile lichen on the rocks of the burial chambers of our Bronze Age ancestors will continue to spread like glorious, radiating stains.

These, in truth, were always the real survivors anyway, tolerant of desert heat and arctic cold, of irradiation, pollution, and even being shot into space … so coalmining's brief century of much gentler poisonings has left little more than a mark on them.

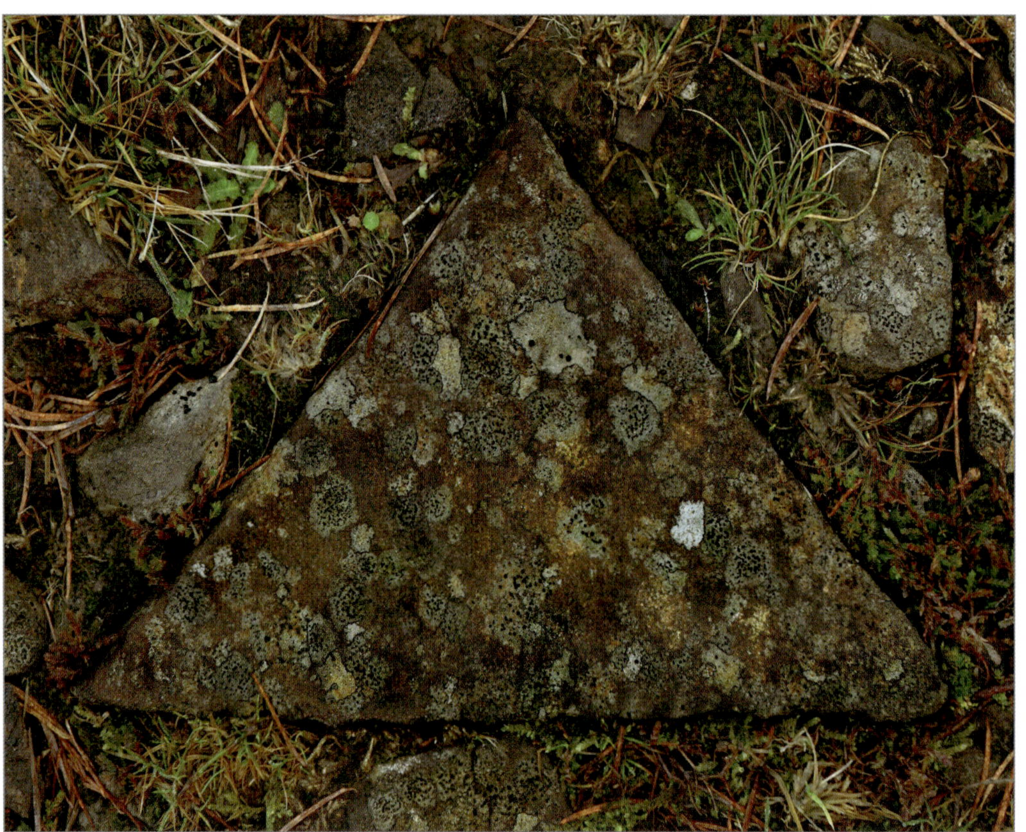

lichens' rich variety of colour and shape

Trying to describe the seemingly-infinite variety of shapes lichens create will always prove as unprofitable as our efforts to locate the one true source of the river Garw. You might just as well ask what shape water is: lichens, alongside all liquids only being definable in relation to where they are to be found. Their colours and countless contours appear like maps of countries, road atlases, cities, moonscapes, firework displays, the universe.

They were the product of the union of fungi and algae, as the first organisms to be established on planet Earth some 600 million years ago when green rootless algae began to move out of their shallow waters to try to make a living on a scorched and desolate land. Fungi provided the algae with roots to grip tight and flourish, in a process named in 1877 by German botanist Albert Frank as 'symbiosis'.

In a 1987 interview – just two years after the closure of the last pit in the Garw – Margaret Thatcher proclaimed that there was *"no such thing as society"* just individuals and their families, ushering in a decade and more of the politics of individualism and of greed.

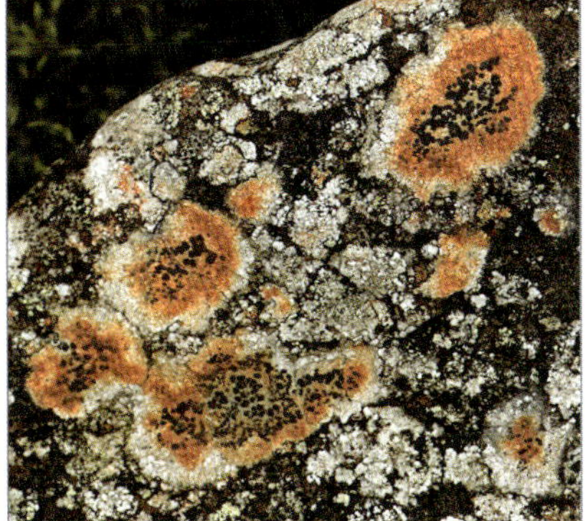

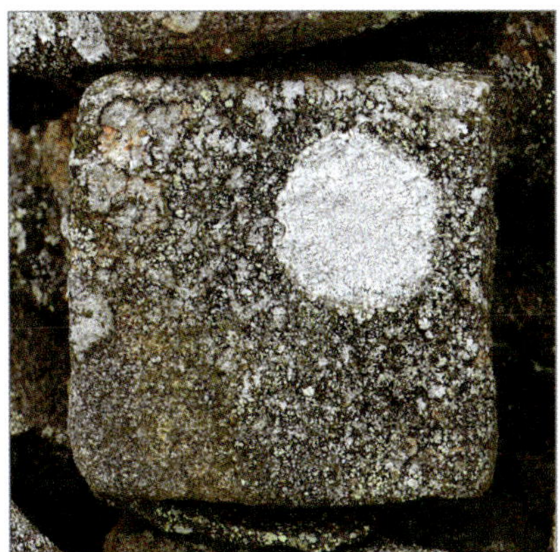

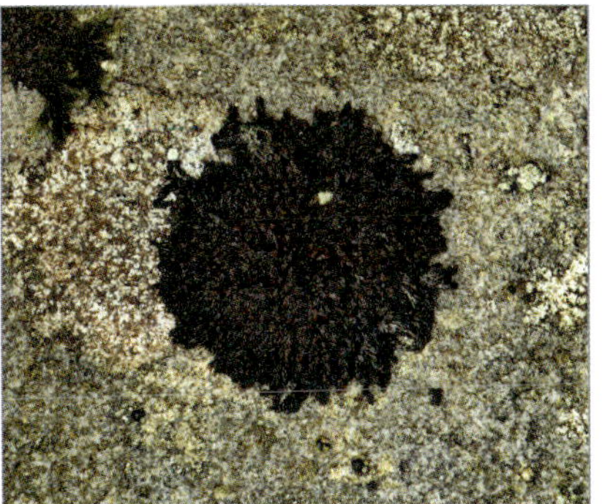

A similar debate is raging concerning the nature of lichens and of the myriad other formations of the fungi family. When you look closely at these ancient organisms, it's difficult to tell if they are single creatures or a vast collective; individuals or one being, grouped closely for safety.

Ninety per cent of the world's plants depend on mycorrhizal connections (*mykes*, Greek for fungus / *rhiza*, root), linking them in vast underground networks with nearly every organism, passing carbon, water, nutrients like phosphorus and nitrogen, and even alarm signals, back and forth, through their elaborate circuitries, in what Richard Powers has termed an "underground welfare state" (*The Overstory*, 2018).

English botanist David Read named these fine tubular structures that branch, fuse and tangle in an almost-infinite filigree, the '*Wood-Wide Web*', challenging Darwinian hegemony of the 'survival of the fittest' as the best description for the workings of the natural world, as well as Adam Smith's championing of selfish individualism in a free market.

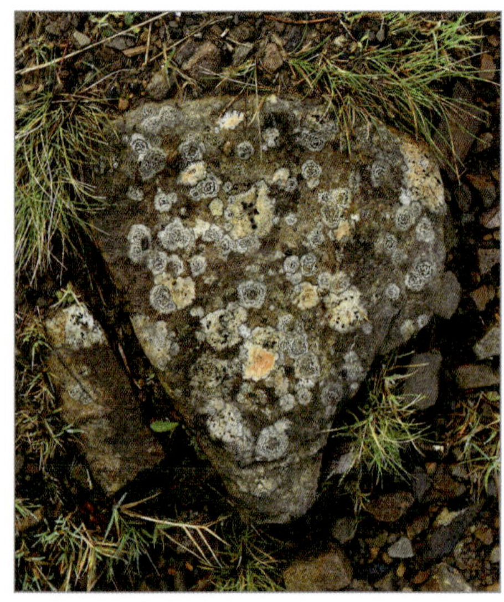
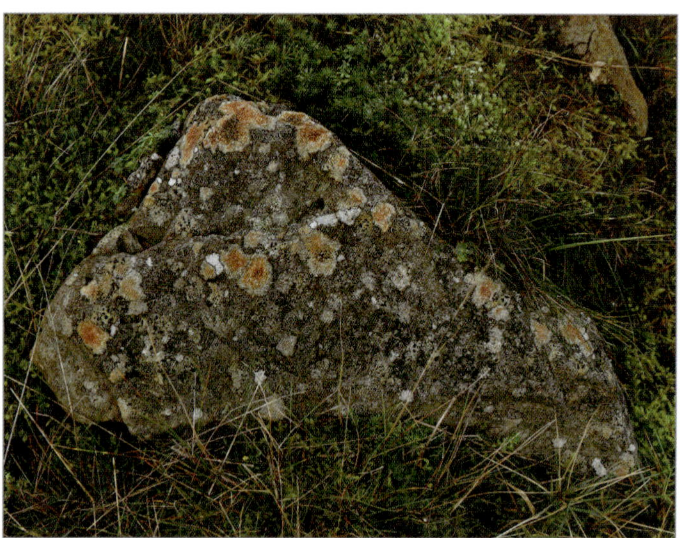
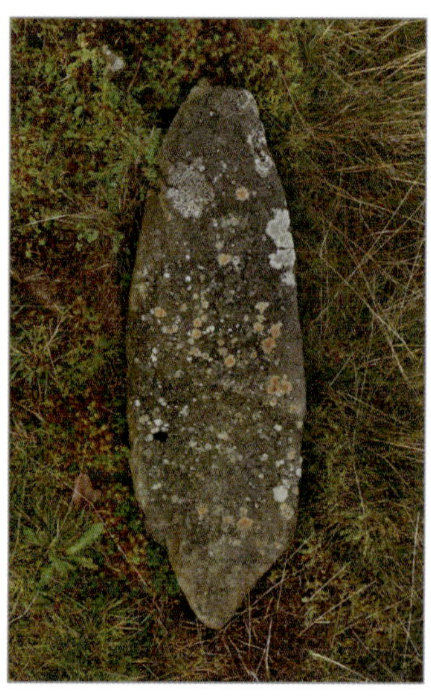
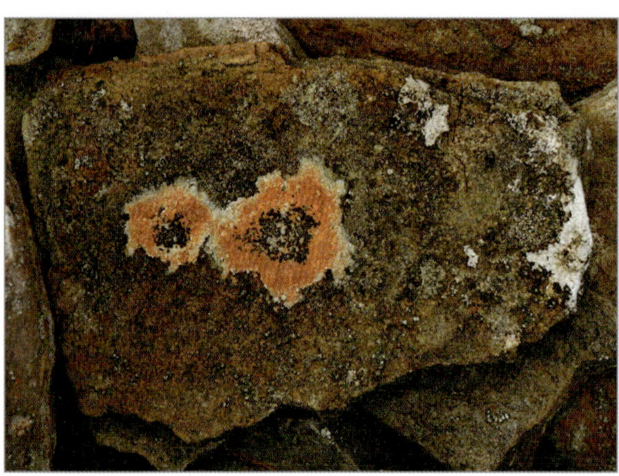
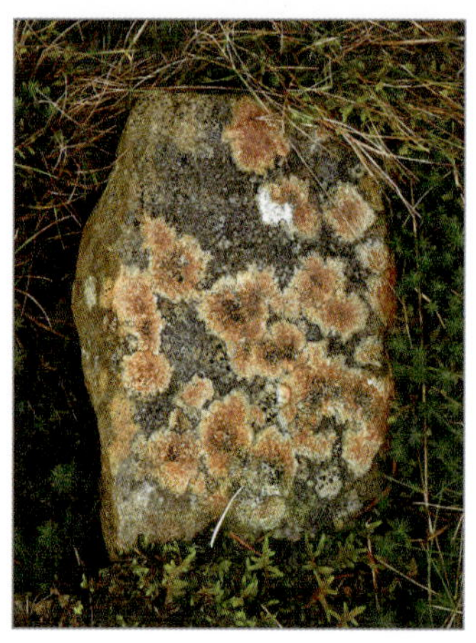
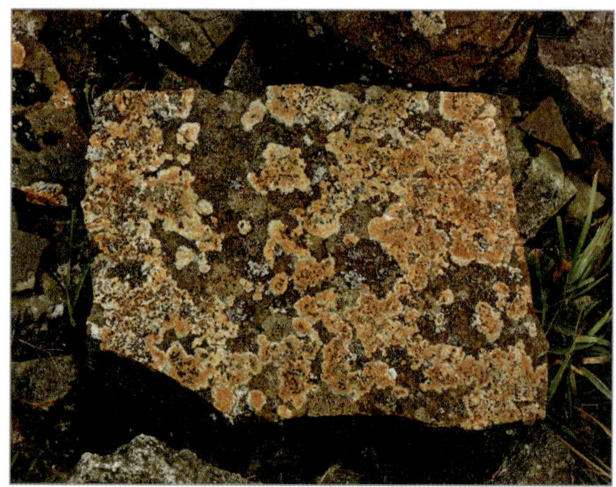

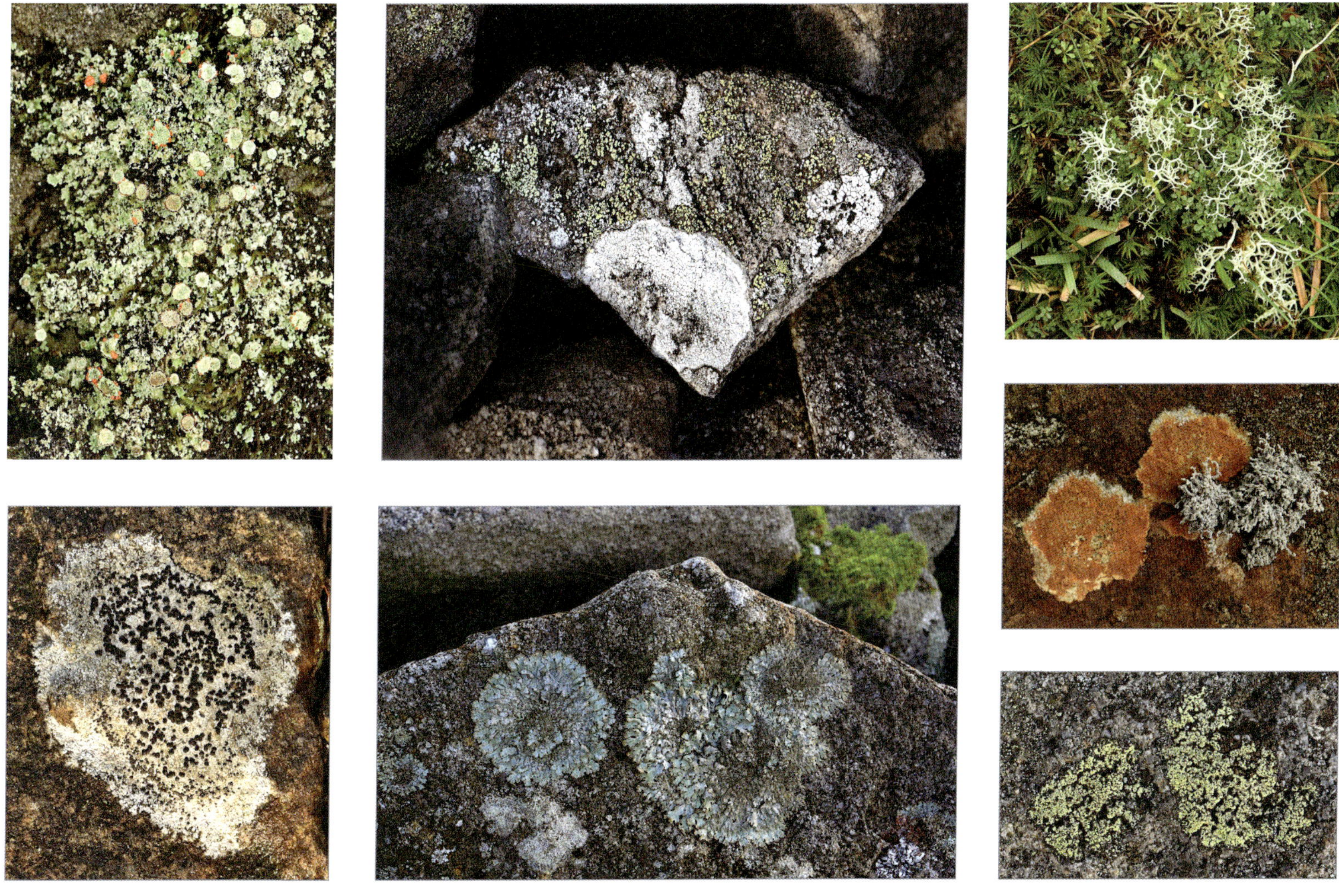

These lessons are crystal clear, it seems, within the smallest and the largest of things.

Intensive commercial forestry practices which select and plant only what is thought to be the most profitable of trees – expelling in the process most species of bird, mammal and insect life, and ripping up much of the land's underground communication and support system – have resulted in less lucrative yields with much more vulnerability to disease … as well as featureless, dark and silent arboreal deserts.

In *Braiding Sweetgrass: indigenous wisdom, scientific knowledge and the teachings of plants*, Native American biologist Robin Wall Kimmerer revealed that in her Potawatomi Nation language the word for hill is a verb, essentially meaning 'to be a hill', eternally active, ever changing.

Perhaps, from lichens and trees to cities and human relationships, this is a more useful way to understand and live in our world … better understood not as things, but as processes.

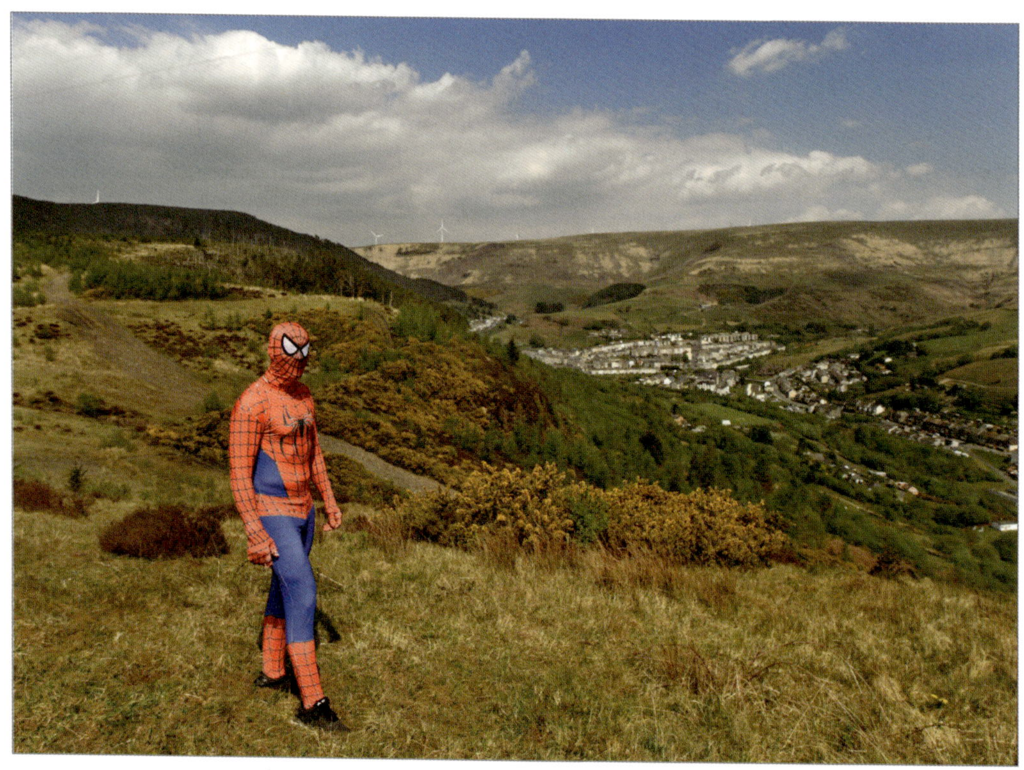

opposite:
Kevin Sinnott's painting, enititled *Superheroes*
(inspired by the work of Richard Durston, above, for children during the lockdown):
Kevin's prints from a preparatory sketch were sold to support a local carehome.

Mutual aid and co-operation were essential for people's survival here, when intolerable forces were applied to lives and to the land during the harsh years of coalmining. The construction, equipping and running of workmen's halls and institutes, and the establishment of mutual aid societies were based upon the principle that the health of the individual was most effectively guaranteed by the well-being of the whole … with no-one left behind.

In this co-operation-for-survival model – paralleled by what we are learning about the reciprocity and even altruism of the superorganism of forest and field – the healthy paid for the sick, the working for the unemployed.

And it is this spirit that is being recalled, in some small ways, in our communitarian responses to the new realities of the Covid pandemic, which only a united, co-evolutionary response will defeat, a reaction which begins, perhaps, to track a faint path towards a new / old future for the people of the Garw, as well as everywhere else.

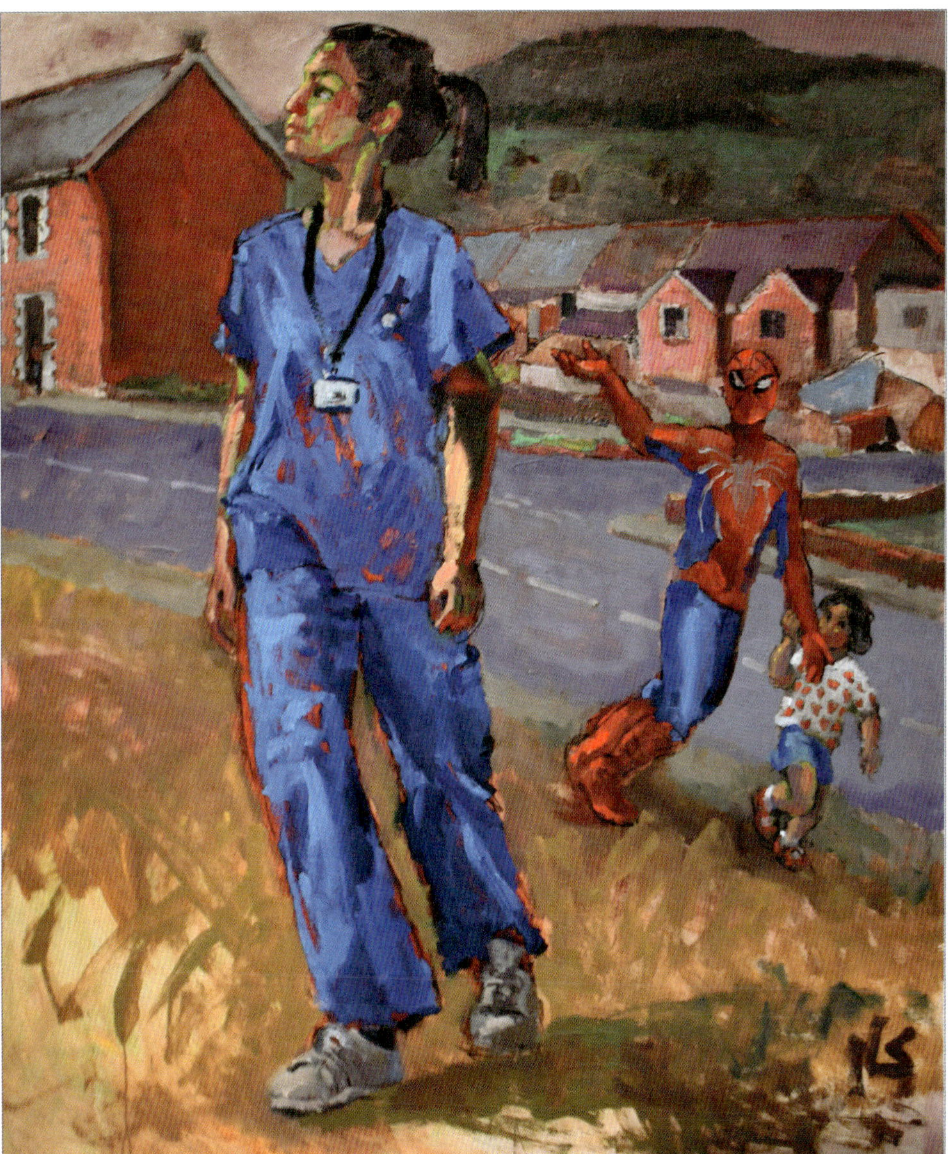

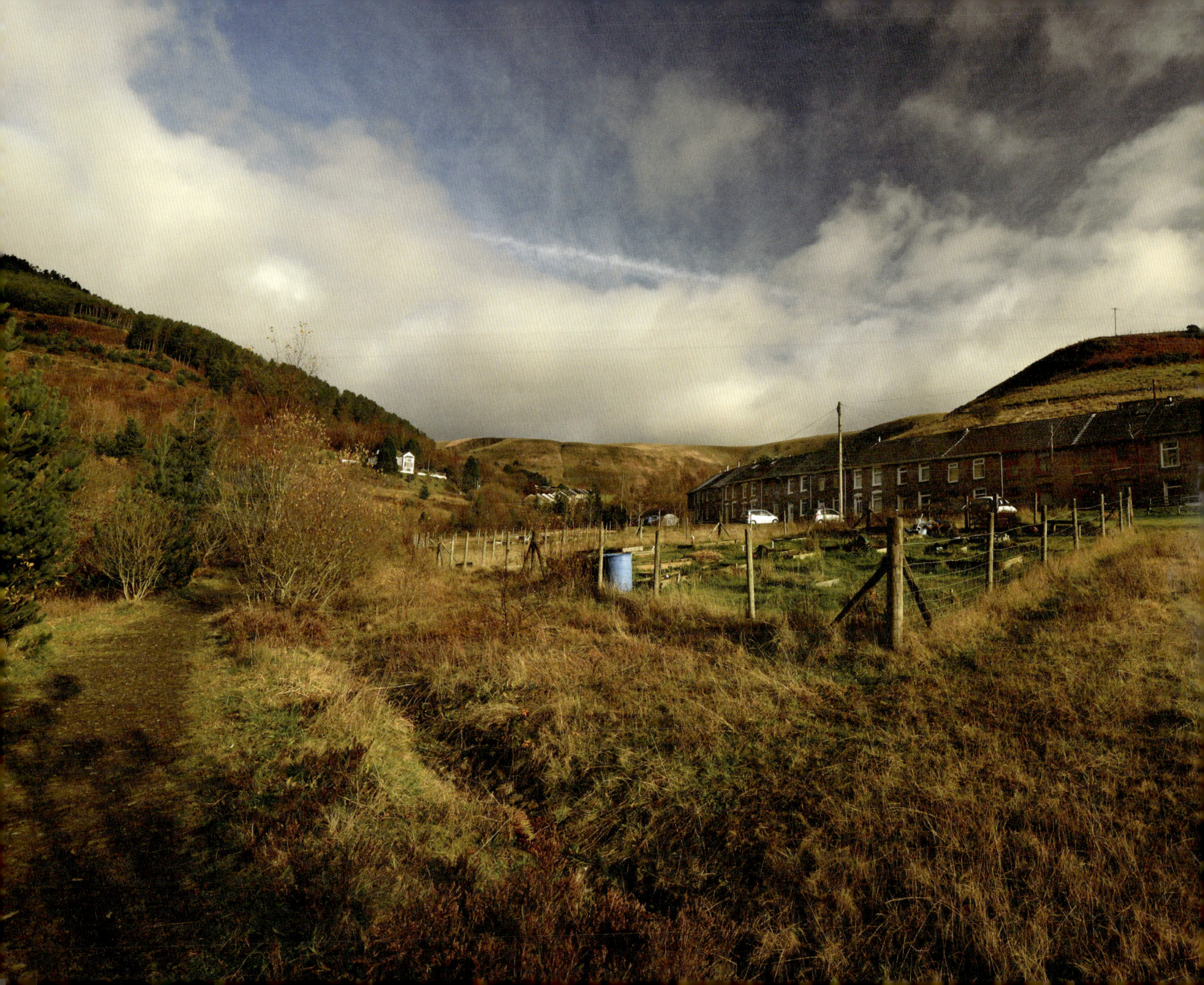

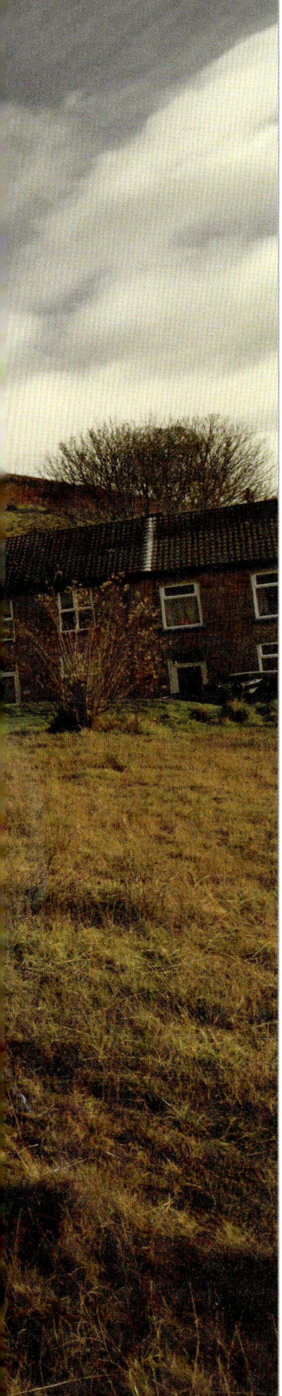

The coal which brought droves of men and their families to this tiny Valley a little over a century ago took 250 million years to create. While decaying trees and plants were swamped and compressed – every twenty feet of vegetable debris producing just one foot of coal – it took us less than one hundred years to exhaust it.

In response to this and much other alarming evidence, and in the knowledge that we had now entered the Holocene Age, the sixth mass extinction period of our planet, American mycologist and entrepreneur Paul Stamets in his March 2008 Ted Talk asked his audience: *"if there was a United Organisation of Organisms … and every organism had a right to vote, would we be voted on the planet … or off it?"*.

The lichen and the rocks of the Garw Valley, its river, trees and hills, its birds and fish, its animals, insects and fungi will win … always were winning, of course, despite appearances.

After taking their beating, it's clear that the earth is blooming again, one blade at a time through our detritus of brick and coal and iron.

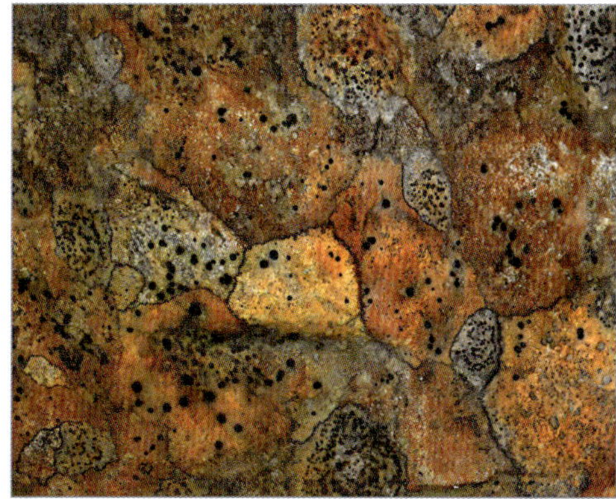

And, as the sun continues to rise and fall over our golden valley, the only real question for us today is whether we will decide to throw our weight behind the inevitably-victorious team … or not.

opposite:
raised bed allotments,
awaiting the Spring,
Railway Terrace,
Blaengarw

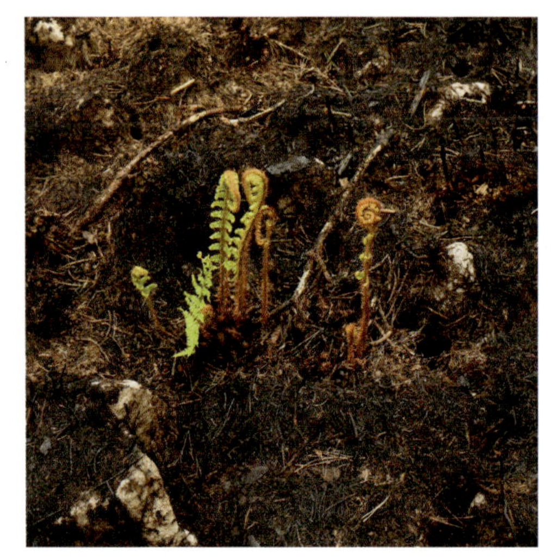